Affable in Adversity
The Bereavement B*tch

by

William Hunter Howell

ISBN: 1499268637

ISBN-13: 978-1499268638

DEDICATION

In loving memory of the adventurer I love and miss each and every day.
The world is a far less colourful place without you.

Oh, and if you're reading this Dad, I'm sorry. I got a bit carried away. I knocked on a lot of wrong doors, went down a lot of dark paths and the need for distractions became a tad excessive.

Basically, I fucked up.

But I'm back now.

CONTENTS

"Every time you are able to find some humour

in a difficult situation, you win."

PROLOGUE

I hate the overuse of the word 'literally', but there is no denying my tranquil blue eyes literally lit up as they absorbed the astonishing magic of South Africa's white beach coast line from seven-thousand feet up in the air. For it was a view only complimented by the astoundingly addictive and juxtaposing red soil that governs the landscape of this fascinating world. It's a view that remains resolutely glued to me. A view that is still so dominating, so decisively delicious, so surreal and so stupendously staggering that I have acid like flashbacks, as if caught in a dream so vivid that my vision is shrouded by a memory of what was indubitably the grand, gracious and ever genial Garden of Eden. This was a sight that caused a shiver to rattle my nervous system and forced my heart to palpitate in a fashion that mimicked a Bakermat tune, no matter how many times I got to scan the astonishing horizon of Africa. There is just a magic to be found here, irrelevant of whether this view was from up high as we danced across the cloudless sky, or whether we tread across this ever-contrasting landscape via the divine medium of foot. In all honesty, it was as if I'd won Willy Wonka's golden ticket each and everyday during the years Dad worked down there. For this life was a roborant against banality and a far cry from the life in politics that I was used to as the child of a European Member of Parliament.

Nonetheless, despite being blessed with this sensational, stunning, unobstructed and godlike panoramic view of Shangri La, it was the view inside the cockpit of 'Mike Lima Delta' that encouraged my beaming lips to uncontrollably quiver with joy, as my heartbeat meticulously matched the wonderful whirring of this Cessna's propeller blades. This view I coyly speak of however was more pinhole than panoramic, the kind of picturesque prospect that could have instigated the peerless phrase 'a picture paints a thousand words' and the sort of sensational sight that made this humble and humorous human understand how lucky I am to be the fastest sperm to participate in that Darwin inspired race against the odds, twenty four years ago.

You see it wasn't the rare but amazingly available grandiose and glorious view of Africa that had stolen my smile, warmed my cockles and made the local vicinities below partially pregnant. Nor was it the state of blooming bliss that was warmly welcomed as I passionately perched in this forever banking airship. For it was instead the look of utter happiness, exhilaration and ecstasy that washed over every emotion of my Dad's being as he sat at the controls of this phenomenal flying machine. I mean I was left in awe of his genuine grin. I was inspired by the glowing radiance that perspired from every part of my paternal parent, seemingly lost in euphoria without limits of what could be achieved in that exact moment. It was as if my Dad was a charming celestial being, soaring through the sky as angelic as a mortal could be,

2

looking out over this picture perfect paradise, soaking up what society calls a wonderful world, but what my family knows to be nothing shy of heaven on earth.

This was the kind of moment that has the ability to wake you up as it drags you into an effervescent dream where absolutely nothing can take the crown away from complete contentedness and undisputed happiness. This is the memory that stands aloof and rings the bells of yesteryear. This is the internal tonic for tired eyes that brings me back to a previous nirvana. This is the dose of medicine that I swallow in the here and now.

However, this wasn't always the case, for this memory was also the tranquillity that tormented my every thought for over four years, relentless in its ruthlessness and impeccable in its precision. The type of reminiscence that was once so regal in its role of retention, at least until one inexplicable 'accident' occurred, and suddenly this miracle of a memory converted itself into a reminder that became caustic, conceited, corrosive and callous, and it is this journey from the gates of Lucifer's lifeless lair back to delectation, exuberance, optimism and mirth that I am to share with you now, and I promise it will be an absolutely no holds barred account of upmost honesty, candour, fidelity, rectitude and transparency.

It's now been over four years and thus I write this recount with the cocksure clarity that can only be pursued by a person who has run from themselves and their demons for long enough for it to become second nature. For running & hiding from such adversity becomes a subconscious reaction, so subtle that even the most astute of intellects could not have predicted nor prevented such a response. Yet in spite of such an overhauling emotional response and in the face of such internal impossibility, there is a twinkling of hope. For the very first time since burying the prickling paroxysms and intrinsic lacerations that such a person has run away from, there is a moment that completely captures your breath. A moment where not only do you realise you've been running, but you are fuelled with the most overwhelming astuteness, and a backbone that triggers your desire to tackle these hardships. All in all, there is an imperative belief and a rotund realisation that one can truly overcome the torment that has been so tender for so long.

This moment is nothing shy of momentous. It's that moment when a person consciously decides to walk through the gates of hell and get in the ring with their invisible devil. Deciding to take the fight to this Lucifer that is so exclusive, you know deep down that despite the ravenous wishes of your loved ones, this is a David & Goliath bout that you are forced to enter completely isolated from help, withdrawn from backup, unescorted and alone. Yet, whilst this unaccompanied battle with your inner Beelzebub is impossible on every betting card, you are stimulated by the physical & emotional pain of the past, with the constant running too much to bear. Fatigued by the exertion of putting on a face everyday, so that those around you don't feel uncomfortable but are instead blissfully unaware. Exhausted by the consequences of not sleeping, either as a by-product to burying such grief or due to fear. Scared of what your nightmares might drag up as your head hits the pillow each night.

It is with this back against the wall comprehension that you're willing to deplete yourself in one last hoorah, an attempt to prevent the on going depletion your experiences have previously proved. Thus without examining even your bare arsenal, you throw every last ounce of energy you have at breaking through the armour of this private Prince of Darkness, whether it takes days, weeks, months or years. There is this newfound determination, this fight in you so tenacious that you will never back down, and after you've tried, tried and tried again, you finally savour success. But this is not a success that is comparable to anything material, nor a comparison to the type of victory that bows its head to supporters, colleagues or witnesses. But rather, this is triumph in the biggest battle know to mankind, a battle so vast and powerful its worthy of any history book. A battle no one else knows about, not its relevance or its importance, not even the fact it ever took place. Yet, you step out of this metaphorical ring, exhausted but victorious, and more aware than ever how hard you've fought. You stand atop of that podium, wearing a medal that only you can see and only you can acknowledge, for that medal I speak of, is clarity, and the adjective I used in conjunction with this purposeful word, was cocksure. Cocksure clarity.

Now, given that I started this intentional combination of words known as writing with a nervy recollection of better times, you have every reason to question my use of the word 'cocksure'. However, you will learn progressively and quickly throughout this 'memoir', for want of a better expression, that my adoration for the English tongue of traditional eras is wholeheartedly a love affair with words that have the ability to describe. Words that present themselves to the readers' soul, the sort that lure's in an audience. However, the emphasis is placed upon you and your imagination, you and your determination. You see, it is your ingenuity, creativity and honesty that truly holds the reins in this encounter, for it is your imagination and determination that animates these sentences and brings this 'book' alive.

So, cocksure: an adjective defined as confidence in an excessive or arrogant way, and that is exactly what this recently sought after clarity is. It's lucidity like I have never experienced before. Or, if I have been partial to such clearness in a previous life, it was a state of mind that was either too many moons ago, or it has been permanently erased from my frontal lobe and my insular cortex, whilst I can be pretty damn certain my limbic lobe has been refreshed too. This is a notion that is supported by my ability to lock away sentiments within my own private 'William's Box', similarly formatted to that of Pandora's. Thus, this 'new' state of mind really is clarity on a level I have never experienced before. Clarity so influential that if an emotional relapse was to occur, I can say with true grit, I am no longer afraid intimidated or petrified of staring my in-house Diablo in the face once more. For this is a clarity worth fighting for, this clarity is more than a word, this is clarity that has made me more awake and more aroused by who I am than previously plausible, provoking me to grab life by its terrifying but triumphant testicles and find out what it really has to offer.

What I am trying to say is, as some kind of reaction to hurtful memories and constant struggles, I hid some part of me away, never fully comfortable in who I was despite my Oscar worthy acting. But now that I have stared down the barrels of this symbolic shotgun, I have not simply come out of the other side as a survivor, but I have emerged as a man, albeit one not willing to grow up just yet. But in spite of my intended immaturity, I'm now a man who has found true purpose, carousing in the kind of happiness that I thought was only part of the Hollywood bullshit conspiracy, and guess what, I am fucking revelling in it. I don't take things for granted like I used to, but I also don't get erratically pissed off by those who do. Yeah things annoy me, but these things are miniscule, like the fact my younger brother occasionally beats me at Mario Kart on a console of my generation, a first world problem to say the least. However, I have learned how to accept and deal with the bigger challenges in my life, challenges that still rear their fuck ugly heads on a daily basis, and challenges I will delve into in due course. But, this learning process, and god damn it, it is a learning process, is one that I have accepted, and in my humble and occasionally fucked up opinion, this is because I have an unfaltering openness with who I am, a pact between me, myself and I based on truth, and strength. A pact that I am not ashamed of despite the stigmas of society

I know this must only be the first step in what is sure to be a marathon, but if I can keep this fundamental building block in place, and honour this pact with my openly ridiculous self, then all the other surrounding issues that have occurred will, crossed fingers, fall into place. This belief of mine is dogged. For I am determined that this understanding will help resolve the detrimental and damning by-products of my internal hibernation, and maybe, just maybe, I will be given the chance to adopt a state of mind resembling something of the scenes before my hardships occurred. However, I am certain that these by-products, whether relationships with family members, friends or lovers, will reach a whole new level, that in my darkest days, seemed like a mission so tough even Ethan Hunt would have found it impossible.

Sure, you can tell me I'm optimistic, but I'll respond by telling you that your observations are educationally pre-school obvious. You see, I like who I am when I'm optimistic because I'm god damn eccentric, ridiculous and happy, and I like what I bring out in others when I'm this way. I revel in the fact that I'm an affably academic rhythmic Romeo who has graduated from the hard knock school of life. I think about my each move, and ultimately, I do what my gut meretriciously recommends because its exciting, yes, but also because I have a wicked good heart, and that alone prevents me doing the only thing I won't do, and that's participating in anything that may harm others. You see this is the acceptance, the acknowledgement and cocksure clarity I speak of. Not cocksure in an arrogant way. No. Cocksure in an excessive way, for I have never experienced euphoria the likes this, and I'm cocksure in an arrogant way that I don't ever want to lose this idyllic balance of transparency, or betray the harmonic deal I've struck up with myself that harbours the gods honest truth.

Anyway, now that I've transformed into an overweight polar bear and broken the ice with my spiel about striving for clarity, it would seem I have also relinquished my attempts to avoid clichés by stating there is light at the end of even the darkest of tunnels. What's more, I proclaim it is positively possible to experience the personal phenomenon of facing your fears, which in more cases than not, is a fear of your past or at least the trepidation of getting back into bed with a specific and harrowing event that altered both you and your perception on life.

Yet despite beliefs of the contrary and the monumental Herculean task that lay await, I boldly believe you can in fact return from the dark side of the moon, and return a victorious Gladiator. But in order to reach this stage of survival, it is a necessity to accept that your life has been remodelled, shuffled, adapted, spiked, reshaped, or any other term for altered that you may wish to adopt. For this acceptance of the consequences that inevitably happens in the wake of life changing events, is as crucial to succeeding in the war against your own clandestine calamities as water is to a particularly parched clown fish. Thus, the repeated prescription of trial and error in which I was the sole participant, provided me with one certain answer that aided my conquest to deal with the ever adapting, never predictable consequences of adversity... and that imperative piece of the struggle puzzle is none other than attitude.

I usually don't need to pat myself on the back, at least not when it comes to the subject of attitude, as I'm a silver lining, glass half full, the-ship-is-sinking-but-I'll-still-be-singing-in-the-lifeboats kinda guy, affable in the face of adversity, or at least, I am now. You see before I decided to confront my emotions, I was still that cheeky-chappy-always-happy jazz cat, well I was when swanning around my beautifully amazing and somewhat expansive friendship bundle. However, behind closed doors, both metaphorically and literally, it was a very different story altogether. At times I dealt with my situation very badly. I shut myself off from everyone including myself, abandoning hope, finding myself further from the light than ever before, usually rolling up a spliff or two in an attempt to aid my completely flawed sleeping pattern, disabling any ability to dream or more specifically any dabble in nightmares, and more than anything, to absolutely eradicate the emotions that were eating away at me like a persistent pot-bellied pig. However, I mustn't be too hard on myself, for there were times that I deliberately tried to confront my self wallowing situation, although this would always fail to be a permanent move of dominating substance throughout this chess game that relies so heavily upon strength and stamina.

What I found to be hardest to accept in defeat though was the fact this was the first obstacle, nay, the first time in any area of my life that I had failed. Fuck-a-doodle-doo did this realisation really got on top of me, like some cuckolding she-devil of patronisation and humiliation, pinning me down in the most self-degrading cowgirl-esque frenzied experience one could theoretically comprehend, wrapped up in the tightening thighs of incomprehensive helplessness. The thought of failing at the most substantial and important hurdle I'd come across made me doubt myself in a way I'd never thought possible, and I have a morally correct but bizarrely loose cannon of an imagination.

I lost my confidence, my self-assurance and my social buoyancy, all of which I struggled to contend with. Yet this face I painted on each day when I left the confines of my room, this face that repulsed me so much, this face that I imagine to be a combination of the terrifying Joker and a younger but just as suave Hugh Grant, somewhat kept that fire in my belly burning, kept the embers of hope alive. I was spurred on by numerous factors such as my incredible upbringing, with my lifejacket of nurture keeping my animal instincts of nature alive. I was aided by he ever-loving support of my family and close-close friends. Repugnantly helped by the knowledge that I was, in a way, being selfish with my emotions having seen first hand the suffering of those far worse off than I.

What I found to be top of the relief residence though, and this is possibly less likely but no less relevant, is the clichéd fact that I found a home with words, whether books, articles, sonnets, poems or even quotes. I found help with writing my feelings aware that I was unable to voice them. I found signs of hope and courage everywhere, symbolism on every corner, all of which escorted me through the overdose of petrified pain and the feeling of being a lost boy, bringing me back to this wild party called life... and with this new found clarity and acceptance, I can tell you with unbiased honesty and an enormous erection that this rave is more impressive than ever.

I understand that I haven't really preached what I mean by attitude yet, but that's solely due to my ability to get carried away with verses, thus, I apologise for my digression.

Now attitude is not only how you choose to deal with a situation, but your perceived way of thinking or feeling with regards to a truly significant event or sequence of events. Quotes have always been a way for me to reason with my circumstances, a means of seeing the bigger picture in a new light. Quotes act as a medium able to explain a situation in a way that is both poetic and relevant. Coining something so sensationally yet so simply. Thus with the notion of there being no time like the present, I see no reason to withhold the words Winston Churchill elegantly expressed to me, conveying that, "Attitude is a little thing that makes a big difference." With this honest outlook being seconded by the powerhouse statement Mary Engelbreit confidently conveyed to my conscience once upon a time, stating, "If you don't like something change it. If you can't change it, change the way you think about it."

You see, in my humble, and constantly adapting opinion, sometimes clichés are the most accurate assertions. Don't get me wrong; I'm not saying that these arguably tawdry quotations that have somehow cemented their way into online search engines and books that specialise in 'Toilet Trivia' are, by any means, for everyone. In fact, for a quote to win my heart in the same way that Jessica Alba has in past films, they have to be something special (like Alba in Sin City), and it doesn't hurt to know the context either. After all the context of my suffering is vital to the core understanding, as an onlooker, yet more significantly, context is the tool that's helped me progress. Nonetheless, I've strayed again, so lets take it abruptly back to my outlook on quotes.

There is one conjecture that I swear by, one simplistic saying that I will preach to anyone with absolute conviction, no matter what the situation may be. Whether it is unimaginably colossal or relatively trivial in the grand scheme of life, for there is one quote that has struck the chords of my ever-dissipating ability to provide a positive twist. One quote that has provided a symbolic soda-stream to my faltering facility to make lemonade, and that quote is quite simply...

"It's not about the situation, it's how you deal with it."

To me, this is the foundation, the bedrock, the bottom line, the infrastructure, the heart and soul of what attitude is, and what its infinite ability alludes to. I'm not by any means getting spiritual, or transcendent, nor am I trying to tell you how to deal with your situation, for as similar as it may seem from a peripheral perspective, everyone's in a very different boat, and I am fully aware of that. Instead, I'm trying to simplify what is so crazily complex in the months and years subsequent, that period of recovery that is so hard to identify in a broad church of occurrences, and thus I can only write about what I have found to be helpful, in what I hope is not a vain attempt to help others. I want to be able to assist those that have experienced or are indeed experiencing tragedy, events causing great suffering, destruction & distress, and thus I am in a way forced to write from the first person narrative and relying upon my past.

You see it took roughly four years and three months for me to change my attitude, or at least for me to 'consciously' change my attitude, and to start concentrating on how I was going to deal with my exceptional situation, instead of concentrating on the situation itself. In this decision, I kind of fancied myself as the Tony Stark / Iron Man of my emotional world, like a quick-witted, red & gold wrecking ball that has purpose. (Breaking News: I specifically mean Iron Man as depicted in the first film, the sequel was shit, with the third one just about clawing back some unkind level of kudos.) I was prolonging my torturing adversity, extending my grief and throwing myself down a lengthy slide of excruciating misery, as if this waterpark had replaced the all important H2O with sandpaper and staircases.

However, this wasn't the pinnacle of my pain, for bearing witness to what my inability to cope with such proceedings was doing to my loved ones and those very closest to me was the ultimate destroyer. You see realising that my attitude was causing them more pain than needed and the fact that I wasn't allowing myself to heal, made it a futile impossibility for them to be able to help someone they love so dearly. I either pushed my girlfriends away or refused to get close to them, I took my anger out on my family during a time where we were all grief stricken, and still there was nothing I could do about it at the time, which was like a Rottweiler bite to the balls. I mean these people would do anything for me, absolutely anything to ease the pain, to make me smile and to help me move on, all whilst wanting to move on themselves, and my response at the time was to inadvertently make life an even harder ride, as if I'd taken off the safety belts on the Alton Towers rollercoaster, Nemesis. But this was just the ruthless rut I was stuck in.

Looking back on it now though, maybe I was taking out my agony on those closest to me because of this 1990s Hugh Grant as the 2008 Joker type mask that prevented me from showing my true hurt to friends. I just didn't want to heighten the perception of my pain amongst them. Instead I was hoping they'd think I didn't have a worry in the world, whilst I was in fact involved in a Dr Jekyll & Mr Hyde type battle scenario. No doubt my friends saw me as Dr Bruce Banner, a good-looking, intelligent, witty species of humanoid, whilst my family had to deal with me Hulk stomping the very ground they walked on. I know my family will never cease to be there for me, my number one fan's so to speak, and this instinctive understanding created an atmosphere where my only liberation was to unleash the fury upon them instead of others, not just because it was behind closed doors, but because I inherently believed I couldn't push them away, or exasperate the pain. I was wrong though. I was so very wrong. In fact, Gordon Brown's decision to sell off our gold reserves was a decision that heralded more acceptance than my decision making progress to push my blood relations away.

However, what's worse is the knowledge that I could have prevented all this collateral damage by simply changing my attitude, by not being so dogged in my stubbornness to run away and hide for over four years. Quite simply put, you have to start with yourself. You have to understand whom you are, how you are going to deal with the personal Great Wall of China that you're dealt with, and how you are going to clamber over it, come hell or high water. "Weakness of attitude becomes weakness of character", according that kind of intelligent rock star we know and love as Mr Albert Einstein. For choosing to have a positive & grateful attitude is quite simply going to determine how you rock this one time party that we, under the influences of the English diction, call life.

What credentials do I have when it comes to this unpredictable, unreadable, volatile and arbitrary process called bereavement; well that self-important and stifling shit storm starts here!

"My Father was killed in a private plane crash in Mozambique on my third day at university."

This punchy punch line was the incredibly well rehearsed, straight to the point, and auto-piloted speech I would reel off in preparation for any inevitable & uncomfortable questions directed towards me, more specifically, questions with regards to my Dad.

It is a collage of words that was recited more often than one could think possible. Worn out like a dirty dishcloth or a re-used Johnny and performed with such distinction that the likes of Meryl Streep & Jack Nicholson kept messaging me on LinkedIn for tips and tricks. It was a testament prepared with precision and perfected with practice, never surrendering any more material than required. It became electively drilled into my reaction process, or more accurately, my distraction process. I ensured it held a magnitude that meant the actual content of this authoritative statement had no impact on me whatsoever. Not the slightest tug on my heartstrings, nor wince on my face. Just half a stanza comprised of commanding words, each one staggeringly powerful. Yet, these were words, no, a sentence, nay, a statement that was recycled over and over until its content was nothing more than a hollow shell, like an empty shotgun cartridge. I knew it was a formidable reply just from the look on the question askers face, taken aback by a short but devastating response. It warranted the kind of retreating reaction and illicit look that suggested I'd just used three-digits to finger-ram the quizmasters pet ferret. You see I can deal with any variation of shocked expression; it is the look of pity that cuts me down like defenceless timber up against a salivating lumberjack. Not because I feel sorry for myself, quite the contrary in fact, however, I will go into this in a Mariana Trench like depth in due course.

Anyway, as Billy Wilder once dexterously divulged to me, "Hindsight is twenty-twenty." This is as true as ever with regards to the stunningly sharp response I gave, and occasionally continue to give, although this is subject to two factors. Firstly, the dynamics of the given scenario; and secondly, it was dependant upon whom the unsuspecting participant, the gaggle of individuals or even the 'ménage a trois' I was about to unwillingly disarm, like a Dickensian Chuck Norris who relies solely upon the plethora of his spoken dialect.

Anyway, I now understand why I react with such arrogance in my slick tongue, and that's because it's a defence mechanism. I tried not to let my guard down in any circumstances, including any innocent question, even those that only implied mild curiosity on an everyday level, a question that may only enquire what my Father does for a living, whether or nor He's a keen fisherman or if has more than two nipples. Sometimes I answered in a tone that would encourage those curious George's amongst us to try their journalistic luck, or at least allow them the possibility of further probing into my trauma. But I concede to the fact the majority of instances would instead see me using a resonance strong enough to ensure an abrupt ending to any such conversations, somewhat symbolising the infamous final scene of 'The Italian Job', leaving just enough room for the partaking audience to ponder over the particulars. Arguably a survival technique if you must.

These diminutive, and what I thought to be subtle, self-defences were used to barricade others out of my solo skirmish, thwarting any chance of other crewmembers joining me on my one-man canoe that was allegorically caught up in a Lunada Bay Wave, or some relevant scene from the Wahlberg / Clooney movie 'The Perfect Storm.' I thought I was protecting others from a pain by keeping silent. I wanted to chaperon all others away from a torture, for it was a discomfort so rife I wouldn't wish it upon anyone, not even those I downright distaste, not even the egotistical Cristiano Ronaldo or the fame hungry 'glamour girl' Katie Price. (Just off topic briefly, but as a freedom fighter and an enthusiast of the Queen's English, I am perplexed at what fragment of this recognised waste of space, formerly known as Jordan, is glamorous! Nonetheless, the show must go on!) However, I understand now that whilst the road to safeguarding others from my bore was paved with good-ish intentions, it was also a detrimental road that worked hand-in-hand with my subconscious in a partnered attempt to close myself off.

I was so worried about opening up to others about my tribulations, as if a sordid clam, that I got lost somewhere along the way. So lost that I found myself in a self-summoned Fort Knox, somehow preventing even I, Billy the King, from hacking into this emotional safe. I was scared that the more others knew about my circumstances, or if these others even knew anything about it, I would put them in an awkward situation. I get embarrassed about imposing something upon others that they are not ready for, something they may not understand. I was petrified and tongue-tied to be the sole creator of an uncomfortable atmosphere. I was alone, possibly by choice, possibly because I cared about how people would perceive me after being dumbstruck by such a broadcast. I didn't want others to distinguish me for what I was dealt with. Yet, it seems I have never had a problem with people distinguishing me for my unnecessary Spike Lee / Kim Jong Il glasses, my dangly earing, attention seeking haircut, flamboyant dress sense or my even more extravagantly loud Jack-in-the-box type personality, which brightly sparkles like some wild Prince of the un-Princely. But, in spite of this constant show, a show that is similar to that of a male peacock, with reference to both the feathered bird and my system of seduction when it comes to sexual philanthropy. The truth, however, is I was afraid of anyone sneaking past my innately high-tech security structure, unless I knew I had absolute jurisdiction over the printing of such sensitive articles.

Nonetheless, I asked my younger brother to give these ramblings of a mad man the once over, maybe even venturing into the unknown with a voice over style oration, out-loud in his head, akin to those Raoul Duke moments in Fear & Loathing. However, his preferred process is not of relevance here, what is though, is the fact that He tells me how things are straight up, no bullshit, with no lingering in the lounge or beating around the bushes. You see, this young squire, who I will patronisingly forever see as my little brother, is seriously switched on and knows exactly how to deal with the frequent balderdash I spew, electively ignoring my knack for wordplay, ignoring the flair, the genius, the elegance, mastery, panache and the pizzazz in which my sun rises and sets.

This time his feedback was somewhat different though. Maybe its because this was the first time I'd conveyed my emotions with him whilst sober and void of any intoxication, that his opening gambit included words like emphatic, unique, excellent and impressive. Words that, for the first time, made me believe I could comfort others. Made me believe my method of writing could highlight the plight of pain whilst encouraging a smile, allowing the reader to wade through the eccentricity and idiosyncrasies in order to actually find something in which they can relate. Something that communicates to the emotions they are feeling, or have felt. I want to say, "Even if this only helps one person I've done my job." But fuck that. Writing isn't my job for one. Writing is my way of portraying what I cannot say aloud, not with the same conviction, glamour or razzmatazz in any case. Thus, the whole point in me getting my sweet little cheeks into gear, and actually writing this tale was to tell the truth, the whole truth and nothing but the truth so help me God (who I envisage to look like Dennis Hopper) whilst this scribble is in place for my benefit as much as yours.

It is for this reason I will continue to take this self prescribed honesty pill, and state that the ambition of my scribbling is to help as many of the helpless as I can, to try and provide hope where it is needed, to idealistically appeal to a congregation of the masses. Bell curve is a phrase I want to avoid, because everyone's situation is different, whether your struggle is bereavement, divorce, dealing with the illness of a loved one or anything. My motivation lies in the knowledge, that through my pain, I have the potential to ease the pain of others, it's just whether I want to try for the stars or not, and whether it happens with this first attempt of unconventional healing, or not, this will not be my only unconventional pursuit of bettering myself, and trying to help others do the same. But Jiminy Cricket, I have spiralled off topic again, addicted to words like a Shakespeare-esque Tim Buckley, so its time to hitchhike back to the relevance of my brother and his critique of my opening gambit.

He didn't hesitate to praise such workings, but there was also no signs of Him dilly-dallying when he said some parts were too dense with chitchat, I was possibly preaching a pinch to much, it was too dark, sometimes scary, and perverted by other similar styles such as my Russell Brand bravura of depiction. He is right, of course, he always is. I always listen to what he has to say, his point of view and his opinion. This is probably due to the fact he's switched on academically, but also because he's in tune with the ways of the world. However, I felt it necessary to clear the murky air that was suffocating my decision to illustrate in this way.

So, let's start off by excusing my style of 'preaching' such resonance. As I have touched on formerly, it is hard to write from any other perspective. However, at no point do I intend on telling you how it is, because I can't. Instead I can only write about my experiences, from my perspective, allowing an insight into how I have come to terms with everything, and I keep my fingers crossed whilst holding onto a four-leaf clover that you will be able relate to this journey. I only know what I've experienced.

Next is the argument that the narrative is too dark. Simply put, being in a situation of despair, no matter what the specifics are, is a dark situation. The only way I could write this was to start off by delving into a place that I was scared to go back to, and that is a dark place. But, its also only the beginning of what becomes peculiarly positive, and thus this narrative stance will progress and blossom in a way that's comparable to a flower, or more equivalently Emma Watson, Alexa Vega or even Joseph Gordon-Levitt. (All of whom I would happily wake up next too, even though they were upsettingly ugly kids. Whilst the pillow talk possibility with JGL is very dependent on my inebriation levels.)

I wasn't a depressive, a downer, a threat to society or a monotonous drifter, wandering a bleak landscape, absent from all happiness and glee, with no knowledge of how to smile. In fact, due to my ability to chuck all negativity and callous emotions into a hidden and unbreakable safe ninety per cent of the time, I was the embodiment of merry. For sake of context, its that uncomfortable time again when I have to toot my own saxophone for no other reason than to ascertain the state of my mind, body and soul I portrayed for that ninety per cent, hardly containing the Cheshire cat grin that has always played the leading role in my ensemble of features. So in a flurry of adjectives to describe my mood that was so clearly contaminated with positivity, I exposed that Sunday-best side of myself, in which I am a jubilant, perky, effervescent, upbeat, nonchalant, affable, sprightly, chipper, passionately whimsical and an animatedly lustful gentleman that far prefers being high on life, wrapped up in the golden ride that cloud nine vivaciously offers, than that of the prickly flipside. But, as much as I would love to remain forever an optimist with my head in the cumulonimbus, it is far from the purpose of this scripture. For my sole aim is to benefit those who need it, in their dark times, especially as I'm of the opinion that no one who is high on the natural heroine of life is in need of a helping hand in dealing with such euphoria. Yet more specifically, the kind of euphoria that is associated with rewarded certainty, like 'Chunky Monkey' ice cream or something 'Very Berry' in one's immediate future, for that's the extreme level of euphoria I'm sermonising.

MY HURT, MY PAIN, MY STORY

As I stated earlier, my tactful yet insensitive and inbuilt response, which didn't stretch further than declaring, 'my Father was killed in a private plane crash in Mozambique on my 3rd day at university", only allowed the listener a limited insight into the terrifying truth. A truth, that once I let it get hold of my cerebral cortex, became an incessant and irresistible cramp that no amount of electrolytes could counteract. In any case, now seems as good a time as any to suck it up and do what I have not been able to do since that life-changing event which took place on September 20th 2008.

This 'thing' I speak of is opening up. Putting my memories, feelings and despondencies out there in the universe, presenting a part of me that I've hidden for so long. Exclusively endorsing my emotions the freedom to wander around in the public domain, exposed for all to see. You see, unleashing my intimate outlook is that something, I don't know what exactly, but that something I needed to do in order to once again safeguard my progress, cementing a consequential act that has the capacity to help others. A quantum leap of selflessness into a sea of emotional uncertainty, all for those three sisters I have grown so fond of and all of whom I never want to stop sleeping with; Clarity, Acceptance & Progress! (Ironically, 'Clarity' does actually sound like a devious & dark-haired damsel I definitely, maybe would.)

Nonetheless, my new playground was to be set amongst a backdrop of dreaming spires, and located within the recreation yard known as Oxford Brookes University. This was eye's on stalks crazy scary though, for I didn't know anyone when I started at this establishment of further education, but then again, that was one of the reasons why I chose to attend such a school. It was the excitement of uncertainty, the thought of fresh acquaintances, and the chance to explore who I was without any vices. So my Mum and my unofficial step-dad, Harry, were the chosen compatriots who dropped me off, assisting me through the standard sequence of signing in, locating the room I would spend the next year dwelling within, and lending me a hand with the unpacking of my unnecessary collection of belongings, all in the name of a bullshit ritual, one set up by the powers at be, and one that we all have partake in.

I say it like I despised it, but I didn't really. Yes, it was a boring and tedious task, but it was somehow adrenaline-charged and nerve-wracking. This non-stop fun was then followed by my interpretation of 'The Last Supper' although the setting was one I believe to be somewhat different from the bible, yet better than what Jesus supposedly dabbled in on his last night. I mean I did the whole restaurant thing, great food, fine wine, good company, toasts, speeches and the clinking of champagne glasses, or at least this is the blurred evening I remember. However, it's not blurred in the way that I was used to, which is usually as a direct result of mixing hops, with grapes, and the throwing about of spirits here and there. But rather, it was an evening blurred for another reason altogether.

You see, at this meal, or in fact just before, whilst I was enjoying a cigarette in a magnificent courtyard, I received an international phone call from Dad. My Dad wasn't there to drop oneself off at Uni, for he was on one of his frequent business trips to South Africa and Mozambique, dealing with timber, diamonds, Jatropha or whatever. However, he nonetheless gave me some fatherly words of advice in his husky voice, whilst he also lovingly took the piss out of me a tad as I was attending the Oxford 'polytechnic' and he was a graduate of Teddy Hall, a college of the actual Oxford University. However, he then seemingly broke character a bit, with his very last words, and moreover, very lasting words. Words that croaked out, words that I always strived to hear. Words that due to their tone, context and rarity, were genuine and heartfelt. These words that echoed down the phone as Dad spoke to me were, "I'm proud of you Will, and I love you, now remember one thing... Work hard in the morning, play hard in the afternoon and seek nothing but damn fine company in the evening." And this, unbeknown to me at the time, was the last time I ever spoke to my Dad.

Now don't get me wrong, I'm usually the first to jump at the chance of calling something horrendously Hollywood clichéd, but this wasn't. This was a jubilant moment I can take comfort in, an occasion I do take comfort in and a celebratory scene that I am lucky I can celebrate. It's hard to explain context to others, but when the candle goes out and reality really kicks in, I believe you only need to be able to explain it to yourself. However, to keep this context uncomplicated and short, the uncompromising step-monster, Ayesha, had quite simply prevented me from living with my Dad for the last 4 months of his life, and subsequently and for obvious reasons, this is the only regret I have in my life.

However, as I stated, the fact this was my last conversation with my Dad was unbeknown to me at the time, thus this memoir must continue accordingly. So, two days after that feast fit for any variation of King or Queen, the 'rebellious' and 'maverick' side of my personality reared its rather good-looking head. You see I broke the rules like some immensely mild Scarface. I mean, I acted in a way that any immature, MC Hammer influenced you-can't-touch-this type of nineteen-year-old chap would have. I ignored the pathetic policies and the rueful rulebook of my campus that stated no overnight visitors were allowed within the confines of one's room and I did the polar opposite. I became a felon by welcoming my then-domestic partner, Lily, to my new abode for a long weekend, all the while keeping my middle finger up to the irrelevant commandments of my university halls.

Apologies, for such a hype-erecting-build-up to my mischievous ways, but I couldn't avoid creating an anti-climaxing crescendo, somewhat like the first time I saw a picture of Kate Middleton's pixelated boobs. Anyway, I don't remember what the missus and me did on that Friday night, for my memory of this evening is rather overshadowed. Instead, I only remember fragments of the following day, fragments that are etched into my memory. Fragments that I can still see now, with a clarity and astuteness so sharp, that, at times, I find it hard to differentiate between the past and present.

I remember getting ready to step into the shower, about to step under the warm, relaxing and purposeful waterfall, before I saw an incoming phone call from the then unaccepting Ayesha. In fact, such a call was a modern-day phenomenon as rare as small pox or Dodo dandruff. Nonetheless, I ignored it, too joyful to voluntarily put myself in the firing line of a fall out with my Dads wife, or consciously jump in the way of an inevitable bad mood bullet. So, I carried on with my medial task and I got into the shower. However, upon my exit, and after the subsequent grooming that is associated with a metrosexual male, I received another incoming call from Ayesha. This time round I reluctantly answered my out-dated Samsung, but nonetheless I answered it. Anyway, all I can remember of this conversation, crackling in the light of poor reception, is hearing her Zulu accent and the devastating words, "Your Dad... involved in... train crash." Struggling to understand, I asked her to repeat this mayday call. "Your Dad has... been in a train crash!" That's the full extent of the details I was given, thus immediately confused by the fact I heard train. You see, I knew my old man, and he was a notorious adventurer and fearless adrenaline-junkie, who wouldn't take a train in Mozambique, ever.

Nonetheless, I didn't know what to do. I didn't know who to call or where to look. What's more, I was also trying to explain what I had heard to my better half Lily, whilst hurt by the knowledge that I didn't have any answers, for neither her nor myself. I was completely lost, but I was not without hope, for I was used to the rebellious lifestyle of my Pop. Anyway, I grabbed my out-dated mobile again, putting the receiver to my ear in a modernised attempt to call my Mum. Just from her voice, her rickety unsteady voice, I knew something was up. I can't remember all of this discussion either, but maybe this is a direct result of me blocking out some of the more harrowing moments of my past.

Maybe it was due to the scale of shock that had paralysed me, as if I was under the influence of an emotive puppeteer. What I do remember though, is some of the reproaching clarification I needed to hear. However, this clarification simply amplified my understanding, nay, my need to be worried. I was in completely unfamiliar and foreign territory and deep behind enemy lines, for I had never needed to be worried about my Dad before. There was this history of car crashes, motorbike mishaps, combine calamities and plummeting planes, although the latter was in 1981 and thus before I was welcomed into this wonderful world, so I guess that's why I wasn't required to be worried about such a devastating wreck of an aircraft crash. But this time, this time I did have that worry, trying to control that aggravated vexation. For this breaking news couldn't have hit me harder if I was on the receiving end of an unexpected Haymaker from David Haye himself.

I remember Mum told me my Dad had been involved in a private plane crash in Mozambique, and that there was an optimistic one per cent chance of my hero surviving. I couldn't control the waterworks. There were tears streaming down my face as I unwillingly continued to unsteadily hold the phone to my ear, trying to find any hope or assurance in this tirade of unhopeful and down right pessimistic information. Even now I struggle, for this personalised newscast was so agonising that even now I cannot find the right words. My back hit the corridor wall, whilst I simultaneously dropped my phone as if being riddled with fifty rounds of 'Tommy Gun' fire. Slow motion yet frenzied. The only thing that was missing from this apocalyptic scene was the visible blood trail as I slid down the white vertical partition, paralysed by shock. This was a combination of reactions that should never be proficient in real-life, but instead kept to the cinema screens, akin to the lobby scene in the original Matrix movie.

I was lost. I was completely lost. I was with the one person I wanted to be with, but the one person I didn't want to involve. Absolutely alone, absent from my friends, whilst geographically distanced from my family. I was heartbroken by the fact I wasn't there for my Mum, and struck by guilt that I couldn't embrace my younger brother Oli, for he was the one person that mattered the most to me in that overwhelming instant. I didn't want to be there to bullshit him and say everything would be dandy, but instead to ensure him I would make it as tolerable as possible. I wanted to be there for my Mum, for despite the fact my parents were divorced, they had an incredible bond, the ability to console in the other during their time of need, and a common focus in doing what was right for my brother Oli & of course myself, and thus I knew she would have been as hurt by this horrendous news as I.

I had no one at University to abruptly approach with this abrupt news. I wasn't friends with anyone yet, or at least I didn't have any friends I was close enough too, and even if I did, I didn't know how to annunciate the news I myself had only just heard. However, I knew I had to, so in a raffle style process of elimination, I pretty much just pulled a name out of an upside down top hat. I got the words out and told someone, eventually, although there was not a lot of detail to accompany this shocking sentence. This upsetting experience, where I was forced to spill the most repulsive beans, was then followed by a truly traumatic train ride, one that takes the top spot of any troublesome train ride competition. Lily and I had a four-hour journey that allowed my imagination to run a riot, depicting what I thought to be unimaginable scenarios. You're right though; the one per cent chance given to my Dad should have prevented any glimmer of expectation or hope, as it was a miniscule chance indeed. But, given the participating party, or more specifically the fact that my Father seemed so unbreakable, this cursory chance usually bolstered my ability to smile in the face of such apparent adversity. Nonetheless, I don't remember any of that joyless journey.

It's possible I was pondering in silence. Maybe I was trying to silence this subject in favour for trivial chitchat with Lily instead. Maybe it was a combination of both, riddled with moments where spoken encouragement was needed. However, I can recollect one image, an image that has stuck with me in the same way I've retained the memory of sliding down the corridor wall, unable to stand any longer. I remember looking out of the train window only to witness a by-plane, much like the Piper Seneca my Dad would have been in moments earlier, with this symbolic picture flying alongside us, following the blueprint laid out in front of the train, following the tracks as they cut through the countryside. I was rendered utterly immobilised to this symbolic distraction, defenceless, unable to look away, greeting the warm tears as they rolled down my face, like trickling pearls of memories, annexed to my tenderly benign cheeks, imprisoned by the grooves that were etched into my skin.

Next in the memory bank is my arrival into the nippy Norwich railway station, setting the scene for my next nostalgic flashback. There I was, walking towards my 'stepfather', Harry, who was stood shoulder to shoulder with other familiar faces, overwhelming my emotions with the mortifying mural that decorated their saddened appearances. An hours excursion by car subsequently ensued, riding shotgun with Harry trying his best to keep me optimistic. However, even his smokescreen wasn't as thick as it could have been; yet this was possibly a purposeful effort. Once again my memory is flawed somewhat, with gaps like a Swiss cheese, ostensibly overwhelmed by the situation I guess. However, I do remember Harry telling me of a heart-to-heart chinwag he had with my old man in the early days, a tête-à-tête arising after Harry told my Pa of his blossoming romance with my Mum. Dad's response, "You have my blessing, I just don't want to lose my boys." Well I can safely say we'll always be his boys.

This spontaneously necessary journey was long, full of trivial talk, skin-deep trifling, moments of meaning, waterworks stimulated by painful ponderings and a blurred awareness of my surroundings. But still, all I wanted to do was be there for my brother, Oli, to hear the shocking story from him, to hear his voice, his thoughts, to clutch this blood related pillar of mine, and with just a look, make the perpetual promise to always be there for one another, knowing it was me and him against the world now, forever cementing that you and me against the world brotherly bond.

I stumbled through the door, my body crumbling under the weight of what was becoming more and more apparent, only to be welcomed into the warmth of my home, which understandably and blatantly bared no warmth at all. For the first time it was an unfamiliar shelter and nothing more. But in spite of all this, I carried myself up the stairs, into the kitchen, and embraced Oli, a hug that showed emotion on such a level that even the Ernest Hemingway's and Jack Kerouac's of this world couldn't have captured, for its true meaning was superior to any combination of words.

It is a brotherly bond that has always been there but rarely spoken about. Combined with a sincere love, stability and strength that showed an equal support and acceptance, knowing that whatever the next page of this inevitable horror story displayed, it was to be a battle fought against the odds, a battle where us brothers resembled those brave Spartans that were faced with an enemy army of limitless proportions. A tsunami of hardship was sure to ensue, but as unprepared as we were, this bond settled me in for the lengthy storm that was undeniably approaching. It may seem like an oxymoronic statement, like jumbo shrimp, open relationship or acting naturally, but it was comforting to hear the uncomfortable news directly from my brother, albeit flaky in its detail. It secured a bond that will always prevail, unlike the family fallouts of others, the type that the modern day has come to accept as the norm.

Anyway, I'm sure I wasn't expected to sleep that night, which is lucky because if it had been a module or exam in sleeping (and I'm certain there probably is a university or college somewhere that offers such a prestigious degree) I would have failed, spectacularly. Moreover, with nothing but the knowledge of a plane crash, an uncertain list of passengers, the knowledge of some fatalities although no names attached, and the scantily slender chance of Dad defying the odds again, it was a night of who, what, where, when, how and what if's.

When the following morning finally dawned on me, I was lost preparing myself for reality, trembling from exhaustion, for I was physically and emotionally fatigued, watching the sunrise through the bedroom curtains, urging me to rise in a similar manner. I then headed upstairs, about to completely cover the coffee table in house phones, mobiles, pagers, laptops and homing pigeons in the unbearable wait for any additional news. However, as I arrived on the first floor, I was drawn to the living room by nothing more than quiet chatter, only to find my sensational soldier of a Mum accompanied in an unobtrusive conversation with Harry and my Godfather, Guardian and Dad's best friend, Paul Whittome. Even to this day I couldn't have wished to wake up on that Sunday morning to the comforting arms of anyone else but

PW.

Unlike the arty aspersions of independent films though, which ceaselessly cast visuals of rainy days, weather-beaten houses of distress, billowing whitecap waves or whatever heightened falsifications they choose to characterise, my remembrance of this reality is admittedly more absent, but nonetheless unfeigned and candid. Nevertheless, it didn't take many ticks of the clock to receive more news, in which my well-founded family, whether immediate, extended or those that were adopted along the way, we were all rocked by the newly established and horrifying verification. There were no survivors out of the six passengers on board the light aircraft. This included the vindictively validating news that we lost our good friends Johan and Louise, and the earth-shattering confirmation of my Dads death. Fuck I wasn't prepared, and I tortuously recoiled at the fact I was ruthlessly prevented from saying goodbye to him. I was riddled with emotion, but stabilised by my upbringing, for I knew deep down what Dad would have wanted me to do.

My first thoughts, be there for my family, and more specifically to dedicate myself to my two younger brothers, Oli then 17, and Zack then 6 months. In fact, my only thoughts consisted of them. I can't make comparisons, nor take any level of credit or praise for the way I dealt with those days and weeks after this tragedy. You see, in my intellectual imagination, I acted this way inherently, but I also acted in a way I believed most people would, with heart, like always. It is so impossibly hard to covey a lot of what was occurring at this time, what I can convey though, and convey with earnest conviction, is my pride in my family. The way we pulled together, albeit in our own fucked up family way. Proud of the way my brother Oli characteristically became his Dad, becoming a mature adolescent and a wise fatherly figure in much the same way it was indigenous in me too. But witnessing this first hand was something unforgettable and truly exceptional. I'm proud of the way my Mum became the rock, never once floundering, and always showing true grit. In all hell raising and rock n roll honesty, I'm epileptically proud to have friends and family like we do, for everyone proved they are more than supportive, comforting, generous, caring, responsible and first and foremost, unfaltering, and in a time where there was nothing to prove.

As you can imagine, I loved my Dad so very much. He was my rock, my go to guy, the answer to any and every problem. He embodied the wise words I often required, and there was this noticeable breath of fresh air when you were in his presence. He was intelligent, caring and committed. He would give you his full attention, his full support and you could be damn sure he would be on the touchlines of every sporting event Oli & I were involved in, no matter how bizarre. He had this warmth that was so unique. He was a determined and ambitious man, someone whom would always find a way to succeed in his task, and he was possibly an exception to the conventional policies given he was a maverick of his day, acknowledging the rules, but bending them at every chance. He was the kind of Father that would always be on the side of the teacher in any mishap at school, and more often than not, he was right to do so too. He could be short-tempered of course, and on occasion he wouldn't hesitate to crack the whip, however, he would always feel truly awful and maybe even a touch guilty about it afterwards. He was the kind of fatherly fellow that encouraged his sons to stand on their own to feet and to fight for what they believed in, which inevitably created numerous Good Will Hunting type scenes. Unfortunately I don't mean that in a school janitor mathematical genius sort of comparison, but in a confrontation of obstinate and inordinate minds sort of way, a close quarter combat of words type scene, comparable to that of Robin Williams versus Matt Damon.

But even with our differences occasionally slipping to the surface, Dad was a sincerely caring man and an unquestionably loyal friend. But most of all, he defined what it is to be a family man, the epitome of what a Dad should be, at least in my biased opinion. He was the type of guy who would leave all his hardships and bullshit at the door, a protector and a fantastic Father. I accept I may have weaned out numerous negatives and bad memories, sticking to my stubborn wishful thinking and optimism, but that's just who I am, and that's probably a result of my unpractised reaction process. In any case, whilst I would like to make one of those humorous comparisons I am so clearly addicted to, one that would inspire you with a daft and eccentric understanding of this man, I simply can't. Instead I can only construe him as an exclusive rebellious individual, an unprecedented exception, a novel in his own right, and quite simply, a one off unique being, the polar opposite of a dial tone and the embodiment of a perpetually consistent adventure.

As always, it's a long-shot-toss-up-type guess as to why I'm opening up via the time old medium of putting pen to paper, but there are some vague reasons that I can just about make out in this crystal ball of mine.

The fact this method is a first for me could be introduced as one reason, for it is a means of exploration, and one that each of us is allowed to travel down. However, I only suggest this for I really am aware of how unbreakably hard it is to open up verbally, and give some oomph to the thoughts inside your head. Another figurative image materialising in this Mystic Meg scenario is one that revolves around my own personal gamble. You see if I lay it all out for all to gander at, if I do the one thing that scares me most and become the open book I've turned a deaf ear to for so many moons, then I'm promisingly progressing, whilst you may also be able to deduce and recognise the pain I speak of, a win-win situation, and one that is making my Calvin Klein Y-fronts more than just a wee bit wet.

Now I'm not saying that my experiences or situations are in the same ballpark as yours, not by any means, but they could damn well be part of the same sport. What's more, and at the very least, such honesty could be gospel proof that I'm not a vacant carcass completely stuffed to the brim with bullshit, but instead it shows that I have indeed suffered like you, providing some sort of grandiose grounds for invisible trust. I accept I'm not the most idealist concept or mirage of what a councillor should be. I accept that at the infant age of twenty-four, I am arguably too young to be a representative of this weight-on-the-shoulders kind of role, as if trying to be some sort of copycat Atlas. But in spite of all this, I couldn't justify not saddling up and at least attempting a shot at the greater good.

I've just about tried every other hackneyed and prosaic technique, so why not attempt a selfless act, reliving my pain to ease that of others, offering a point of view that makes this mandatory space-shuttle ride towards helping others seem worth while. This is especially true given I know how it feels for happiness and clarity to seem as though they're located in a galaxy far, far away. To me, its trial and error on a grand scale and an attempt to shoot for the stars, because even if I only make it half way, I can still revel in the knowledge that I've escaped that secluded Sauron inside and tried to do something much bigger than I. Maybe it's self-important, but because my wounds are still wretchedly raw and my healing process is still so present and relevant, I am beginning to have a buoyant belief that maybe I can step up to the mark and embody a new approach, simply knowing that you, the bibliophile, are helping me as much as I hope to help you. Anyway I've wandered off topic, again.

So, the ensuing weeks and months, after my Dad was killed, became participants in an estranged epoch, which I preferably refuse to put a time frame on, for I view this period in my existence as one blurred and frenzied circus of life lessons, like an unidentifiable jungle with hostilities at every glade. You see, as a family we had to deal with media questions and presumptions that appeared to concentrate on the fact my old man was a former Member of the European Parliament, fixated on the political history of his life and almost shelving the notion that he was primarily a Father, husband and family man. Then there were the crash scene investigations and the consequential reports of these unwanted groupies. On top of this we had to learn how to deal with the consistently nauseating contagion of perception, knowing that each excruciating element was glued together by the speculations of external parties. It was like an unsympathetic and suffocating Spanish Inquisition for fuck sake. Worse than all this though, was the fact all of the afore mentioned were being dragged out and muddied by the corruption that riddles the South-East African authorities, with lawful and political perversion so rife it could've be confused with the conspiracies of 'Serpico' or 'LA Confidential'. It was a long process that seemed to be overhauled by obligation.

I had to weather the storm of bullshit procedures, and persevere through the relentless onslaught from the said factors above, both unethical and misunderstood. It was a cancerous concoction, a bottomless cocktail of delicate discomfort, cumbersome situations and saddening retentions, all elongated by a dishonest system. In addition to this, the CSI reports, insurance schemes and news broadcasts were all accumulating my agitation, whilst there was plenty of bitch-slapping bureaucracy that couldn't see the damage it was inflicting, such as the attempts to get my Father's body back from Beira (North Mozambique), the search for the truth of what happened and why the plane fell out of the sky, to name just a few. Of course I was aware that none of this red tape or paperwork play dough was going to change the past and nor was it ever going to ease the aching pain, but that truth didn't help either. Don't get me wrong, I know this sort of form filling official procedure is necessary, but it's methods of administrative speculation is exceptionally extensive and bitterly cold hearted.

'Bitterly cold hearted' may seem a tad harsh given these persons of authority simply have a job to do, but to me, my chosen words don't do their speculative and damn right disgusting research enough damning justice. No words possibly can. You see, I remember receiving a bible thick documentation from the CSI team, the one that was meant to supposedly clarify why the plane dropped like a rock from thousands of feet up in the sky. There was a lot of jibber jabber in their document, the formalities of formal dialect and the standard beating around the bush of governmental organisations. Now I don't read my utility bills properly. I don't read the T&Cs of any contract I sign, so I probably don't own my own soul anymore. Hell, I don't even read the short but sweet messages in my Birthday cards (I simply open them upside down and pay attention only if something cheque shaped falls out). But this document, this I went through with a fine toothcomb and a microscope. And what was the calculated outcome of the authorities' scrutiny... the pilot Johan 'Rooikat' Wessels was at fault and main reason for the plane's crash.

Bollocks. Complete and utter made up bollocks. I knew Rooikat, I've flown with Rooikat numerous times and I even lived with Rooikat and his wife. He was the opposite of the statements made, with the report stating he wasn't licensed to fly the plane that crashed. Now that's some serious scraping of the barrel and analysis only put in place so they can point the finger elsewhere, a notion that still hurts a lot today. Rooikat was an unbelievable pilot, and that's not just coming from my first hand knowledge of him. He was a former military pilot and had accumulated more than 518 hours in commercial flight time. For both these reasons, I don't think experience can be questioned on any level and I still find it so brutally painful to think Johan's name was thrown about amongst the reasons for the plane's demise and the deaths of all on board. The plane's left engine was one-hundred-and-eighty flight hours overdue a service, a major fault, and that's where the buck stops in my opinion and in my heart. The inconclusive investigation of the SA authorities proved very little to me, very little except the level of corruption that is strife in Africa, and this went on for over three years. Three years of ferocious fuckwits covering their own arses and three years of cold-hearted deductions that ensured the mourning process was dragged out and complicated by more than semi-perpetual anger.

Nevertheless, the day after Oli and I received the chilling confirmation that cleared up the murky waters of the rumour mill, we had a television interview, throwing us into the deep end of an emotional response but enlightening us to what our Dad's political impact meant to others, whilst also proving there really is no rest for the wicked. Credit where credit is due though, for these reporters, anchors and interviewers were all respectful and delicate with their line of inquiry. Christ on a punctured unicycle, even the boom dude was on best behaviour. Now of course these questions had been conversed a touch prior to the lights, camera, action and clapperboard moment, but even so, it was news that was steak tartare kind of raw to my family and I. Quite simply, it was a gut punching phenomenon and a hard-hitting bottom line that shattered my family's world, far more than the notion of it being news for the general public. It was a fragile first interview at a fragile time, but it was handled with heart, and for that I am grateful.

Now I am not oblivious to the surreal, for I myself find the memory of being questioned and quizzed by a TV crew for the six o'clock news unbelievable, but the context and practise was no different from what I still experience now. I mean, broaching the topic of 'my Dad was killed' with anyone is daunting, browbeating, consternating, intimidating and thwarting, whether it involves friends, lecturers, the parents of perspective partners, interviewers, The Biker Mice from Mars or any other acquaintances. It drags up the same disdaining emotions, but it remains unavoidable for us all, no matter who the recipient.

Anyway, once this uphill challenge was out of the way, it was onto the next confronting task, although what faced us next was akin to 'The Travelator' from the 90s TV show 'The Gladiators', the only difference being this one seemed insurmountable. What is the task I speak of? Funeral preparations. This is an event which offers that fucked up feeling any teenager would unwantedly endure when having to attend the funeral of a loved one, especially a precious parent, and witness the horrifying moment they are placed in the ground or charcoaled in an oven.

This was not easy, not only in the emotional sense of such dictation, but with regards to the organisational and administrative skills required. It demanded and commanded a nerve of steel, for we had to keep a level head in the face of such a paralysing realisation. I can't thank those who helped enough though, for we had a great 'team' around us, a flamboyance of family friends organising what needed organising and patiently dealing with the red tape. Their involvement was seemingly innate and their assistance became second nature, such as getting Dads body back from the authorities in Mozambique to the shores of the UK, and then to the humble hamlet that I call home. People really stepped up to relieve as much of the burden as they could, knowing that Oli and I had our own provisions. These were probably just distractions from the actualities that were swallowing us whole, but nonetheless they were provisions that were categorically crucial, morally of course, but on a personal level more than anything. These included the decision-making processes of what hymns should be squawked by the congress, the seating plan, the flowers, the readings and who was to orate these readings et cetera et cetera.

This isn't easy. In fact it's worthy of any antonyms of the word easy, for it's conceivably the most arduous thing you may ever stumble across. I'm not referring to the coordinating, management or technical support of such an event, in which you essentially become nothing more than a ruffled and rattled roadie. No, I'm referring to the emotional weight that will get on top of you at frequently fucked up intervals, much like a menstruating mountain moose, and a male one at that. But don't fight the feelings that get thrown about. Cry. Shake. Weep. Yell. Just let it out. Let the tears flow like Sutherland Falls. After all, everyone is there to help you and to be there for you. They are trying to take as much of the pressure of you as possible. They are taking up tasks that they may have never previously done, and what's more, they are doing it above and beyond their ability, all to ensure the celebrations of this loved ones life are perfect. But despite all of this, what their true skills consist of, as your closest friends and family, is their ability to be a shoulder, to comfort you and let you know that they will be here for you every step of this shit-storm journey. This is a gut-wrenching time of newfound heights, and as such no one expects you to be handling it in the same way a robot would, without any reaction.

However, this is easier said than done, for the hardest part now is to allowing yourself to react emotionally. I mean, that bag of useless pride needs to be dropped dude and the daunting realities that are covered in some sort of bubble wrap of shock need to be embraced, for your own good. It doesn't matter whether you are a fifteen-year-old bereavement casualty or a ninety-eight year old survivor. Accept any help that is offered from others. Accept that this is an emotional time of exceptional destitution and thus allow yourself to express such feelings. In fact, I beseech you, don't try and hide your feelings, and definitely don't try and hide from them.

Don't get me wrong, my telepathic abilities tend to falter a tad when they are required on a grand scheme, thus I am unable to speculate at which principal pain and upset you found to be the toughest to endure during those first days after losing someone. Mine, however, was the eulogy, or for want of a better word, my tribute, weeping over which words would be closest to providing absolute justice. I'm just grateful to my godfather and the fact he was there to comfort my nerves, enlightening me to the fact the congregation would to be the most sympathetic crowd I would ever speak in front of, with these words alleviating my worries no end.

However, the on mass audience wasn't the foundation to my tensions, unfortunately. Instead my anxieties were based around the fact I just wanted to do my Dad proud. I wanted to portray his uniqueness in a way that would promise the audience more than justice, not with the flurried flair of words that could distract the listener from what I wanted to say, but to enthral and enchant them with the actual truth of my perspectives. No doubt this was a pressurised ambition, especially given my Dad was an orator by profession, for he was a politician, a speechwriter, a no-notes-speak-from-the-heart type of dude, and he showed this competent capability of his at the funeral of my grandfather, his Father, who had expired only six months prior to the death of my Pop. It was not a challenge, nor was it a way for me to compare myself to him by any means. Instead, it was a way in which I could equate, to know I had made him proud, to know I had done his spectacular life more than genuine justice.

Anyway, funeral day is like surfing a tsunami of emotion, with waves of uncontrollable sentiment breaking around you without warning, rhythm or regulation. There's getting into that lifeless limo with a precession of teary-eyed family following the body of a loved. There's a predestined route of black cars that steadily rumble down memory lane. The promotion of an undisturbed silence made up of flashbacks and comradery, a family so together in proximity, yet separated by the thoughts of each individual, so close and yet so far away from one another. There is the arrival at the church, the pictures of sadness splattered across the familiar faces that you regularly frequent, as well as those that you don't. There are those smiles of reassurance that you politely return, not realising your reaction, before you step into the awe-inspiring volume of flowers that is simply a veneer to cover up the true sadness of such an event.

I remember being arm in arm with my brother and step mother, Oli and I flanking Ayesha side by side, supporting her I guess, whilst inhabited by the pain that such a day brings, and encompassed by the fear of saying a personal goodbye for the last time. I remember this unlikely threesome following the coffin as it paraded down the cobbled and stony path towards the weather beaten arches of the Church, before simultaneously taking a large inhale, looking at one another sympathetically before we stepped into the overcrowded lions den that was unhesitant in stirring up the anxiety within. But more rousingly, there was a wave of pride that shuddered around my body. I guess it was just seeing the sheer volume of people who came to this holy construction to pay their respects, for seeing first hand the vast impact this male parent of mine had had on so many was exceptionally emotional, yet it was also somewhat encouraging, as we walked down the aisle towards the front row seats of this funeral for a friend.

As has become so common amidst this frenetic time of my life, my capable memory is limited to narrowed specifics, thus I can only remember certain parts of this significant service. However I do remember choking up as I tried to bellow out the lyrics to the hymn 'Jerusalem'. I remember my brother's bravery in standing at the lectern and magnificently orating Dads favourite poem. I remember walking out of the church at the end of the service to Toto Africa (A song that I previously loved and now subsequently cannot listen too) and I remember every second of standing at the pulpit, looking out across the nave and delivering my very personal tribute.

I started strong, for I wrote the eulogy in such a way that it would ensure such an assurance, looking past the crowds to the back of the room, knowing the inevitably teary outcome should I connect with a familiar face of vulnerability. However, as I went on, getting to my relationship with this rock of mine, it became tougher and tougher to stay resilient, with my pronunciation reaching Usain Bolt speeds, witnessing the nerves arise to such an extent I would have made King George VI seem as confident as Barack Obama in any spotlight situation, at least that's how it felt from my standpoint.

I was trying to fight back the sniffles and cries of a heartbroken son, all the while ensuring my voice propelled the eloquently meaningful words, as if I was a jacked up gramophone that could expose true heart. In hindsight, I guess I wanted to be in control of what melancholy I exposed, wanting to seem robust and immovable, but that's not who I am. You see, this is no time to put in a Daniel Day-Lewis type performance, but rather it is a time to embrace your emotions, promoting nothing but a sincerely authentic tribute. A homage that has been tidied up by thoughtful words and delivered by candid and bona fide expression, equitably bearing all, not for the spectators, but as a last hoorah from you to your loved one.

But now that I have shed some sort of light over this discursion of mine, and highlighted my plight as a notable need to establish some sort of new and internal relationship of truth with myself, I feel serenely comforted. What's more, I believe that once I have inaugurated this mentality into my every day being, I can then try and encourage others, that are in a similar ball park, to do the same, maybe even providing some kind of direction to those that are lost. Thus, with this in mind, the next step I am to force upon my unwilling self is one of sharing. So to kick off the proceedings, and in a similar way to that of any school bell style distinctive ringing, let me share with you my eulogy, my salutation and adulation, and what was ultimately my tribute to the man I knew as Dad.

Eulogy

My Tribute

"Paul Howell. My Father would be so proud of his constituency to see how much love and support his name still brings even after 14 years out of the political limelight, and the affection showed by everyone reminds us all why he loved Norfolk with all his heart and fought for it with all his might.

My Mum, Johanna, was a huge part of my Fathers life during his political career and the two of them were very much a team, travelling to areas such as Russia and Belize together, with Mum behind the scenes but still a great factor in Dads success. She tells me of my Father's political career and his concern for others, points he would talk to me about. He was among those who highlighted the plight of the minority Kurds in Iraq and Iran, terrorised by then leader Saddam Hussein. He was the first European Member of Parliament to visit Chernobyl in the aftermath of the nuclear disaster and sympathised with the local Russian population and those affected. He also successfully campaigned in favour of getting Europe to ban the importation of seal cub pelts from Canada. Closer to home, Dad was completely engaged with the outer harbour project at Great Yarmouth and was involved with Bernard Matthews regarding the Caister Lifeboat.

As you can imagine, my memory of Dad as a politician is very vague and only from old newspaper articles, the internet and from what many people tell me, including my. Father from time to time, can I truly get an idea of how much he loved politics and how much of an impact and difference he made throughout the World, never forgetting Norfolk. However, I do still have some memories, brought back by old photographs, of me on the canvassing coach in my 'Vote for Paul Howell' and 'Vote for Dad' jumpers, next to 'The Team' all with matching tops with the same support shown on both the jersey itself and in the pleasure shown on all their faces. It is as much these moments, why my Dad was in love with what he did whilst making a difference.

These memories I have of what I can only describe as my Hero and Idol, are all of this colourful, energetic, fun, larger than life man who made the most out of everything and ensured that everyday with him was going to be an adventure or as once described, 'a successful disaster'. And to compliment this enthusiastic and entertaining side of my Dad was this amazing level of intelligence and inspiration, he was my 'go to' man, as there was rarely something he didn't know, but when there was, Oliver and I would let him know about it. He was the life and soul of the party, a breath of fresh air with his cheerfulness and warmth. Yet amongst all this, there was still room for this fearless maverick who had a real love for uncertainty, and ensured there would never be a dull moment with him. It is easy to see why he was such a huge impact on all of us and why he will leave an enormous void in our lives.

My Dads life turned out with all its twists and turns and ups and downs, and that was a constant if not a guarantee. However, he would always ask the rhetorical question to Oliver and I in his defining low growl, "You wouldn't want a boring life anyway, would you?" to which we would both reply, "Dad we are Howells and more specifically your sons, excitement is a certainty."

On the subject of family, it is imperative that I note where a great deal of my Dads strength and happiness came from in the last 3 years, and that was his everlasting love for his wife, Ayesha, and youngest son, Zack, whom he loved with everything his heart could give, and Oliver and I are very proud to call Ayesha our step-mum and Zack our brother.

Everything valuable about life, and how to deal with the rollercoaster ride of living, was taught to me by my Father. But as well as this he showed us how to deal with the more important aspects that only experience can teach. He taught me to stand by what I believed in and to never leave my principles, even if it's a disagreement with your own Father! A lesson I paid a little too much attention too! He taught me that honesty and loyalty are two of the most important principles to live by, even if that means you must stand-alone. He also taught me to keep my chin up and smile, no matter how tough the situation. To never give up, something my Father passionately lived by. These are all lessons my Dad would still stand by today and just some of the reasons why I am so proud of him. But above all else he was the perfect model of how to be a devoted Father and taught me that no matter what else is happening in your life, your family comes first. It is this lesson that he proved to us every day and every night, and showed us, is the most important one of all. To a lot of you he was the flamboyant, charismatic European Member of Parliament and Strasbourg's Mr Norfolk, but to my brother Oliver and to myself, he was simply Dad, a fun loving Family man, who we will never forget, and I am immensely proud to be son, of Paul Howell."

Christ the mangina rocking cosmic cowboy, this cohort of phraseology, commonly known as a eulogy, that has acquired squatters rights and taken up residence on this formerly blank page, still manages to crack me open four years on, as if I've been reincarnated as a boiled egg of emotion, sat at some table during a rousing brunch. Anyway, I will be the first to admit that I am usually better with my choice of constructive criticism, but some times a self-pieced synopsis of one's own work simply needs a little spice of subtle profanity. However, I will accept the fact that my use of expletives could be misguided, and if so, I will extradite myself immediately if not sooner. It's just that I find this crazy little thing called life a little easier to swallow once you equip a bantam quip and furnish a smile in the face of misfortune. You know, a little witticism here and a touch of tomfoolery there just to help the medicine go down or something.

Nonetheless, I appreciate that you, the individual who is reading this unregulated rant of goodwill, will have most probably been through this piercing procedure known as a funeral yourself. You may have even recited a tribute, passage or reading, and remember that heartache like it was only this misty morning. However, it is also just as possible that you found it too hard to electively open up in front of the sympathetically staring eyes of this kind of congregated colony, understandably choosing to be all ears and all heart at the event instead. Whatever your decision though, my point is, this bollock punch of a process is now a memory, heavily accentuating the past tense, and thus promoting the idea that there is little need to dwell on such a fucked up festivity. Now, I'm not saying or even suggesting you have to forget this moment ever happened, or even ignore its very presence, not by any means at all, I just want you to concentrate on what comes next instead. You see, if you believe such a move will benefit you in the solo salsa that is the bereavement process, then go with the current you beautiful salmon you, just do what you believe to be right in that wicked good heart of yours.

Of course, you may well be at the same stage as I, willing to try anything to move on and find peace. Like I said, my telepathic skills aren't a full strength currently, so I can't tell if you have kept a copy of the eulogy or not. Nor can I tell if you have been blessed with an eidetic memory similar to that of Mike Ross' in the hit US show 'Suits'. But, what I can tell you is that I have found great resolve in my unwilling step to re-read what I wrote over four years ago. You see this trip down the old dusty path of memory lane somehow unearthed a piece of me I thought I had lost in the sands of time, forever. Thus I implore anyone who is struggling with there own personal antichrists to explore what was said in those days so proximate to your loss, and those days when you were so emotionally rife, for there is absolute veracity amongst this unforgiving pain of the past.

However, now that you have some idea of what I went through and how I was smashed in the face, gut, rib and heart by the bereavement mallet, I believe it is time to delve into what is important... The weeks, months and years that followed. The decisions I made and the processes I pursued in an attempt to find peace with myself, a means to laugh and joke in the way life intends and how I got to where I am now. Thus there seems no better place to start than at the beginning, at year one.

"Whenever you want to achieve something, keep your eyes open, concentrate and make sure you know exactly what it is you want. No one can hit their target with their eyes closed."

Paulo Coelho

YEAR ONE

I had changed. I had become a shadow of my former self. Nay, I had become a shadow of my former shadow. I had become hyper-cautious. I suddenly wanted to be the exemplary model citizen. I wanted to be the epitome of all things good and I completely converted to this new way of existence, like a born again Druid and absolutely ardent about it. I wanted to be whom I thought my Dad wanted me to be, and at the time, I thought this to be a goodie-two-shoes-rod-up-the-arse-straight-up-fucktard type fella. I felt guilty for smiling, and I became guild-ridden for laughing. I struggled to have fun because I foolishly accepted fun as shameful behaviour, and this, may I add, is perpendicular penguin shit!

I mean, when one suffers from the aftermath of a loss, as catastrophic as it may be, feeling bad for having fun is not culpable under any condition, far from my-all-ears-chinchilla. You see enjoying your only shot at this life is the only wish this lifeless person in question would want from you. This loved and loving person would want nothing more than for you to maintain an optimistic outlook like never before, and rejoice at what you have, not what you have lost. I know how hard it is to accept this as acceptable, so much so that I'm not going to push the old glass half full or half empty philosophy in your face. However, I am going to state that we should be outlandishly screwball grateful we even have a goddamn glass in the first place. For it's not whether your perspective is optimistic or pessimistic, or whether you see the glass as half full or half empty, but rather the observation that there is clearly more room for a tipple in this glass of yours whatever way you look at it.

Anyway, I went back to Oxford town on my nineteenth birthday, you know one of those birthdays that you wish you could ignore, like the dreaded 50th that so many delightfully despise. Nonetheless, it seemed to be a landmark of some negative significance, for it was a birthday that landed three weeks after the consequential death that collaterally killed something in me too. I didn't know anyone at Brookes, so I can empathise with any feeling of lavish loneliness as I was living in hermit like hibernation too.

Hibernation gives you time to think, and I never saw this as a good thing because I over think. I over thought everything, with thoughts on how I could have prevented what had happened pretty persistent, whilst my other serious thoughts concentrated on the fact I had changed. I knew I had changed and it crushed me so much. I was no longer this reckless kid who enjoyed pissing off his parents whenever a chance arose, or the type of boy who didn't only paint the town red but painted it every colour within the royal rainbow. I was no longer chasing those beauties of the opposite gender as if some sort of rabbit in the height of spring. I was no longer crashing numerous cars in numerous seasons and I was no longer seeking attention at every street corner and each philanderer promoting party.

You see, prior to the plane crash, I was a real livewire, a little rough round the edges but I had stars in my eyes, and yet not one person at my temporary home of education, full of strangers, knew me as this rebellious rooster. It felt as though I was literally stuck between a rock and a hard place. I wanted to be the arrogant me I was so in love with, but I didn't want to draw attention to myself for fear of questions being asked, starting on the back foot by placing strangers in an awkward situation and afraid of the pitying look that had become all too common. I mean no one wants to start a friendship by having to answer any curiosity as to why you're being sheepish with the words, "Oh me, I'm just dealing with the extremely fresh loss of my Father who was killed without warning."

In a way, I was vigorously dragged into seclusion to deal with life after Dad on my own, literally behind closed doors, not knowing how to approach people, not knowing how to ask for help or seek support from others, and ceremoniously conscripted to wear a V For Vendetta style mask that bared an eternal smile that flipped the ugly truth on its head. You see this disguise of mine was purpose built and designed to protect those on the other side of my cheap bedroom door as much as it was put in place to benefit me too. It was that friend that I loved to hate, a means for some part of me to get on with my day in the magnificent sun light hours, before I had to lace up those metaphorical boxing gloves of mine, ready in time for my brawl with those personal demons that showed their faceless faces at night. Like 'Marky Mark' I ended each evening swinging blindly.

Its devastating to be unaccompanied and abandoned like that, but it was also the only discovery I had made that allowed me to continue with my newly shaded life, and yes, it sucked cockle-cock. I mean it was a vicious cycle where your temporarily contented elation is also the grounds for your detrimental melancholy, knowing exactly how the following rotation of the earth's axis would solemnly pan out. Knowing almost exactly what hardships I would be faced with during the day, and almost exactly what torment I would be faced with at night.

As a result of this stress, I suffered from insomnia for those initial eight months after Dad left the festival, a condition that was most definitely spurred on by the result of copious catalysts. Nonetheless this was a bastardly bizarre phenomenon. In fact, this sleepless slag had obviously been well researched by Chuck Palahniuk, because he fucking hit that nail bang on the head when he penned, "With insomnia, you're never really awake; but you're never really asleep" infamously used in 'Fight Club', because that is exactly what was occurring, a mist of uncertainty where the days had no beginning and no end.

Looking back at it now, maybe I should have used this chronic sleeping disorder to my advantage and become an educated Rolling Stone and standard bearer, demoralising the 38,000 other students with my ability to party rock the house like LMFAO for some 240 straight days. In fairness though, this socialising solution to keep up the riot, was in fact suggested to me by misguided movement of misfit mates. But, as always with this mourning flex, there were far deeper reasons as to why I didn't jump on the first year gravy train that passed through every station of debauchery, ending its journey at either Kings Cross St. Pussy or at a traditional al fresco Turkish restaurant, the kind that is more famously known as a kebab van.

But in the hope of understanding why, lets analyse the stimuli that viscously bent over my first year experience and fucked it so relentlessly. The first would seemingly revolve around my inability to control the recurring night terror that so vividly plagued my slumber. Now, I can't remember if the dream itself was pernicious to my siesta, or whether it was the fact I was too afraid to nod off as time went on, scared of what this recurring and fucked up dream had to offer. Either way, this dismal dream is the defendant on trial here no matter which way you look at it. The vivid nightmare itself, however, I do remember, and the short story version goes like this.

I was in the plane. A fly on the wall of the cockpit, eyes focussed on my Father, never breaking my awesomely attentive concentration, loyal to the last moments my Dad was given. Now, I don't know the details that cloud the realities of the crash, such as the allocated pews of those on board, but I have always imagined my Dad being in the co-pilots seat. Maybe this is interconnected with the fact he was an ex-stunt pilot, but whatever the actuality, this is how my nightmare dreamed up the spontaneous seating plan.

Moreover, the dream was made even more harrowing by the fact I was witnessing the hallucinated sequence first hand. I was watching the familiar faces of those passengers on board, the people I knew so well, watching them enjoy the coastal skies of Beira and seeing them share smiles of blissful appreciation, at least before I was made privy to their transformation of expression. You see, these ever-familiar faces of delight turned into hysterical trepidation, screaming and yelling, crying and quaking. Then, just as I brace for the inevitable impact that I had braced for so many times before, a wave of calm sweeps over my old man's expression, a picture of love, eyes of a man who has lived a life in the moment and as a result managed a smile of exaltation, and this is the very last image that is etched onto the retina and optic nerve of my dream like state, before I jump-jolt awake as if struck by the lightening of reality and attacked with the defibrillators of actuality.

The impetuous emotional riposte of such a repetitive practice is a contradiction in its own right. You see I despised the unwelcomed invite to this last dance that was forced upon me, as you can imagine. But I simultaneously thrived off this contingent chance to see my Dad one last time, even in spite of the upsetting context, all of which created a mindboggling oxymoron of torment. However, recollection has encouraged identification, and this is a tough segment of the healing puzzle, and in my opinion, just a piece of the puzzle. But you cannot be fully complete until every piece has been located and accepted, or at least this is what I found my erratic arrangement of trial and error to bestow upon my solitary saunter towards the greener grass. Anyway, lets delve into the implicated impossibilities of insomnia and the invisible infection of instability, both conceptually and physically.

Dead on one's feet. Burned out. Fatigued. Overtaxed. Exasperated. Run down. Haggard. Fucked. This level of exhaustion is a first-class stone in ones shoe. I mean, even my capacious courtship of the English jargon falls short of any attempt to portray the true effects of such systematic sleeplessness. You yourself may have managed to avoid this prickly plague of having your eyes constantly open, and thus managed to avoid any suffering from such a burden, thus for want of accuracy, I will try my best to enlighten you. I will try and paint you a minimalistic picture of the effects of insomnia as if I'm some sort of Barnett Newman of the vocabulary world. So lets delve into the fucked up furore of this feebleness.

Within the first couple of sleepless days your eyes struggle to focus, and after several restless rotations of the sun and moon, one begins to hallucinate. Unfortunately for the psychedelic souls amongst us, these hallucinations do not occur in a fascinating fungus induced type way, but rather they appear in an involuntary and draining type fashion instead. But these desirable facts can take a backseat quickly, for insomnia and hallucinations are not as fun as your festival mentality may claim, as the following attention-grabbing headline of vigilant insomnia will ensure. For after eleven days, there is a likely chance one will finally getting some Zzzzz's, however this is a sleep you will most likely not wake from, for eleven days without sleep will end in the everlasting silence that death guarantees. That's how harsh this chronic torture is.

Its fair to say I didn't experience the eleven days of blurring visuals before hitting the death bed, but rather that I'm just mad into knowledge, and what's one meant to do if he canny sleep and if he canny rattle his brain for a certified answer that he requires.

Anyway, the reason I'm still alive and kicking despite having insomnia for two-thirds of the year is simply because insomnia takes numerous forms, all orbiting around the no sleep ideology. It's a lack of sleep, whether this is due to disturbing interruptions or an unbridled inconvenience when it comes to falling asleep, leaving your mind to wander, ponder and traipse into the dreaded lost ark of endless envisaging. Maybe it's waking up too early or the periodic abundance of consciousness in the depths of darkness. Whatever form this whore called insomnia adopts, its something many of us have encountered, whether man or woman, mermaid or merman. However, its duration of stay is never signalled. It could be an overnight stay, frequenting bi-monthly like some travelling Godmother, or it could over stay its welcome, like some blue-eyed au pair girl called Cressida. But whatever the score, you have got to trust me that it's not always short term.

I had insomnia chronically, or in other words, almost every night for over a month, at least that's what the term chronic is defined as in this perplexing context. I was on an addiction fix of less than two hours sleep a night, every night, involuntarily deciding I could sleep when I was dead. You know, a live-hard-die-young-you-only-live-once kind of sleep restriction, and unfortunately this became severely second nature. I had to learn how to deal with this incessant fucker on a daily basis, whilst I was also learning to deal with the bereavement ball-slap, as well as ensuring I kept up with the vigilante free Spiderman routine of wearing a mask, all of which took a lead role as I attempted to keep up with my seldom studies. It was a wank-wallowing-witch-hunt I'm telling ya.

Conclusively, this was a somewhat tricky juggling routine, especially when one has had little to no sleep. What was the first attempt at a remedy, well I was prescribed Benzodiazepines such as temazepam and loprazolam, which essentially transformed me into a ranch animal of some kind, pumped full of tranquilisers that endorsed calmness, relaxation and sometimes sleep, without the fun that is promised by some tranquilisers such as Ketamine. I also dabbled in the newer Z medicines, which included names straight out of a Star Trek movie, such as zopiclone, zolpidem and zaleplon.

Not only were these pills about as fantastic as forced anal, but they royally fucked me too, so much so they were on the brink of becoming a culprit far guiltier than the cruel insomnia itself. I mean, every morning felt as if I had been hit in the cranium with a primitive rock of unrelenting giddiness. Fuck, I was scared shitless of this miniscule but mindboggling medication that fisted my face every day, but I was in such a sleepless state, I was willing to try even the most amusing of techniques. So much so in fact, the next stop on this coach ride for the tossing and turning was located between Cognitive Treatment Town and Behavioural-Therapy-on-Thames. Moreover though, and what I came to learn shortly after my arrival into these metaphorical medical municipalities was quite simply which techniques best suited me, and the winning technique that had the most luck was none other than the stimulus-control therapy. I warn you though; it's a weird one.

Stimulus-control therapy ultimately aimed to do what should have been wholly natural to pretty much every human, mammal, reptile and insect, associating the bedroom with sleep. This natural indulgence had clearly been lost in translation somewhere along the way, with the majority of the blame surely going to my uncontrollable cock and sleepless libido. I mean the change from this room of sleep to that of no sleep wasn't exactly altered by my lust for studying or World of Warcraft.

Now, I'm not saying stimulus-control therapy simply snapped me back into recognising that there was in fact a bed in the middle of my room and that this piece of furniture had a primary purpose that involved and promoted sleeping. No. But rather it inspired a way for me to block out the nightmares, and that was to watch something on a screen while trying to pass out, such as a movie, or porn, or a porno movie or whatever.

In my circumstance though, I turned to two very different but equally surmounting TV shows. The first was made up of the dynamic quadrangle of Vince, Eric, Turtle and Drama, all of who are more universally known as those guys in 'Entourage'. Whilst, the second orgasmic ritual jumped into my world disguised as the handsome, dazzling and rough round the edges fella named Hank Moody and his charmingly repugnant existence in 'Californication'.

To me, these were my methods of escape, my fuel and my desire. They acted as the flickering spark that allowed my imagination to run a regular fucking riot every lonely evening. Of course this obscure method of weaning out my strife with snoozing didn't work every night, not by any means. But it did assist me in overcoming the internally sleepless disagreements I had on those nights that I was alone, although it did have the unintentional by-product of getting me strung out on an addiction to HBOs 'Entourage' and Showcase's 'Californication'. I can't sell these tekkers to everybody because it's personalised experimentalism. But, what I can say about this visual distraction, which became so familiar to my agenda, is that it's a technique I still use today, four fucking years on.

I guess the unrighteous route of drinking myself into an epileptic state with a conclusion imitating Tinie Tempah's debut song title, was not really an option to me. Yes, I had become too sensible to take a trip down that slippery slope, but I was also very aware of my fragility, and thus the barrel or distillery I had the potential to backward two and half somersault with pike myself into, For this would have acquired an almightily botched landing without a doubt, and for this realistic reason alone, it was kind of taken off the menu.

Anyway, I wasn't aware of this unscrupulously decadent path at this stage, thus I avoided almost all those poisonously delicious cocktails that are so wonderfully packaged in bottles, cans and creatively designed glasses for another reason altogether. You see I was scared of what alcohol could do to my façade, viewing it as the kryptonite to my smokescreen, and the only thing that could make my concealed lacerations transparent for all to see. I didn't want to become 'that-guy', the fella who didn't get on with alcohol, with each shot forcing moisture from my eyes and uncharacteristically becoming that cheerless chap who'd be known as the emotional wreck on the public party scene of fresher's fun. It was like a variation of Jesus infamously turning water into wine, except my party trick was to turn all alcohol into gin.

What's more, and on top of this temporary scaredy-cat outlook upon one of life's great pleasures, it is safe to say numerous snifters of firewater was, and remains to be, rather unfavourable to my nights sleep. This is not simply because one's sleep is interrupted by the sudden bolt upright awakening and the unconditionally gagging for a vessel full of ice cold Adam's ale, all in the vain effort to counter-attack the Ghandi's flip flop situation that dominates one's mouth. No. Instead it's more due to the fact that, any sleep I may have been getting at this restless time in my life became even more sporadic when I was nothing shy of three sheets to the wind. Don't get me wrong; a single nightcap will do wonders in seducing the sandman, but anymore more moonshine than that has quite the reverse effect.

One second let me just pop my pretend PhD cap on before I take on the disguise of a blasphemous science professor. There we go.

So, this is categorically nothing new to you liquid experts, but it is pretty easy to pass out when one is seeing double, whether this involves your bed, someone else's bed, a bath, floor, mantelpiece or even the top right shelf of a chest of drawers. However, this type of dormancy is actually a thief, for it steals from the forty winks that usually kick-starts the shuteye of your nocturnal cycle, commonly referred to as the dream sleep. This is then followed by a fragmented fuck up in frequent awakenings, caused by the body metabolising the liquor in your system. What's more, this mainly comes in the form of recurrent trips to the little boys room, usually for a tinkle, although any bodily function could show its evil side, at any time and from any of your orifices.

Moreover, and in addition to this by-product of ethanol, one can also expect snoring or wheezing, the sweats, perpetually aggressive headaches, arousal, nightmares and insomnia. The latter two side effects on this list speak volumes alone, especially given that I was battling with bad dreams and jousting with wakefulness. Thus, my decision to stay away from the juice and repeatedly retire early is fathomable.

The exhaustion I felt in this first year, a combined result of insomnia, emotional stress and keeping away from the beautiful immoralities and dependability of illegal remedies that glowed green like a collection of fire exit signs, were unfortunately not the only hurdles that had to be faced. Bastards. No, there was also anger, infuriation, petulance, antagonism and hostility, which were all inconsistent partners-in-crime at this time, and occasionally continue to be, whilst the extent of this damage was ultimately unknown to the majority shareholder, that being me.

I was angry at the world. I just couldn't help but think, why the fuck had this happened to me, and how the fuck was this fair. I mean, I'm a good kid, all right I may have inadvertently nabbed a 'Peanut-butter KitKat Chunky' from the local Spar shop once upon a time, but this retort from Karma was massively over the fucking top and melodramatic. I never took this anger out on my friends, but then again I wasn't close enough to them in the initial year of my university life to do so, although this was possibly a choice I consciously conspired and crafted. Nonetheless, like everyone, I needed a way to release this anger, and regretfully my targets were limited. What's worse though, these targets were also the last people I would ever want to be on the receiving end of my cantankerous rage. The recipients I'm talking about are my family.

You see I would seek comfort from my Mum in those days when I couldn't keep my hurt bottled up anymore. But she was also the one who took the full brunt of my painful release too. I guess the reason for this reaction is that there was no one else I was comfortable around, nor close enough with to let the cracks in my venire become visible. However, she should never have had to deal with my fickle furores, especially for as long as she did. I mean I could have got on the blower to the Guinness World Record guys n gals, for I am pretty certain there was no one with more pent up anger and aggression than this replicating Hellboy, with the slightest nudge releasing my surface deep slingshot of belligerence.

I would join the party-going hall of famers and smash TVs and launch technological devices at walls whilst ignoring the meticulous methods of Steve Jobs. I would imitate adult Simba as I roared down the phone and I would put Brian Blessed to shame with my spontaneously practised plethora of curse words, with my mother forever retaining the given to her role of victim or scapegoat throughout each innocent occasion of this appalling sketch show.

Unfortunately I don't fully understand why this was my natural response, all I know is, I was bitter. I had lost a Granddad who I was increasingly close too, and then lost my Dad so soon after. It was a situation that was well over my head, provoking a pestilent ire. It's a situation so alien and so incomprehensibly hard, that you desperately want and need advice, but the only person who can deliver that advice you want and need has been taken from you, and that is one of the hardest moments of realisation. Its a vicious cycle, one that is decorated with piranha sharp teeth and trap doors, all of which are located at constantly random intervals, forcing you to pave your own way, whilst you remain constantly kept in the damning dark. Yeah, it's fucked up, but looking back now, it establishes one as Mark Henry kind of strong, whilst it also encourages one to believe you can complete all the 'Bush Tucker Trials' single-handed.

It is far easier to concentrate on the negatives. Concentrating on the ways in which life has bashed you around so dishonourably, as you try and fight back against this tyrannical, irresistible and deceitful presence of the unknown, coerced and circumvented by this schoolyard bully of life. In fact, I'm almost positive a Mr Brightside mind-set is pretty much preposterous when one is this brow beaten. But once again, it comes down to one's strength, tenacity, temperament, demeanour and proclivity, in other words, it comes down to that unacceptable edict, attitude. Now, I know how frightfully fucked up it is to obtain an optimistic outlook for I've been there, and Sister Mary Mother of Morpheus, one can only contemplate and speculate at what you have lost, and quite rightly so. However, this Microsoft outlook we adopt cannot be sustained indefinitely, and unfortunately it is up to you, and you alone, to certify that this doesn't happen, otherwise this negativity and isolation will eat away at you like the eighth plague of Egypt.

You can't just think about what you have lost, for you must remember what you still have left, and once you can comprehend this, well then you have to carry that fucking flag and hold on to the noble notion that we know more substantially as gratitude, and then you must never let it out of your deathly vice like grasp. It doesn't matter whether this gratitude refers to your parents, parent, brother, sister, hamster, pelican, Louboutins, Nintendo DS, family or friends, it just matters that you appreciate they are still alive and kicking, and that they need you. Hell on high, I still have my David Attenborough collection of awesomeness and this has given glory to my gratitude and defined my appreciation of what I still have in this wonderful world of worries. Yeah, it's a small slither of a silver lining indeed, but it's a silver lining nonetheless.

As the audaciously awesome Abraham Lincoln once proclaimed to me whilst I was a touch tipsy at a party, "We can complain that rose bushes have thorns or rejoice because thorn bushes have roses." And if that doesn't give you an enormous erection whenever you're feeling a little stig in the dump or a tad lower than usual, then just remember there is some youngster out there right now getting caught jerking the gherkin by his dear old Madre. I mean ouch dude.

Anyway, this far from foolhardy fresher's foxtrot of mine was totally lame, at least in the carefree carousing sense, but then again, that nine-month party that everyone else was basking in was also an insignificant three-tier trifle compared to what I was faced with. You see I wasn't running away from the reality of it all at this stage, far from. Instead, I was trying to grab the antelope by the antlers so to speak. What I mean is, I was using the new-born inspiration that courses through the veins of a person in mourning. I was using this newfound desire to better myself, for the sake of those I loved and those around me more than anything. I was harnessing the power to fight the things that later had the power to crush me.

You see I was studying in the city my Dad studied in, and studying the subject that he later careered in, politics, whilst I was also taking on political campaigns in his old constituency. I can only presume this wasn't coincidence and that it was in fact an attempt to get closer to the man I was now forever further away from. I'm no psychologist, but it doesn't take the combined scrutiny of Sigmund Freud and Carl Jung to work out my intuitive thought process in these decisions. Look, I was by no means the solemn bee in the hive. In fact, I've always harnessed an infectious smile that mingled with an uncontrollable chortle, the sort of happiness that could make Voldemort roll around in the aisles. However, I still had very obvious issues, and issues I wanted to resolve despite being lost in the woods when it came to knowing how.

What's more, Oxford was a four-hour journey away from home, no matter how one looked at it. Whether cruising along in Mufasa, which was my beaten up Peugeot 206, or electing to take the railroad. I was also aware of the burden I was becoming on others, thus I chose to never open up to my new-fangled playmates and bosom buddies, whilst I was simultaneously closing myself off to both my Mother and Lily, believing it was unfair on these beauties as it wasn't their problem to deal with. I was basically becoming ever more unforthcoming with my emotions. Hush-hush, tight chops and zipping my lips, you know Mum's the word and all that, only I couldn't even give her the word, not unless I was truly having a turbulently turd-soaked type of bad day.

I am lucky to have mother which such unconditional love dominating her kind heart, for it seemed she would never leave my side no matter how much I closed up. Unfortunately, I took this incredible trait for granted. This was also apparent with Lily, a girl so stunning her face could cure cancer, a girl who had seen me go from care-free, rebellious and charming, to padlocked, inaccessible and cavernously deep within an 8 month period, almost trapped by her moral code to keep her hand clasped round mine given what I had been through. That is when counselling came cartwheeling into my calendar, and it really did clock in cartwheeling, for it rapidly became a bi-weekly spectacle of help, and a medium that did genuinely help, like a Jim Davidson's Generation Game of Memories, minus the Operation Yewtree scandal of course.

After a couple of sweet counselling sessions though, I found there to be something weirdly accommodating and strangely invaluable about talking to an external party, or what is essentially an inquisitive stranger showing off their multiple certificates, acclamations and commendations, all of which are displayed in the arrogant fashion of plastering them across their usually mundane office walls. You see, counselling is a form of pragmatic accommodation and a confession box without the religious extension. It's a medium in which you are encouraged to voice the pent up antagonism that seems so insufferably hard to declare elsewhere. As I keep stating, I was all for the false guise and trying to act as cool as a cucumber, or more accurately, I was trying to portray myself as a Caucasian Lenny Kravitz.

But in this purpose built room of private exposure, my masquerade was turned into an epoch of total truth telling, as if another lie to myself would ensure my nose elongated in a Pinocchio motivated fashion. Counselling made me ball out the tears, whimper and weep, cry the nine bar blues, jowl and sob. Fuck, I hated that counselling shit. I hated having to rely upon someone who wasn't me, specialist or not, for brandishing my inner most secrets was totally tormenting. It was also alien in its presence, for I was having to open up to a woman, and whether the lights are dimmed or not, when I'm left alone with a woman, I've usually undone my belt and all three trouser buttons before the door has even shut, for I'm all for being naked and then hopping on the good foot to do the bad thing. However, this was a type of nakedness that even this patron of passionate procreation wanted to avoid.

You see, once you arrive inside this magnolia decorated building, you linger nervously in the waiting room, reading leaflets on depression, pregnancy, substance abuse and gynaecology or whatever, all the while anticipating the moment your name will be read aloud so that you can walk, run or crawl towards the basilisk free and ever-bland chamber of secrets, dreading the defenselessness of todays appointment. You tell yourself 'I won't crack this time. Today I'm a completely closed book.' Then you participate in the standard meet and greet with the familiar face that knows more about you than anyone else, even that teddy bear you have confided in for over a decade. After this you flick your eyes around the room only to see that sweet smile of assured trust, as if symbolising the calm before the storm, for this most random of associates is about to probe you yet again, and not in the good way that you're imagining, for usually my prostate remained ignored.

Yet you're still confident there is no way this counsellor is going to break through your concentrated chainmail guard as you sit down and prepare to dismiss this experienced shrinks' attempts. The therapist would then ask something cock-clown simple like, 'So, how are you feeling this week?' Ah, so you're trying to break me down nice and slowly are you doctor, like some sort of enzyme. With this tactic now more than apparent though, I'd answer her short line of enquiry with a textbook riposte, not lying by inserting a wisecrack counter such as, 'feckin awesome, I'm cured of all my ill emotion', but instead, employing a hasty and honest response like, 'I'm alright thank you', summing up one's mood as quickly as possible. And that's it. I would leave my confession as ambiguous as possible.

However, after this declaration has been made, the situation suddenly becomes a silent competition with this professional challenger just waiting for you to delve into a rigorous conversation about your emotions. It is a stalemate though, for I would remain strong and keep fighting off their tactics, refusing to speak, move or even blink, holding my ground with no intention to crumble… then Wham! (Not the band unfortunately.) I would break down with upsetting gusto, and involuntarily open up wholeheartedly. An odd feeling to say the very least, for it's incredibly hard to put your weight on someone else. It's horribly unnatural to throw your shit at an external being like some sort of capuchin monkey, unleashing all the troubles you've kept deep inside for so long, the troubles that were swallowing you limb by limb, the troubles that you didn't know how to deal with despite your best efforts to remain Mr Solo Dolo.

There is an explosion of feelings, a real heart to heart that takes only the slightest nudge of encouragement, knowing that the emotions you've concealed from the wandering eyes of others, still remain under the table, hidden from view. Of course, this is a practice that's a million miles away from easy, with a trip to Jupiter seeming a more likely venture. But Christ Almighty would I feel larger-than-life after each session, as if I'd just been to moneysupermarket.com, for now I felt epic! However, this is not a notion where I felt fantastic as soon as I stepped out of that cubbyhole of confession, ready to get on with my day. No. For a reflection period is necessary more times than not, you know a touch of time to truly allow the weight to lift from my crumpled and sore shoulders.

Now, I am aware of the stigma that, quite rightly, coincides with counselling, but I still stand by using this service for what it can offer you. It doesn't have to be taken at its laughable face value, and it doesn't require you to bring your bag of pride in with you, in fact I'd recommend leaving that suitcase of self-sufficiency outside the room for an hour or so, surrendering yourself to scrutiny completely, for what is usually no more than sixty minutes.

My advice, you should try and mould this beneficial experience to cater your needs and make it worthwhile for you. Look, I hate preaching, but nonetheless, like Martin Luther King Junior, I believe. I believe we must accept the fact that, those of us who are suffering from any bizarre form of bereavement, divorce, separation, depression, alcoholism, low self-esteem or even G) all of the above, need support. And whatever this support structure may be, compliance of this fact has been as rewarding to my healing process as blowjobs have been to universal sexual progression. Formidable comparison: No doubt. Unnecessary imagery: Probable. However, when it comes to accepting the need for any sort of abutment, blowies are the only impacting similarity that holds enough equipollent justice.

Of course I'm not the only organism to entomb his emotions and consign any delicacy to the grave inside. But, I am a Jedi Master of such a practise, somewhat resembling a six-foot-one-inch translucent and colourless Yoda with a 10th Dan in the Martial Art of Dissimulation and a 10 inch... Nevermind. It is with this hard earned degree that I can argue that a counselling session here and there, or therapy thrice a blue moon, wasn't enough to dismantle my hard earned skill, but it was enough to make me feel something again. For feeling numb gets tediously lacklustre.

Odd as it may seem, but it was simply tip top to teem with tears every so often, mimicking Made in Chelsea's Louise Thompson, although her tears are far more recurrent than mine, which shows her resilient strength of character. I put my hand up though, for I didn't let this liquid pain flow from their tear ducts anywhere near enough, and to be honest, I still don't.

I don't know why I ridiculously sought to surf down the same route as the emotionless Tin Man, for crying and showing emotion is far from the weakness I thought it was. In fact, allowing an overhaul of feeling makes you stronger. You see, each time I slipped into my designated alcove to avoid others seeing me upset, I would promptly collapse on my bed in a ruckus of distress, snivelling and sobbing, privy to streams of tears duplicating the Thames, Seine and Limpopo, all of which lead to an overflowing estuary where my head rest on my pillow. Sometimes I hold my bedside photos of Dad, other times I re-watch the news reports of the funeral or the initial report of his death, for this is the only video footage I have of him, the only chance I get to see him animated, and the only chance I have of hearing that distinctively low voice of his. Occasionally I have to break a lifeless object, you know like throwing my TV across the room, punching the door, snapping a tech-deck, punting a Furby or going George Foreman on the tail end of my mattress and pillow.

It just breaks my heart every time I accept my Dad has gone, thus I never wanted to accept it, instead I would try to keep hold of that ever diminishing one per cent chance He was given so many years ago. But, once that grieving gust has passed and the reservoirs have dried up due to draught, this rush of relief sweeps over you. The aftermath of such emotion brings to light how much such an expressive moment was needed, reminding you of how long you'd pent up such trauma, and how long you had refused to allow yourself a release.

♦

I mean, the process, the combination of counselling or its alternatives, and the reflection and acceptance of it all is an elixir. It is a remedy, restorative, organic, free and a process that doesn't require the involvement of unpunctual drug dealers. It's a cure-all even if only a quick fix, a temporary dabble in au natural pharmacons, an indispensable weight off an otherwise diligent mind. Quite simply, it acts as a lily pad, a stepping stone to acknowledgement, and one that is not solely designed for you to speak your mind, but to give you the strength to keep on trucking. It is a service that is there to supply those in need with enough determination to identify, pinpoint, distinguish, alter, amend, diagnose and decide what is best. It is a fucking means to an end of this sad sweet tale of woe, with the results of such sentience making me wetter than an otter's pocket.

Moving on is such a complex concept though, undependable and intricate. You know you need to move on, but you can't, for an entire host of reasons. There is this ethical obligation to your moral compass, one that emotionally steers you down a path that suggests it's wholeheartedly wrong to progress. This is the 'fun guilt' clause that I touched on earlier, the belief you shouldn't be able to smile, because the trauma of bereavement is anything but smile worthy. What do I say to this? I say you should raise your middle finger up to this cock and bollocks notion, and give it an almightily enthusiastic salute, for no matter whom you have lost, or whatever the situation may be, your happiness is paramount, and that's the bravado fuelled bottom line.

The ability to beam a smile should not be wasted, like Lindsey Lohan on a Friday night, and no matter whom the other parties involved are, even if they are the accidental antagonists of your hardship, they are sure to prioritise your exuberance and gaiety as a principal priority. So all together, lets raise that third digit of ours, you know, the fuck you finger, and lets unanimously direct it towards the calamitous and ill-fated feeling of guilt, and lets do it with a Cheryl Cole influenced winning smile.

I guess the other thingamajig that prevented me from moving on as quickly as one would have liked or hoped, and a contraption that propelled me deeper and deeper into a closed off life, was familiarity. I'm referring to the constant reminders that have that X-Men ability to blend into day-to-day life, but invade your personal space on certain occasions and getting right up in your face on others, offering absolutely no opportunity of avoidance. For these little indicators, which are so irrelevant to the thousands of additional by passers, are the one's that somehow manage to hit you like a round nose bullet to the heart, directly hitting the very nerves that have become so delicately instable.

Unfavourably I was privy to these perturbing intimations on a day-to-day basis, and thus I know first hand how much they can affect the healing process of grief. You see, throughout my first year of struggling I had to battle with flashbacks that came with the zone in which my dormitory and landing were situated within. The place where I received the devastating news for the first time, the memory of collapsing against the wall and falling to my knees in a state of shock as if I was the recipient of multiple stun guns. Then there was Oxford town itself, which was an exquisite and magnificent memorial to my Dad, given it was his University City in my eyes, with the constructed route into this stunning metropolis taking me right past the gates of his old college, Teddy Hall. I also had to tussle with my chosen subject of study, which was enough to throw me off balance, for I knew full well what the impact of certain political suggestions could have upon my steadiness, meekly admonishing me without notice.

These three trinkets were all significant throughout my entire time at this educational facility, for each day I had to walk past these gestures that brought my etched in scars to the forefront of my attention, Monday to Friday, and then Saturday and Sunday. Fuck-a-duck, these soul-shaking reminders didn't even take bank holidays off, the hard-working-overtime-seeking bastards. But it went further than these direct links to my past too, for things that only resembled my Father's initials or my family name, all became influencers beyond their wildest dreams, with P&H logistics obtaining the unparalleled ability to set me off. Fuck, even the independent butcher, Arthur Howell's, became an aching Achilles' heel of my wavering vigour.

If anyone knows of a technique to overcome these recurring reminders that evolve into more than niggling flashbacks, please let me know. Whether these techniques are credible, tantric, meditational or otherwise, please don't hesitate to plaster it across all of JCDecaux' billboards, nationwide. For as far as I'm aware, such experiences that are so dearly personal, cannot be overcome, overlooked or ignored, but maybe we can get used to them. You see, they trigger something inside us, something no one else can notice for they would never spot such trivial insignificants that so blindly choke us. Our ability to see what we don't want to see becomes irresistible.

"Vision is the art of seeing what is invisible to others" or at least that's how Jonathon Swift made himself known to me, only the art I'm questioning is more like an imperceptible battering ram of Roman rule, and a battering ram that others can't detect, establishing grounds for an argument that suggests this could have been the first stealth invention.

Like many, I've had to come to terms with what is gospel, you know that disconcerting truism, 'what will be will be', for the balls deep truth is that there is no escaping these unforgiving memory motivators. Instead, one is forced to soak up this private pummelling and learn how to deal with it, without guidelines or textbooks, and manufacture our own method of damage control. You have to become well versed in the underlining issue that we've waded through for some duration, you may even need to crack open another bottle of that fine beverage known as attitude, and go bottoms up on it.

What I try and do is, I try and make each reminder into a positive memory. Not a flawless plan I know, but it gives me a reason to reflect on the impossibly perfect times of my life, the times I may have taken for granted back then, but smother me in bliss now. I guess everything comes down to perspective and how each of us spunky spider monkeys choose to deal with the hand we've been dealt in this unavoidable game of Texas Holdem. I mean I don't want to be destructively effected by everything. I don't want to sit around waiting for the band to get back together when I know this world tour is over, albeit after one sensational sequence of gigs. Personally, I much prefer using my optimistic twenty-twenty vision to see the sunny days even in overcast conditions. But that's just what I do. I try and see the silver lining that is always there, for I have accepted what has been lost and celebrate what I have left, and I enthuse over what I still have to achieve, gain and experience, all the while never forgetting those who aren't able to continue partying with us.

I concede that I may have made things more detrimental than they ought to have been, especially regarding my decision to hide from the pain as much as possible, and becoming increasingly afraid of these horrific hallucinations of my past. Maybe its because I had to deal with my feelings all Hans Solo, and was cornered off by these invisible bullies, that I allowed the voices of the past to get under my skin more than I should have. I could deal with the flashbacks Oxford had to offer, as they were mainly about receiving the news, as well as the subsequent bureaucracy and events that followed the death of my parent.

You see, for me it was going home that kicked me in the ball-bag. For going back to the county I was brought up in is what had me most terror-stricken, or more accurately, scared shitless. Going back to my native land, or that bump on the east coast was unbelievably tough, and I emphatically empathise with those who had no escape rope like I had. I mean, the sheer presence of my recollections here were enough to drop me like the Berlin Wall, for I would be overrun with memories of what seem to be a far less complicated time. When I was at home, everything brought on evocations. My entire childhood and my teenage years were brought into question, and these reflections were far more powerful and far more uncontrollable than those accustomed to Oxford.

Everything with my dear old man was an adventure of unpredictably. Beginning, middle and end, and I wouldn't alter this no matter what the enticement. But, it has meant that I have had to deal with the unlimited memoirs of my memory and the unconstrained stories of family and friends, stories that have to be shared. Then there is that forced smile that I have perfected for whenever one of Dad's legendary sagas pops up as an inevitable conversation piece. It's not that these stories don't make me happy, because they fucking do. It's more because I blocked them out as much as possible and thus a forced recollection is somewhat painful. I guess I did this so that when I'm reminded of the evil event, or in a way asked to recite it and thus dwell on it, the facts becomes a non-fiction of tragedy, no matter the genre of the original tale.

I still find it hard, even now, when I'm swanning around my homeland, trying not to be frustrated by the lengthy healing process, but instead accepting that it is a lengthy healing process. You see identifying the reasons is the hard part of this salvage process. It's one part of the procedure that hits me like a Dwayne 'The Rock' Johnson 'Peoples Elbow' because of my ability to compartmentalise so efficiently, my ability to block it all out. I've always been good at this compartmentalising contraption though, pigeonholing my emotions in a John Depp style of method acting, dividing my emotional capacity into sections and categories, sub-sections and sub-categories, allowing me to run and hide from the truth of actualities. But I assume this is relatable to all. It's how we're taught. Even from at a young age its, this is how to behave with grandparents, this is how to act at a friends house, this is how to behave at school and with certain strict teachers, this is the way to behave with my quick to snap Dad, etcetera etcetera.

Then after he died it became, this is how to act around friends, strangers, lecturers or just about fucking anyone in all honesty. However, this had it's own set of unruly repercussions. For on those occasions I was home, which would either be during the ridiculously extensive university holidays or the odd weekend, I came to realise I was now afraid of my humble abode, and that I was worked like a dog just to cope with the thought of any mental breakdown that could competently lie in wait on the horizon, like a striped leopard amongst the tall grass of Norfolk's savannah. Here I would struggle to catch those much-needed Z's more often than ever, but worst of all, I was releasing my indignation upon my family.

My uneducated Ivan Pavlov-esque understanding suggests my immediate kith and kin unsurprisingly reminded me of my Pop. This was hardly their fault given the automatic and default DNA placed within them. However, I just wasn't aware of why I was maddened at the time, and more appropriately, I wasn't prepared to accept that this behaviour of mine was in any way my fault. Instead, I found it far simpler to buy a first class stamp and send the accusations elsewhere, anywhere, so long as it wasn't to the correct address and post-box of culpable acceptance.

However, what I have learned now is that there is no hiding from the thoughts of the past. You know, that figure in the crowd you think is your lost loved one, or the voice you sometimes hear in the wind that says they are near. It's a talent you may be professing you attain, but sooner .or later we all get caught out for pretending, its just on this occasion, you are only conning yourself Mr Frank Abagnale Jr.

Look, I get it, its hard, in fact I'm sure being water-boarded seems like a more fruitful option than that of addressing your emotions and tackling the memories that eat away at you on a very daily basis. However, you have my word, take in these remembrances and cry at the at the stories you wish you could relive, but then accept them for what they are and laugh about them. Then laugh with others over their biographies, for these chronicles are there to ensure a smile, yet always remember that these memoirs only supply what you want them too. They can be cheerful or gloomy, and they can be very different depending on your mood of the day, of course. But ultimately, you're the narrator and you set the tone. You set the approach. You always have and you always will.

Moving on, for want of a better phrase, the rest of that initial year seems to have an undertone of discomfort and resentment. There were days where I couldn't face the world. Days where I would bolt my door shut, staple the curtains closed, switch my portable telephone device to airplane mode and land punches on any item of furniture, essentially becoming a catastrophic black hole of bedlam. Yet, there were also days that saw me enjoying the ecstasies of spring, snakebites at the sports bar, Frisbee, footy and rugby in South Park, and of course chit-chatting-and-kit-katting with those I had grown so rousingly close to. Of course, these chinwags were almost always frolicsome and inconsequential, I mean its not as if we ever discussed the plight of the Kurds in northern Iran whilst completing an al fresco centurion challenge, but hey ho, that's just the way aha aha I like it, aha aha. I guess I was just enduring what everyone endures, everyone who has ever strolled across this bountiful planet, for I had my ups and downs, good days and bad, almost working as a referee for my mood, allowing the good days to be placed in a bap and chowed down without grace.

That virgin year however, does bring about those days of destructive domination, or more accurately, those memorable dates in the core calendar that you are personally aware of. There are those obvious days, like the date of the event in question, such as that of the plane crash in my case, the pertinent Birthdays and of course the family day of Christmas. Not so much Easter though, oddly enough.

Then you have those holidays that have been composed and commercialised by the capitalist corporations of America, such as Grandparent's day, Secretary Day, or more appropriately, Father's Day. C'mon though, that's not a day, is it? Is it really? Either way, this imaginary day is like a karate chop to my sensitive scrotum, with this short synopsis reducing me to waterworks alone.

I think about my Dad everyday, of course I do. But on this Americanised day of celebration, I am in a way guilted into pissing more tears than usual, which is probably a result of my morally correct standing and the way I was brought up. But still, I dread this day. It cuts me open in the way those actual days of substance do. It prevents me from surfing the wave of slumber the night before, and envelopes me in an emotional response on the day itself, from dawn until dusk, without fail, every third Sunday of June.

Between you and me though, it is as normal as muesli to miss someone you loved, so you can rest assured it is routinely run-of-the-mill to have a regally rough time when these significant dates do indeed arrive on your doorstep. I mean, minute-to-minute, I can never guess what fickle feeling I'm going to pick out of this packet of emotional milk chocolate 'Revels', with a selection of all-sorts dictating my spirit on such match days. All I know from my own meandering experience is that there is an importance and a need for wholly emotive explosions to blast out of us from time to time, a need to do the necessary and participate in the prerequisites, whatever that means to you.

I guess my routine has changed in conjunction with the way in which my ability to deal with the situation changed. I mean, in that first year I was all about following my perception of what was right, doing what I should be doing, and clocking onto my quintessential inkling of how I should portray myself to others, acquainted with the knowledge that I was one of two chief representatives of my late Father. After all, perception is reality right. With this in mind, I found myself dressing up in Sunday best on a day-to-day basis. I would conduct myself in a way that wasn't true to who I was but rather what I thought Dad would've appreciated. This included going to church on Christmas Day and even

Easter Morning (albeit after the ritual egg hunt that still hasn't become extinct despite the fact I am now a mature member of society. Banging!). However, these 'traditions', if you will, have all been reformed over the years, although this is without a doubt due to my being more cognisant about life, traipsing upon a new era of questions, and interrogating the blatant bullshit that seemed more extraneous, even laughable, than I had been able to realise in my earlier years of narrow-mindedness.

Unlike those customs that I touched on above however, there is one ritual that had unfortunately been practiced less and less, most probably due to my own inability as opposed to that of my new eyes-wide-open stance. This formality I speak of is the ability, or more accurately inability, to visit my Dad's grave. You see, in that first twelve-month cycle I had no qualms with such an endeavour. In fact, simply setting foot in that Christian burial ground had the faculty to fuel my determination, as if it were a high-octane fuel source that would ensure the excursion towards my ambition would not be halted prematurely. However, this is a gut punching and significant step. Expressing lyrics of love to a headstone, a symbolism of what is eternal. The involvement of a character that can't console your pain with conversation anymore, yet you still let that person know how much you adore them with verses of affection so strong the words themselves sound unspeakably lame. Then there is the gripping of bouquets of flowers, in which their colours extravagantly exemplify the season on hand. What's more there was also the telepathic communication with my younger brother, with each of us standing aside to provide the other with space to say our own private piece, with the glazed cherry on top of these scenes coming in the form of a rare brotherly hug.

Yet in spite of all this heart-warming participation, I stopped myself from visiting that churchyard, in which Dad was the guest of honour in my eyes. A route I subconsciously went down for no deliberate reason, other than it became part of the collateral damage that was encouraged by my emotional pigeonholing. You see, when you visit the resting place of someone you loved so dearly, one really does realise the vast reality of it all, with each visit edging you closer to the cliff of acceptance. As if each visit is a pitiless woodpecker, an unavoidable what's what that is punishing you, preventing you from running and hiding from it all. It was for this selfish reason that I started making my pilgrimage less frequent. Unable to believe what was clearly gospel and not wanting to lap up what was clearly the real McCoy.

I have spoken to others, both friends and acquaintances, those whom have also lost a parent, many of who have also been unable to amble into God's acre, knowing how hard they will be struck by the infallible truth. I guess this stems from the fact that you cannot play hide and seek with your emotions, and concurrently visit this hallowed ground, I mean that's chalk and cheese right there. Thus, when this first year was over, and I was shipped back off to get in touch with my studious side, in a time when my university course actually began to count for something, I realised I could no longer tango with both the Alsatians that were pulling me in different directions. So, with my stubborn subliminal self, assessing the deep end that I had so suddenly been launched into, my submerged mind simply decided to run from it all, and without my conscious being made fully aware. I presume this was ordinary though, for I was residing in a city over one hundred and eighty miles from home, and surrounded by friends none of whom I had a bond strong enough with. Well not strong enough for me to divulge what was really going on under my exterior.

I had one saving grace though, one which stayed in the perfectly carved shape of my smile inducing Lily who had, bizarrely enough, picked up the patience to stick around despite the obvious modifications that I had undertaken, with 'Pimp My Personality' having been very counterproductive. You see this blonde haired and tenaciously tanned beauty was the only person who could prevent the pain at the time, a muse for my happiness and a reason to flail my fists as I put up a good fight against my struggles. But this was inevitably a one-way street, for unbeknown to me I was heading the other way and towards the derelict district of despair, yet unwilling to hear that this saunter was chapter and verse. As you can imagine, this haphazardly forced Lily into a confusing continent of confusion, where each word and action hung on a brittle, vitreous and delicate shoelace of discontent, steadily promoting solitude as the reign of silence became ever more supreme. Consequently, it was only a natural response for me to sprint off in a temporary bout, with nowhere to run, and absolutely nowhere to permanently hide.

To conclude though, that first year of dealing with death is so foreign, not foreign in a trying to find a tapas bar in Costa Brava on a winters Thursday type way, but in a floundering and ferociously fucked up way. It's a learning curve that can't be represented on any excel graph, for not even the impossibly steep north side of K2 is comparable to this precipitous adventure of woe. This is sincerely trial and error on a grand scheme. It's a solo journey that makes the expeditions of Sir Ranulph Fiennes seem like a Monday morning commute into central London.

Then there are the subliminal changes in attitude, the kind that only the rad vision of hindsight can hope to offer. It's a year of entirely new day-to-day dealings that we're forced to deal with, witnessing our emotions being tossed about like eggs, flour and milk on Shrove Tuesday. It's a bloody period of ostentatious obscurities that suddenly become the norm, for they somehow seem to fall into the 'everyday bullshit' column. Yet it doesn't stop there, for we are also made to deal with the tumbling moss of day and night, which rolls into a cohort of colours due to the absence of any visible sleep pattern, positively providing no recess for the distressed.

But let me identify the bullet-points and highlight the cliff-notes as much as I can for you squire, starting with the observation that you have to deal with the consistently persistent nightmares that curse those individual minutes of sleep you maybe lucky enough to dabble in. There is the flurry of counselling and therapy, mundane rooms and clock watching, Yet tears are shed and shoulders are sought, all of which are unwillingly hauled out of you by professional strangers who are educated in awkward silences, but boy-o-boy are these techniques tip-top and efficient. Then there are the gremlins and trolls that get under your skin like well-hung gnats at an autumn barbeque, presenting themselves in very different forms, disguised as flashbacks and everyday reminders, unnoticeable until you notice them, and once that happens there's no turning back Scotty, just the ability to tame those tigers.

We have to learn how to grit and bear the feeling of being truly alone, a feeling forced upon us by the lack of dress rehearsals and absolutely no way of knowing how to boldly approach others with our torment. I mean, you can be packed in a room full of party-going-familiar-faces yet be completely isolated, a loathsome loneliness within a chock-a-block crowd, and then there is that look of pity waiting for you to drop your guard on that blue moon occasion, ready to pounce on your vulnerability. That moment when someone hears about the tip of the iceberg regarding your struggles and tries to understand what you are going through without any understanding whatsoever, naively looking at the insignificant beliefs that are pencilled in on paper, fucking frustratingly feeling sorry for you. Yeah, the gesture is kind of course, but the execution of such a look however, is tormenting.

Moreover, and taking it to account all of this cowardly horsecrap, I must emphasise how critically crucial it is for you to acknowledge that there are no regulations or rules, no guidelines or formulas that you can purchase on Amazon or eBay. Instead, we are quite simply without chapter and verse when it comes to this inoperable hunt for a broad church remedy.

There are many trials and tribulations on offer throughout this time, and I am positive that I have barely scratched the surface of what is on sale in this department of derangement. What I do know though, is that it is impossible for one keep their head up all the time, but then no one expects that of you, and you shouldn't expect that of yourself either. I truly mean that. For this is not about pride anymore. This one is about that inner strength and that ability to take the punches, for life is not about how hard you can hit, it's about how hard you can get hit and keep moving forward. For nothing and no one can hit as hard as life, or at least that's what Rocky Balboa taught me. You can throw jabs, hooks and uppercuts all you want, but when that ring bell approaches, all it comes down to is durability and the capacity to find your opponents weaknesses, the flaws and faults. However, and trust me when I say I passionately hate this cock wad of a cliché, but your biggest obstacle is accepting that 'you are your own worst enemy.'

I really am eternally sorry for those foul-mouthed words, and I promise I will wash my mouth out with a combination of shampoo, soap and an unhealthy helping of shame. But that is it. You see, the attitude you adopt in this almighty bitch slap of a time period is crucial to you salvaging the happiness you feel so distant from, for attitude is quite simply the king dick of recovery mechanics and is the missing piece of this proverbial puzzle. However, to submit a more simplistic synopsis, removing the riddled way of my writing and eradicating the ballsy banter of my biro, I will finish of this chapter with austerity. Thus, and conclusively, when I look back at this sensitive stage of my survival, it is without doubt that the most esteemed principle I learned was the authentic, valid and dependable fact that there is no right and wrong in life, instead, there is just the consequences of our actions. Amen.

"I was more addicted to self destruction than to the drugs themselves...
something very romantic about it"

Gerard Way

YEAR TWO

As you may have guessed by now, I have no plot or plan when it comes to this scribbling away of mine. I have only an ambition. A blind vision scrawled on a blank page, an exposure of something personal and an exposure of somewhere deep enough that it could be mistaken for a soul. It's a brutal yet beneficial procedure, for pondering over what I have exposed on this manuscript allows me to better understand myself, and allows me to use my experiences to aid others where conceivable.

With this in mind, now is the time for me to dive into the 'Dark Ages' of my historical narrative, a period where I struggled with my reliance upon drugs, and thus I must bare an authentic nakedness that feels shockingly similar to skinny-dipping with a tiger-shark, whilst I continue to clutch onto this quill and ink of mine with both hands. Not a euphemism.

It is with this conceited courage that I can confidently kick-off the this years ceremonies by declaring that this was a year no less foreign than its predecessor, with each day throwing up a challenge or two from the unexpected. Nonetheless, this year was also an extravaganza of such great heights. I mean what's not supreme about living in a house with four of your closest pals, all bringing a deliciously different ego to the table, all wonderfully ridiculous and affably awesome.

It was about as close as one could get to disgustingly perfect. Yet there was a flipside to this bronzing penny, the opinion that none of these chaps possessed a personality that my fragile facility could truly rely upon as a listening ear. However, this accommodating set up also had its pro's, such as providing me with an exhilarating extent of escapism. Broadly speaking, this house-share was a Harry Potter fantasyland type holiday park, only one with fewer wizards and conjurors and more copulation and sheer animal magnetism.

You see, during my first year at this free-for-all uni I felt like a member of the unlucky poultry clique, chilling in a battery cage, all cooped up in my single room and able to shut everyone out whilst I handled my horrors in a hermits habitat. Second year though, tittie-twisting time capsule, this was the premier league of tomfoolery and solace, a crazy carnival of fireworks and friendship, with the opportunity to lock myself away both rare and intermittent.

I could reside in my bedroom for those minutes or hours of hurt if I needed, and loosey goosey caught in a noosey did I need it occasionally. I was still partial to times where I didn't want anyone to know or think I was 'damaged goods', occasionally dropping points in the good fight and sporadically loosening my stiff upper lip. Nevertheless, these strategies of running and hiding were subject to change, for there was nowhere to really bolt the door and secrete myself, I mean c'mon, I was living with four champion chaps who fortuitously never allowed me such a prospect. What's more, I cherished their company and adored their antics. I loved the fact our house was the hub of attention, the go to place, never empty and always full of members of our ever expanding ensemble of friends. The sort of time in one's life that makes you realise its better to be absolutely ridiculous than absolutely boring.

Thus it was this persevering rapport of friendship that allowed the shadow of the sundial to continue its orbit, ensuring I stumbled upon a wayward segment of me. What I mean is, I actually found that always-up-for-a-giggle-the-night-is-still-young-lets-see-where-the-flotsam-and-jetsom-takes-us-tonight part of me that I was certain had been misplaced forever, with odds that surpassed any 250-1 probability. Nonetheless, it is safe to say I went off the tracks a bit, with this being the most reckless chapter of my story to date, but I can admit that now, for I am neither proud nor ashamed of this effervescent epoch. Instead I believe this is a process where one has to find him or herself, where one has to deal with their shit in accordance to whatever their personal path to righteousness may encompass.

Anyway, I remember how it started. I remember coming out of the mundane confines of my bolted room of apprehension and transforming into the confident chap of constant chuckles, in a scenario more accustomed to my former life. I remember the introductory few weeks of this second year of study. I remember sticking it to my first year mentality of guilt fuelled fun, or the lack there of. I remember being the 'boring' band member of the household cavalry, embarrassed by my inability to fully commit to frivolous festivities, more afraid and petrified than Gloria Gaynor ever portrayed. For it wasn't until Lily finally blew the full time whistle on our relationship that I found a new path, a path that was spectacularly lit up by disco lights and mirror balls.

Fair play to her though. I mean she knew I was in a rut even when I was painfully unaware of such observations myself. She recognised the only way I could locate my lively self again was to terminate the ever-dissipating connection we once had, a connection that was squandered by my selfishness in a stint of strife. Thus, I can only applaud Lily's bravery and gallantry, not only for doing what had to be done, but also for the way in which she executed it. She knew the only thing that would shake me up and kick start my lust for life was to crush the only stabilising factor I had left, her. She uprooted the only foundation that still stood when Dad was kicking about, and this was the straw that broke the camels back and threw me down a route where I believed anything worth doing was worth over doing, a dangerous mentality for a chap like me.

Yeah, the break up was fucking rough, but it was also fucking right. You see she had been there when I got the news about my Dad being killed. She was my support over those initial weeks and months when things were so daunting. She was there for me during that entire first year, as my rock and judge-free counsellor, and as a result I had become completely dependent upon her, and fuck was that an unfair evolution that transpired. Thus on that day when I was cordially invited to have face-to-face, heart-to-heart, chitty-chatty with her, I knew what the inevitable was, mathematically calculating what the options were, yet unable to embrace the brace position and set up a crumple zone. Once again my memory is struggling with the specifics, but I remember being sat opposite, hand in hand, steadily coming to accept what was just around the corner on the 'second hand' of the 'fuck you' clock.

This tête-a-tête was trivial to start with, with us discussing the weather and the fact my favourite colour is magnolia or beige or whatnot, and then without due care or warning, boom, Lily just burst into tears, with sincerity shining through her increasingly watery eyes as she explained her beautiful reasons for closing time. She explained she had to call a close on our time together so that I could go out and find happiness again, so that I could seek the enjoyment of life like I used to as the ambassador of amusement and so that I would no longer wallow in the daunting defeat of death. It was a selfless act to ensure I found my feet again and made me remember how lucky I was to still be here and to still have what I have. It was a gallant self-sacrificing dance to make sure I revelled in the ritual of this righteous party once more, rising from the ashes of desolation like the Phoenix I am, and boy-o-boy did I do her well wishes proud, whilst also honouring the antics of Anthony Kiedis and Michael Peter Balzary. I went fucking nuts.

I learned from this most beautiful and bewitching of breakups though. I learned that it is almost impossible to be aware of the day-to-day changes that occur to one's personality; at least it is impossible to realise from a first person perspective. For it's not like witnessing changes to a third party person, or analysing someone from an external standpoint. This is unsurprising though, for it is the little things that creep up on us and become routine and slowly alter us without even asking for consent. What's more, it was these surreptitious monotonies that I hadn't noticed, but others had, and even though they had, how were they to notify such a fragile being of said alterations?

It's a tricky business of course, but I believe it is still something that needs to be brought to attention no matter how delicate the situation. The key here is the way in which one goes about such a challenge that is clearly commendable of any 'Crystal Maze' episode; otherwise the person in question will be forever stuck in an unpleasant state of luxury free limbo.

Anyhow, this sudden self-dependency was terribly tough, for I was lost and out of my depth, somewhat embodying the Nirvana baby from the 'Nevermind' album cover. It wasn't an idyllic scenario, losing my old man followed by being on the receiving end of a good old-fashioned break up flex. However, the hardest and most troublesome part of this separation was the new notion of being on my tod for the first time since I landed in this puddle of piss. It was the first time I had felt absolutely alone.

I'd never had to be self-reliant, self-sustaining, self-supporting or any other term that implies a solitary life with the front running word of 'self'. It wasn't so much life without a girlfriend that was harsh; it was a life without anyone to turn to and my inability to approach the subject with anyone in the outside world. That was what triggered a transition in tact, forcing me to become more closed off than ever before, for I was unwilling and unprepared to take on the turbulence I was sprinting away from. Instead, I invested in an upgraded mask if you will. Trying the latest model in numerous veneers. Trying out different personalities in a bid to adapt or die. I mean after all, I was a young man or an old boy, desperately trying to hold everything together whilst it was falling apart. But this was as far from easy as one could possibly imagine.

This surreal situation required compartmentalisation so grandiose that even the rock star rebel of the silver screen, John Christopher Depp II, wouldn't have been able to keep up. This was a nocturnal year where everything had an unlit and eerie tinge, as if this time in my life was taken from some sort of film noir scene in which the majority of my hazy and deranged recollection seems to be backlit. But what choice are naive 'casualties' like us given. It's Run DMC tricky to explain, but self-sufficiency, to me, meant seeking out new ways to wear this makeup that so obviously oozed a narcissistic confidence. Fuck, this even included the introduction of my foolhardy disguise known as Hunter.

However, this alter ego was an advocate that enabled me to enjoy the sinful and mischievous nightlife again, an alter ego that wooed and courted with the best of them. One that revelled in a mentality that was strictly against anything platonic, enforcing a sort of touching but no talking manifesto. This was the measure of my fear, and the extreme extent of those personal barricades I had erected during a time that seemed to be one giant rave. It was a phase that was fuelled by drugs, or pretty much anything that could kill off my emotions. It was a phase of sharing laughs with everyone and anyone, and living in the moment, a moment that was siphoned from the 'swinging' 60s. This period in my life was almost a testimony to Fleetwood Mac, only on a very tight budget. To describe my mentality in one syllable, I was glib.

Now don't get me wrong, I would love nothing more than for you to get your kicks out of an autobiography about a Rolling Stones sort a protagonist, scribbling down the escapades of a folklore legend, for that's what people want to turn the page and pore over right?! The kind of jukebox hero that centre pieces a bacchanalia type festival filled with guitars, drums, drugs and a never ending line of ladies with neck down alopecia. A revelry spanning the decades, where the heavy bass lines are unforgiving, the riffs keep on ripping and one-night stands refuse to get any older. But to write this would be flat out fiction, perjury on a private scale, a personal betrayal. For the nitty-gritty truth of this fable is rather far from an elaborately glamorous story of rock royalty and beat boxing bullshit. In fact, I'm pretty certain this story won't get the guys hard or the girls wet, although in this day and age one can never be too sure.

Instead, this is the recital of a year that was dark and dingy lit by the soft glare of glow sticks and fucking stellar fun. But it was also nonetheless deeply damaging to the healing process that seemed to be ever depleting.

It was as if I was being swallowed up in a vortex that had little structure and little care, gobbling me up as if there were a red light district hooker named Destiny Flower at the end of my average sized dong. Lectures became more and more of an effort, and to an extent irrelevant when looking at the grand scheme of the universe, as did the thought of counselling. Mighty dick and balls, even reflecting on the shit storm that was so scorning in the prior months took a back seat on the to-do list. I would do anything to avoid the harsh heartache I had become so in tune with, absconding the hard-core facts of what reality had churned up. Simply encouraging myself to take a Greg Rutherford length leap in the wrong direction.

Sweet Child of Chewbacca, this year's unpredictable process is a Richard the Third to explain, but nevertheless and as always, I will attempt to articulate such arduousness as best as possible. Now I am fully aware that I am a lucky lottery winner, at least in the sense I had a sensational support structure in place when the plane crash happened, a support structure that was nothing shy of an absolute blessing. (A strong word for an atheist I know.) It was a support structure that meant I always had someone to lean on, especially when that impetuous volcano of anger refused to lay dormant for any longer, ready to blow in a rare eruption of emotion. Again, not a euphemism.

However, when this foothold was removed, in the form of being 'dumped', I had no one to blame but myself. I blamed myself for the dependency I had become such good buddies with, and the weakness I had adopted in the form of reliance upon someone else, and this changed me completely. I became cold, not in a refreshing Jean-Claude Van Damme Coors Light kind of way, but in a White Witch of Narnia with an erection type way. I could no longer commit to any member of the fairer sex for fear of that dependency rising up inside me once more, like a suffocating sandstorm of subjection. I couldn't allow myself to like any 'special someone' again, for I simply saw this as an act of unkindness, and an in humane act of torture.

I told myself this over and over. Yeah, it's plausible to argue that this was a fraudulent mindset, but it was one that had grounds. You see, I thought I would be unleashing the torment and trauma that had become my life on anyone I got close to, for this trauma and torment had become my true character, unfortunately. In short, I saw my issues as exactly that, my issues and that is a state of mind that sucks. I just thought it to be impassionate and corrupt for me to hurt anyone else in such a way again, especially as this sort of pain is a pain that far outdoes that of conventional relationship problems.

Baring none of my secrets became the potion in my Dr Jekyll and Mr Hyde scenario that was clinically condemning. It's a bizarre philosophy fo sho, the belief that you have become a burden on others, but a belief that also seemed to be a common denominator amongst similar individuals and more specifically their tales of hardships, nattering's which were hard fought for to say the least. I mean there seems to be this unwritten rule that more and more people seem to unwittingly adhere themselves too. This philosophy where you won't help yourself by allowing others to help you, instead believing you should struggle in silence for that's what you deserve. A pot kettle statement to say the least given I was, and probably still am, the Ambassador of such an unspoken organisation. I get it though. Everyone has their own problems, so why in heaven or on earth would I consent to complicating the lives of others. Why would I intentionally throw shit they don't need into their already muddied mixing pot, which is probably just as full to the brim as my own. With this in mind, there was absolutely no way I could adopt this logical approach with regards to those I really cared for, which is a paradoxical outlook but nonetheless the grounds behind my theory.

I'm certain it's completely normal to feel so desolate in a completely abnormal circumstance. The kind of feeling that your raunchy relationship with the contemporary world is tenuous at best, and you have got to trust me on this, for it's absolutely customary to believe you are burden especially after what you've been through and the so-called baggage you now carry. I promise you such a feeling is clearly understandable. I mean it is très difficile to open up to your friends, or even your family, for dropping your guard is a huge step in which you must be completely willing to do so. Yet despite this obvious movement, it's the sandbagging norm for one to be complicatedly unwilling. Unwilling to bare anything never mind everything, and to anyone never mind someone.

Yeah, I'm sure I've already referenced this next point but I've discovered it's worth reiterating whenever the opportunity rises. You see, when you've been knocked down time and time again, it takes it out of you more than you can know, mentally, emotionally and physically. It becomes hard to dabble in what others see as the simplicities of life, and this very much includes asking for help, or even accepting help, especially given pride has the awkward ability to imprison and impoverish almost any individual.

We all want to help others, but we'll refuse help when it's offered to us. Why is that? Are we too good for it? Is it because we've come through so much alone we believe we can continue on in the very same way? Is it a stupidly misjudged perception? Or is it the ever present D) all of the above? Quite frankly, I don't fucking know. There isn't a fact sheet available at Borders, and I don't seem to have any scientific answers readily available. Instead all I have is advice, and my advice is... if help is offered, take it, I mean we all require it for fuck's sake. It doesn't mean pouring your heart out to everyone, nor does it mean you are weak. In fact it shows the exact opposite. It shows sense, wisdom, understanding and it defines courage, and I can only wish I had accepted this during my time of need, instead of digging a deeper and deeper hole that slowly swallowed me up like a theoretical and less proficient Sasha Grey.

The key to coming out of this mother of a mess is openness, which isn't exactly easy given one of bereavements biggest bitches is that of being completely closed, so I think we have the right to call this situation a conundrum. Yeah, strangely enough, talking and openness are pivotal pieces to this peculiar puzzle, but don't get me wrong, it's easier said than done, especially when we're as tender as we are. It could take time to feel completely comfortable with someone again, and even more time to assess the unrivalled means of addressing the issues at hand. But if you are not ready then you are simply not ready, and you may need to address this pain in the sanctity of your own company.

However, if you want to dip a toe into what I believe is the next stage of progress, just remember that you don't need to sell the whole story at once or alert the media, just take it easy. Start with what you're comfortable with. Even dabble in a drip feed tactic if that's all you can manage. Now I'm not trying to be patronising, not in the slightest, but from my experience, if help is offered and you need it, I would recommend you take it, or if you're not feeling like your normal bubbly self, then just give someone a heads up that this is the case. This will only encourage you to keep taking baby-steps, but it will also allow others to be more approachable, letting them know you may need a shoulder, whilst also saying good riddance to the effervescent eggshells that can duly develop in your silent suffering. In the end, the choice is yours. It always will be, for only you know when you are ready, and only you can truly help make the decisions to help yourself.

Anyway, on we must go, for I can't sit still or hit pause, which is kind of a cross to bear. So lets delve into the role of dress code and music. Now this may sound irreversibly irrelevant, but bear with me. Now I had always been a bit kooky with my style of dress, a huge fan of accessories, sunglasses, wrist bands, beads and earrings, and whilst this hasn't wholly changed, the way I wear them has. I guess I used to be a follower, albeit one willing to make the flavour of the week his own. You see, first year of Uni I was bunked up with the public school lot, so a tweaked combo of Jack Wills and fake Polo Ralph Lauren was my foundation in an attempt to fit in, even though I tried to change it up a touch so that this lame style seemed to be riding a wave of acid in my case. Then there was Radio 1 on the wireless, and the Radio 1 playlist dominating my iTunes, which proved to be a far from strong look, and was one that was distanced from anything truly individual.

Then second year came through the letterbox, addressed to me in an enlightening envelope, filled with the first step away from being a sheep and more towards the role of cattle keeper or shepherd. Freethinking is the phrase I'm looking for. I was introduced to hip-hop, jazz, garage, remixes and refixes, whilst my ability to express myself through threads became more acceptable. In addition to this, one of the best things to come out of this Tim Burton inspired mother of all soap opera's that I was heavily involved in was later found guilty of also being one of the worst things. Nevertheless, I can't be a hater for something that started off as innocent, awakening and a doorway to some sensational 'had to be there' stories. You see, I found a friend in Mary Jane and her powder pals, all of who helped me expand consciously and evacuate emotionally, but there will be more on this party scene shortly.

Before this rave occurred though, I had been engulfed by an entity where everything revolved around the fact I had lost my Dad, not just due to my mentality, but it seemed everyone had an idea of the struggles I was faced with. I began to notice that people avoid mentioning keywords in conversations for fear it would upset me and instead they would look at me when a 'slip-up' occurred, cementing the fact it would now be a discussion even more uncomfortable to approach in the future. I felt like the black sheep who shrouds the local proximity in awkwardness, a Michael Cera shaped smoke grenade that leaked out Asperger's.

Furthermore, my ability to grab 40 winks continued to wilt, overwhelmed by the quarantine that was quashing me ruthlessly, an imperfect isolation. It was as if I was being dragged further into the depths of darkness, giving up the good fight in a sense. Of course I went out and enjoyed what this traditional town of randomness had in terms of flashing lights, enjoying the metropolis of those mock Mahiki's as much as the polluted anti-establishments of the 'alternative' and 'underground' scene. It was as if every scene was becoming that much more conventional, yet everywhere was littered with the friends I had become so fond of. Then once the lights came on in the club and the music was cut, the masses would start to seek a house, any house, just a place with a roof and an attitude that would allow the late night to linger.

It was late nights most nights, and every morning I would subsequently ignore my right to start the day with muesli, fresh fruit and natural yogurt, throwing my middle finger up at this champion breakfast that is traditionally accompanied by a pint of apple and mango juice and voicing the words 'fuck you' at the idea of a stable run to the gym, for knocking one out before participating in more sleep seemed to be far less hassle.

You see, experiencing what this life had to offer, a life I had never experienced before became far more important than lecture halls and library books. I can understand why this chemical change in me occurred though, and that's because my Dad was killed unexpectedly at fifty-seven years of age, and thus the way I began to think and the way in which I viewed the world competently changed. Change that death surely imparts on almost everyone. I just felt differently when I woke up and looked out of my window, for now when I'm laying uncomfortably on my deathbed, I can confidently say there is absolutely no way I'm going to regret anything I've done. However, I can be cocksure that I'll be riddled with regret when it comes to almost everything I haven't done, and it is for this reason that I'm drinking in almost everything this bar has to offer, benefitting from the bump and grind of the ball, and enjoying each moment this length of string known as life has to offer.

Deadlines weren't missed and extensions weren't taken, I simply took responsibility for my antics and the buck stopped with me. But I didn't give the educational experience of university my all, for I could only see it as petty when compared to death, and of course the subsequent challenges that death churns up for the living to deal with.

Now there's a sentence, or more specifically a word I'm far from fond of... comparison.

I just refuse to create ripples in the unforgiving and much mistaken ocean of comparisons, opting for context instead, with the need for context unrivalled. This principle comes from my well-grounded credence and belief that context should be awarded with a majority shareholding in the sympathetic stages of understanding bereavement, for no one can truly empathise. What I mean is, I saw my state of affairs as a challenge, in the same way that someone who has fallen out of favour with their best mate would also be faced with a challenge, or whatever the ultimatum may be. Quite frankly, there are no comparisons to be made, especially if you haven't been through even slightly similar shit, as it is quite literally incomprehensible. Full Stop. But it doesn't stop there, which is why I grabbed the word empathy by its emphatically empty bollocks and pulled it into the limelight to be interrogated.

I have numerous friends who have lost their Dad, or Mum or some significant other. Some of who were lost suddenly like my Old Man, others who witnessed death take control of their loved one through illness. Yet despite the hardships each of these people has faced, none of these riffraff persons would ever give you reason to think or supposed that they had seen the serious shit that they have. These people never allow anyone to assume they have suffered the un-telling abuse that death imparts on us. But what's more, none of these wonderfully impressive and awe-inspiring people can fully relate to one another due to the crippling notion of context, in which I mean the by-products and knock on effects that are so specific to each person.

Fuck, I can't even compare my standpoint to that of my own brother's.

As much as I love him, and as much as I want to, I simply can't empathise with him entirely, even though the actual event is linked to us identically. I was at Uni, he was at school, I am older, and he is younger. I don't know his burdening context. Nor do I know his demons, or the sequence of events that progressed, the support he had or the loneliness he felt. What's more, and despite the fact I have been subject to the following, I have a very limited idea of what it has been like for anyone else who has lost a parent, agonised at the hands of a divorce, had a Mother who has suffered from a chronic illness for the best part of a decade or witnessed alcoholism attack a loved one, etcetera etcetera.

The fact each circumstance is so isolated and so specific is what makes you the lead character in this pillaging pilot, a proverbial pilot that implemented no auditioning format whatsoever. You are the only person who can choose how to survive, choose how to fight the good fight and choose how to seek happiness again, as hard as that is to hear. It is your attitude that requires moulding and, unfortunately, there is no other craftsman able to help with such an unambiguous sculpture, for this is downright distinct to what you've been dealt. However, whilst this paragraph of realisation is as critical to the curing procedure as Bruce Willis is to saving the world in Armageddon, it would seem that I've digressed. So, in an attempt to get this diesel locomotive back on track, lets progress.

I went from being emotionally sealed behind a closed bedroom door, to extremely emotionally closed behind an always-open boudoir door. I had this newly discovered fear of missing out, a numbing gel that kept my mind away from the migraines, keeping me busy enough to ignore the problems that were very much there, but problems I didn't want to greet nor even confess to. Yet this was only made possible, albeit involuntarily, by the company of others, which sort of became a personal amalgamation of Calpol, paracetamol, ibuprofen and codeine. An ointment if you will, nay, a banter balm, disregarding the possibility that I was probably more of a target for the banter. But that's just a positive product of the negative coin, a silver lining adopted in the form of tremendously thick skin.

Of course there were other colourlessly detrimental outgrowths creeping out from under the woodwork without my say-so. In this instance I am referring to my hanky-panky love affair with writing, which distastefully took a back seat position in this emotionless new world of mine, whether it be extracts, poems, short stories, thank you letters or even tongue twisters, these creative mediums were all sadly shelved. Wretched really, for everyone has their own means of expression, an out if you will, and words were mine. But, in this new era of denial, such idioms forced out feelings I fancied forgetting, with feelings making the attraction of cigarettes and booze that much more charming.

It is for this reason those maiden tides and opening weeks of the semester took a new direction and became a ticking time bomb for my emotional awareness. Habitually I was out all night, watching the sunrises with a bottle of spirit in hand, enjoying the fruits of each night until I slammed into the bed of the week, before routinely cracking on bright and early, the next afternoon.

It was during this mitigation period I sambaed into the social side of Maui Waui. I won't deny the fact that I was sheltered as a child, but I cannot shift the blame on to this irrelevance either. Instead I think it was just another step towards fully experiencing what the fantasy factory of flesh and blood had to offer. I never intended my decision to start smoking the sweet wheat to escalate, nor did I realise that it had, but most crucially, I was ignorantly unaware of the effects it was having on my attitude and behaviour. I'm not talking about any immediate or short-term effects, I'm talking about the shit it fucked up in the long run. Maybe it's because my smoking of marijuana went from social stints, to a self-prescribed medicine, to a friend that was there through thick and thin, and then before I could realise it, my habit had somehow become a sly Peruvian night monkey, happily latched onto my back.

Now I'm not looking for brownie points, high fives or even a thumb's up, but I have never relied upon this plant during the day, not at any time in my life. I simply enjoyed it, at first. But it unknowingly became the sleeping pill that previously never was. You see, puffing on a joint before bed was a remedy for wakefulness, but what's more, it had no flipside unlike the Benzodiazepines and Z-medicines I had toyed around with the year before. There was no messed up side effects, no next day grogginess that felt like I'd stepped in the ring for eleven rounds with Floyd 'The Money' Mayweather the night before, in fact there was nothing more than a slight 'stoneover'.

Instead, this herb allowed me to gain some much-required beauty sleep, for it was the anti-Christ of Honda's catchphrase, 'The Power of Dreams', dispelling any chance of vividness in this department of delusions and revelry. Rather it quite remarkably halted the personal pandemic of those unremitting nightmares, the ones that had pounded my lethargically snoozing subconscious night after night. In addition to this, even if slightly off topic, I have to give credit where credit is due because, thunder-banging-ball-bags, chucking chronic coli into the already frolicking fusion of film and popcorn created a world of wonder that would keep even the wackiest of people in awe, even Mr Wonka. I mean, this herb made the visual and tasty experience of movies and snacks even more of an excellent adventure, an escapade worthy of Bill & Ted's undivided recognition.

Thus in my humbled opinion, and given that I had a set of lungs on me once upon a time it is a somewhat grounded opinion, I believe there are three main chapters to the wacky baccy book and its ability to creep into the daily life of any recreational user. The first chapter to me was smoking the mountain cabbage with friends, and more specifically, I was smoking their supply of pot. The next stage was when I started to buy my own stash, getting contacts for dealers, plucking up the courage to call or text these illegal entrepreneurs, somewhat learning the names of different strands, and adding my purchase to the communal chill mix, no longer just rinsing everyone else's. Then there is the final stage, and this is the one that seems to stealthily slip under the radar despite the certitude that it's definitely the moment I will always single out as the biggest banana skin on this fortuitous road to addiction. The moment I am talking about is the moment a person learns to roll a spliff, a blunt, a bifta, an L-plate, a zoot, a fatty or whatever you want to call it, providing the gateway to smoking with only your shadow as company.

This is a Neil Armstrong step indeed, for smoking by oneself is a very different high from that of a social cotch, and a surprisingly slippery slide into reliance indeed. It becomes a time filler, a new perspective, it makes films better and food tastier, it prompts heavy conversations and ridiculous speculation, sunny days become scenically picturesque and rainy days bearable, albeit that is usually because the dreary days are fuelled by Skate 3 and Call of Duty. It anesthetises emotional pain, numbs memories and, at first, lets you nod off into a state of dormancy at night, with the guerrilla threat of insomnia now disparaged most evenings.

Of course I would never encourage someone to smoke this tree of wisdom, but I would also never frown upon those who do. The key is simply moderation, as it is with all things bittersweet, whether inebriants, Turkish delight, the daily grind of work or even exotic escort services, it all comes down to moderation. This is a far cry from my natural mentality, which still strongly supports the belief that anything worth doing is worth over doing. However, and these were vital words that brought me to my senses in recent times, if anything ever gets hold of you in its deathly grip, unwilling to surrender you, or if you ever become dependent upon what is essentially a vice, then drop it without hesitation, walk away or run if you can, and don't look back.

Don't get me wrong, as far as I'm concerned, you can unequivocally enjoy everything life has to offer, simultaneously if that's your preference, however these choices must not harm others. Thus, if the day comes that you need something, you depend on it and rely upon it, then stop. No questions asked. Just make it fuck off, and if you can't do that, then head to the nearest train station or taxi rank and get the fuck out of there yourself. Reliance and dependency upon drugs, or anything for that matter, may not be harming you per se, you may even be oblivious to how it's affecting those around you, but believe me when I say addiction can creep up on your behaviour and relationships like a wrinkly ninja. But let's take a brief hiatus from this subject, especially as I'm sure I'll be swinging back past the BC bud bus stop later on, maybe even on numerous occasions, for it is a topic that needs to be dwelled upon further. But for now, lets move on.

So, as I stated in the previous pages of this rambling confession, this was a period of progression in the best part, even if it was also rooted regression on the emotional front. I mean, one can only survive the trenches of bereavement at an age of adolescence by accepting it for what it is, and to do this you need to accept who you are, and for this to slip into place, it is god damn crazy crucial to learn who you are. Maybe you already know this about yourself, in which case you're likely to be on the beaten path towards the humble hamlet of hopes and dreams and happiness in all its splendour.

However, even after 4 years its clear that I'm still learning, even if I am slightly closer to familiar territory, observing some similarities to my proverbial past after being lost in the woods for long enough to be welcomed by most laissez-faire lumberjacks. You see I became far more confident. I began unleashing parts of me that had been clandestine for too many eclipses, and no, I'm not talking about my penis you filthy minded son of a seahorse you. In fact, I rephrase that latter comment for the sake of my glass half full optimism, substituting the phrase 'filthy mind' and replacing it with 'sexy imagination'. Just another life lesson from me to you, but cradle a cock, I've digressed again for fuck's sake!

So, back to self-assurance, or more accurately the value that I use to kid myself I had, pretending that I was confident during this yesteryear, constantly needing to remind myself that this arrogance was in fact utter bollocks and a futile fabrication. I was in too deep like Sum 41, wearing a nauseatingly thick layer of narcissistic face paint, like the shit scared immaturely mature man-child I was. Yet too this day, people still think I'm blatantly arrogant and a swaggering show-off, but then who am I too tell them otherwise for this was exactly the impression I oozed.

The unvarnished truth however is diametrically opposite, for this spectacle of style I had assumed was nothing more than a weak attempt and disillusion. It was an attempt to restore my cowering confidence that had seen better days, the confidence that had become so incarcerated. Yeah it was a strong sense of 'style' with comparisons covertly made between my attire and that of a colourful bird, but I remain accepting of these accusations. I'm not going to argue against the fact that it may pay to be a wallflower for some of us, but that just wasn't me.

I was far more invasive of people's personal space and harmful to the retina's of local bystanders. Peacocking with my nonpareil wardrobe, the dangly earrings, the unrivalled collection of glasses, some for traditionally sunny days and others for the Geek-chic intelligent look, whilst I also had an adaptable Mohawk for all occasions. Fuck, I even wore a fake bake tan from my frequent holidays to Superdrug and Boots, albeit this pseudo-bronzed skin was fervently forced upon me by the fact I get burned crazy easy, with even the light in my fridge turning my pasty body scarlet red for tittie-twisting sake.

On paper people had every reason to judge me as an attention demanding douche, a conceited and egotistical megalomaniac hell bent on bringing the world to its knees to see me in my glory, naked and consumed in grandstanding. Yet, this crazily colloquial dress sense of mine was all smoke and mirrors. It was a deterrent. It was a distraction that obeyed the Harry Houdini rule of what the eyes see and the ears hear the mind believes, preoccupying the curious in an attempt to avoid the real questions of substance, questions that I wasn't prepared to answer.

I could handle the preconceptions people drew up and aimed at me on a skin deep level, for these were nothing more than super soakers to my rhino hide skin. It was the judgements cast by people who had caught wind of my actual hardships that were damaging, for this is what I was sincerely fearful of, knowing the harmful hearsay practice of Chinese whispers. I hated those piercing eyes of pity that provoked me to state my case, assuring them I was happy, subtly ensuring them I was not in need of their sympathy or compassion. This was not a super soaker scenario. For these were moments more comparable to staring down the business ends of numerous Heckler and Koch's.

I was just out of practice, closed off from the veracity of my emotions, not wanting to know and blissfully unaware. Yet, I was also well aware that these barriers of the great internal reef and the in-house Hadrian's Wall were not as insurmountable as one would have liked to believe. It's inevitable that others had or have similar methods of diverting the curious traffic away from the acrimonious truth, well maybe not similar, but their own methods of dealing with the Curious George's nonetheless. I mean which sensible lunatic wouldn't want to deviate attention away from the sombre negativity that has become one's life, choosing to blind those around us with what's on the surface while simultaneously hiding what's going on inside. In metaphorical terms, I was like a concert security guard, waving the crowd towards the show, whilst highlighting the 'do not enter' signs that prevented the masses from getting backstage.

Just quickly though, let me explain the snappy two-word catchphrase I just coined above, you know, the 'sensible lunatic' one, for this clever combo kind of touches on the very different opinions I had at very different times. You see, throughout this troubled time of life after Dad, the idea of becoming an emotional recluse seemed unquestionably sensible. To reference James Brown, it was a decision that allowed me to adopt a 'get on up' feeling, as juxtaposing at that sounds. It gave me a skip in my step every so often, but more imperatively it allowed others to get on with their lives too. A win-win result right? Wrong.

The damning infliction this decision had in the long run made it an act of lunacy, much like sprinting the first three and half miles of the New York Marathon, full steam ahead, you'll get snagged sooner or later. However, the beauty of Monday morning quarterbacking and the astonishing wonders of hindsight allow me to reassess the pinnacle moments of my decision-making process. So, having delved into the memory vault, I can safely say it was a huge mistake to never wear my heart on my sleeve, irrelevant of the fact this was all I knew at the time. To put it into some perspective, I can safely say Al Gore's decision to not request a full recount of Florida's votes in 2000 was not as ill-judged as my atheistically eremitical choice to suffer in silence. To put it another way, if I could jump into a fully functioning hot tub time machine with the intention of giving my younger self some grounded advice, my advice would be to open up more, and to be more confident.

When I was having a rough day, I should have swallowed my pride and sought the comfort of others, instead of swallowing my suffering and acting as if everything was just delightfully dandy. I should have spoken to a friend about the troubles at the time, for no one knew how hard I really found it, and that's because I didn't want to trouble anyone else. Instead, I would let it build up and build up inside, forever keeping my groundless grin on show, persisting with this method until I couldn't take it any more and I'd just snap, even If only briefly, I would sensationally snap. I would try and make like a tree and leave as quick as possible, darting for my bedroom, the front door, the back door or even the fucking laundrette, anywhere I could lock a door and clench my fist.

My outbursts would be the kind of ferocious furore that would commence with white knuckles and end with claret covered hands. I would see red, both metaphorically and literally, creating a wake of destruction as if I had embodied the Australian devil that resides in Tasmania, unable to control my solitary flare-ups. However, if this quick escape was off the cards then my Slick Rick inspired tongue would find itself instinctively reloading before unloading a verbal assault on anyone I had become even slightly comfortable with, a tirade of expletives, profanities, blasphemies and obscenities. I would just snap and shatter, leaving any swagger, style, ease, calm and collectiveness outside the china shop before I transformed into a brawny bull.

I was delicate. I was very delicate. So much so that my temper could've be inadvertently instigated by little more than friendly banter, yet I'd break, forcefully telling the rabble-rousing Chuckle Brothers in question that I was having a rough enough day as it was, relinquishing momentary malice. Ridiculous right? I mean how the fuck were my joke-loving friends meant to know I was feeling fragile at that specific moment in time?! I was the judge, jury and executioner when it came to the decision to wear a mask, no one else, thus it's hard to place anyone else at fault on any of these hostile occasions. However, what stupidly slipped under my self-obsessed radar at the time was their admirable response, for these friends of mine cared so much. They wanted nothing more than to help, asking if I was ok, asking what they could do to help, reassuring me with the knowledge they were there should I ever need a gracious ear, day or night. Yet, even this unmistakeable wink-wink-hint-hint setting wasn't enough to break through my protective shell.

The bottom line is, I wasn't willing to help myself at this stage. Even when a fluorescent lifebuoy was thrown my way, or when a supporting hand presented itself during the important first steps, I just couldn't face listening to any self-wallowing words come out of my proud kisser. I've learnt from this though, and a word of advice here, if a kind hand comes your way and offers you a touch of much needed support, take it, without hesitation, just take it. Yeah, this piece of advice is a bit rich, especially given that I've only recently begun to take my own advice on this topic. But truth be told, it feels as good as any hand release ejaculation I can remember. In fact the only difference I can think of is that this supportive help I aforementioned takes a weight off your mind, whilst the sordidly mentioned handy take a weight off your balls.

Anyway, it is safe to say that no matter how much time passes after the loss of a loved one, it doesn't get any easier to accept, and you have to accept this. I surrounded myself with the familiar faces of friends by day and randomly haphazard females by night, adopting a kind of Childish Gambino 'fuck Macaulay Culkin I'm never going home alone' type mentality. Now don't get me wrong, this was a distraction that reaped rewards with either constant chuckling or venereal pay-offs, but above all this, it was a distraction that went far above just surface encounters. Looking back now I can assess my actions better, and it is obvious that I was unable to commit to anything during this soul-searching stage of trying to find my feet, and this included a lack of commitment in pretty much every area of my subsistence. Most predominantly though, I couldn't commit to my feelings or my emotions, instead remaining true to my stubborn inability to accept the stone cold truth for what it was.

Of course there were moments, whether five minutes or twenty-four hours, where I was caught in isolation, staring at the photographic shrine I'd put together as a remembrance piece to my dear old Dad. I would stare at these photos, teary eyed, missing the face that memory has distorted, whilst tucked away in my dark room where the curtains were never open and left alone to listen to a sombre collage of Kid Cudi, songs such as Mr Solo Dolo, Pursuit of Happiness & the uncannily accurate Soundtrack to My Life. This is hardly what one would call a commitment though, not unless you count the bond I had cordially struck up with music, for this was a commitment. I would just listen to music with no obvious company, listening solely to the now prominent lyrics, almost ignoring the beat and rhythm, just concentrating on the words written and spoken by the poetic philosophers of our time.

As I'm sure you are aware, certain songs have this magic that brings back specific memoirs. Memoirs coaxed out with verses, lines, codas and refrains, with experiences certifying the notion that certain lyrics will take on a whole new meaning, allowing one to relate to the wise words in a way others may not. It was these moments of independent confinement that emphatically coerced me into a corner, drawing out fervidly tear-jerking moments of rarity. For these deserted moments of reflection where I was upset and on my Tod Malone were as rare as the philosopher's stone, popping up in my existence sporadically. Popping up as often as table tennis and tea parties with the mad hatter do.

But this simply acts as supporting evidence of my tawdry effort to engage in something regularly and for a substantial period. As I stated earlier, there was no plentiful vow between lectures and myself, for I was not ready to approach what I knew would test my ever-seesawing ability to remain strong. With so much pent up despair, even the most delicate of reminders could have sent my world spiralling out of control, and even the slightest mention of politics would have undone all my hard fought efforts to consign my memories to a provisional oblivion. I guess I was just more committed to the reasons that supported non-attendance than the obvious reasoning of educational advancement.

It didn't cease there though, for I couldn't commit to my family either. I didn't go about showing this in an obvious way that would hurt them, but instead in a more sadistically subtle fashion I guess. What I mean is, I stopped going back home, as often as I had previously anyway, and a lot less often than I should have, distancing myself further than the physical geography would allow. I was committed to not committing. I was a delicate drifter, scared and scarred, battered by life, and steadily slipping into the world of an escape artist. I was committed to accidental self-sabotage, having the time of my life in terms of laughs, lust, sex and inebriation, whilst dismissing any evidence of the truth, harbouring a pain so hidden that it deserved AWOL status. To put it more bluntly, I was despondent, a retreating coward, and wholly unprepared to do what was necessary.

As you have probably conceded, I am not writing this as a playbook nor as a timeline of what to expect and when to expect it. Instead, and as I continue to repeat, this is my experience and thus I can only wish upon a star that these notes have the potential to provide a positive impact on you, even if you can only relate to a single sentence, or a single passage in this extensive scrawling, for it could be the passage that helps you progress to the next stage of the healing process. You may have experienced your darkest days straight after the evolutionary event. Maybe there was a specific moment that arrived months or years later, one that kicked you to touch while you were trying to heal. You may have even been wise to the pitfalls, keeping yourself on the straight and narrow, knowing what you had to do, knowing the options you were given and knowing where they could lead.

Maybe you had an amazing support structure and a tight knit family that worked together for a common goal of happiness after sadness. Maybe you are going through the dark times now, feeling swallowed up by a darkness that is so overwhelming you could be stood slap bang in the middle of the illuminated Times Square and still not be able to see the light. In my experience, it was a moth to the flame parody, if the moth was I and the flame was anything that could be drunk, smoked or belonged in the Led Zeppelin book of buffoonery. As long as it encouraged poor judgement and a heavy distraction from the anti-pleasantries life had to offer, I was as keen as a bean.

Obviously such a blow out is not a wise decision, but then the word 'decision' is a loose term when chucked into this context. In fact, George W. Bush was a more competent decision maker than most of us who choose the path of tomfoolery driven escapism. Unfortunately though, I don't know how we can avoid it. I don't know how we ensure there is an end to the downward spiral of sodomising exuberance. I don't know if it was an individual outcome in which the Molotov cocktail of self-sufficiency, bereavement, and non-prescription potions made it a numbing result specific to me. What I hope I can do, however, is let others know about this dark side of this moon, cast a light on the effects of evasive merrymaking and more specifically what these effects can involve.

I'm not saying everyone resorts to booze, smokes the alternative baccy, pops pills and whips out a credit card to line up any prolific powder possible, nor am I saying the twilight of youthful gaiety will certainly result in an addiction when mixed with totally bitching hardships. You see I had a great time! Yeah, I enjoyed my second year at university a little too much, but I was switched on enough to moderate my antics, even if I was pushing the boundaries on a rather regular basis. But despite the fact I was aware of the carefree catacombs and cavorting fissures along this path, I still didn't recognise my new dependency with regards to the night time bluffing of marijuana puffing, and like a mild child of Amy Winehouse I just struggled to say no, no, no.

Of course I encourage you all to have a ridiculously rad rave of a time and to live in the eternal sunset of youthful frolicking, I mean, we only get to enjoy this party once, so why not celebrate it with an eclectic disco dance. However, I will also encourage you to know your limits and to learn when you've become reliant upon something, whether moonshine or substances, for addictions can really fuck you up. Now, weed may not be a gateway drug in every circumstance, but it is a drug nonetheless, one that everyone has tried, and one that tends to have a life expectancy with every smoker. It is a drug that changes perceptions and makes the harder options more appealing and the yearning for anti-reality a tough temptation to battle.

However, I may have to rely upon the gorgeous face of our favourite ex-junkie to get this point across, for this topic was fantastically worded by the always amusing and lucky to be alive rock star of the blank page, Russell Brand. In 'My Booky Wook' (the better of the two autobiographies, although this is an analysis only separated by the 'Dear Katy Past Future' bollocks prior to the prologue) the cuddly sexual predator known as Brand receptively stated,

"We all need something to help us unwind at the end of the day. You might have a glass of wine, or a joint, or a big delicious blob of heroin to silence your silly brainbox of its wittering's but there has to be some form of punctuation, or life just seems utterly relentless."

This literary genius is spot on, especially with his emphasis on the need for punctuation, albeit not so much with his reference to a delectable dilly-dally in heroin abuse. Dick-pumping doppelganger, and by that I mean fuck, for this blunt synopsis is even more accurate than Matt Le Tissier's cracking penalty record.

I guess I see both drink and drugs as good and bad. They can be both treacherous and dangerous, offering frantic frolics and frenetic fun, but they also have the unrivalled ability to create lunatics. I know I am somewhat lucky, for I consistently remind myself not to become a laced up lunatic, nonsensical and zany. I just don't really fancy fucking up my only shot at life all in the name of riotous elation, joviality and the chance to join the legends of the '27 Club'. But I also had to experience this for myself, I had to try and figure this out on my own accord. I have to make my own mistakes and learn from them. I know this will be a scary realisation for my wicked awesome Mother, not forgetting the other incredible and subsequent members of my patient family, but I also know they trust me, and rightfully so. It just pays to be switched on, tuned in and perceptive, and maybe this saved me from the clutches of desolation, but more charitably, maybe this realisation could help others avoid slipping off the rickety bridges that cross the troubled and panicky waters of craving and obsession.

This was a period that was hard to judge. On the one side it was a time of explosive excellence and unrivalled recreation, whilst the other side of this barely buttered toast showed loneliness, regression and emptiness. There was an introduction to intoxication and an extradition of determination, all of which was possibly needed, yet at the same time, not needed at all. It was an oxymoronic epoch, complicated by the overdue need to roll around in the divulged pleasures, whilst straying into an unknown wilderness of temptation. I was closer to friends, but distanced from myself. Surrounded by ladies and gentlewomen, but isolated from commitment or love. It was an eye opener into a world I hadn't explored before, but it was a journey that had removed me from the healing path I had been so dedicated to previously.

Looking back, this was the peak of my unintentional running and hiding, yet the peak of my gregariousness, for I was socialising everywhere and carousing with everyone. I seemingly went from one extreme to the other, always testing boundaries. Of course, this could have gone hand in hand, and it probably did. It was the very best of one world, and the very worst of another, and it is this that I aim to highlight. I mean, you have to make your own choices when it comes to metaphorically drowning the sorrows and swimming in the barrel, but remember, you have a choice, you know your limits and you know the line. Do with that what you will.

It was during this year that I was presented with next frantic challenge of dismay and disarray. As a master of emotional circumvention, it was a bizarre notion to be swapping the chaotic antics of one place, for the chaos of another. It was unavoidable by all means, but it was also needed, even if heading home for the inexcusably long summer break trapped me in a bitter no-man's-land of harsh reality. However, this trip back home stung me harder than I could have anticipated, for this 'next challenge' I just referred to, indecently exposed itself on the 22nd July

2010 when Paul, my Godfather, guardian and Dad's best friend, passed away after a yearlong battle with cancer.

This was a lucid lightning bolt from Zeus himself, one that was sent thundering through my sternum and into whatever was left beneath it. Losing Paul devastated me, for I had become so close to him after losing my Dad. He had become the voice of reason and reassurance whenever I was faced with life's crossroads. Yet, it was also a moment that made me come to my senses in a way. It had this kind of positive impact that made me realise once again how short life is and that there is no equality in the eyes of death, with this nullifying news rekindling my internal fire of ambition and determination. However, it was also a moment that hypothetically seemed to load emotional round after emotional round into numerous theoretical Tommy guns, before riddling me with these tear-jerking bullets in a John Dillinger, Bugsy Malone type fashion. It was a time that provided a step forward in one sense, and a step back in another.

This contradictory feeling deserves clarification, thus what I meant is, it was a monumental step forward in the sense I could breathe again, inhaling ambition, determination, desire and purpose, having figuratively held my breath for longer than Ricardo Bahia, during the months before. I had a re-emerged focused on succeeding, focussed on making something of myself, to do something I loved and make a difference. This, to me, was as impressive and prodigious as the 1969 lunar landing, the invention of nanotechnology and the sheer remarkability that clouds the archaeological city of Petra. It's an overwhelming realisation that blinds you. A moment that helped me realise I was not as dead inside as I had come to believe, a moment where I got in touch with my most lucrative personality traits. I found that fight in me, that fire I believed had been extinguished, the fire that was in fact eternally burning, although it may have been very little more than embers. It is the eternal flame that burns inside, a remembrance piece to the 'known soldiers' that I have loved and lost. This changed me. I was as fun loving as before, but more sensible. I was a livewire wildcard with wisdom, akin to that of Pocahontas, at least if she possessed a Y chromosome and a deeply Caucasian skin.

However, the loss of my Dad's best friends was also a vast step in the wrong direction, choking me even further with regards to my emotional state. It endorsed a further feeling of fear and I bizarrely began to take some of the blame, believing I was jinxed and bewitched. As egotistical, eccentric, grotesque, ludicrous and outlandish as this is, I still understand my trail of thought. You see soon after the bond between my Granddad and I strengthened, he died. I finally heard my Dad tell me those incredulously rare words the day I arrived at university, words of pride and love, words that he said directly to me, and soon after he too was killed. Then in the wake of my Father's death, I grew encouragingly close to my Godfather and guardian, seeking his advice in those situations where I would have previously gone to Dad. He was then also taken from us all too. I blamed everything on myself. Dad's death, Paul's passing, Hurricane Igor, the floods in Pakistan and the famine of Africa's Sahel region, fuck-a-doodle-do, I even blamed myself for the Deepwater Horizon oil spill.

But as ridiculous as this mind-set may seem, when you've been thrown about by the Herculean mammoth known as life in a way that tells you you're nothing more than a ragdoll, it's hard to keep whistling 'Always look on the bright side of life'. I had been knocked down time and again. My counter attacking ability had become slightly less effective than that of Ken Sean Carson, with the only difference being I'm not as smooth as him downstairs, and proudly so. I had suffered so many knockbacks, not just witnessing the magnitude of death on a personal level, but understanding its presence and learning about its notorious unpredictability. Quite frankly, the adoption of any other attitude had been dishonourably dispelled.

I had started to come to terms with the fact I was now part of a family where trivial phone-calls about tis-was were more infrequent than those pieces of negative news that deleteriously hit home with a Derek Jeter inspired precision. Trapped in the kind of scenario where every individual vibrate of my 'smart' phone instilled me with a panicky anxiety, encouraging me to became more and more fond of ignoring calls for fear of yet more merciless news. I just didn't regularly receive the kind of call where my Mum would tell me about the newly built extension Wendy's postman had just had, or whatever the normal Wisteria Avenue mundane monologue usually is.

No, instead of this I would get phone calls informing me of the loss of yet another person we knew or another person we were close to, simply letting me know the date of another funeral I must try to attend. Maybe these phone calls and these days of sadness were heightened due to my experiences, but whatever the case, it seemed as though my death tally was catching up with both my Gran Theft Auto record and the scandalous score of the Grim Reaper.

Yes, such nerve-nullifying news spurred on my ambition and yes I was more fixated on success than before. In some lights, I was now more focussed than any wanky wizard trying to perfect his or her command over the pleb-dazzling Patronus spell, and what's more, I had knuckled down in the self-starting, go-getting, eager beaver and hungry horse sense of the phrase. But nonetheless, I was synchronically closing in on a misanthropic mentality, transmuting into an emotional anchoret or an emotive solitarian. On reflection, this amount of 'bad luck' had sent me into a state of shock. I was rapidly retreating whilst wildly waving the white flag, a white flag made out of any material possible, well anything except for my Y-fronts or boxers for I was so shit scared at this time that these under crackers of mine were no longer a true white.

And what a way to stride into year three… Flypaper for emotionally fucked up news.

"The biggest coward of a man is to awaken the love of a woman without the intention of loving her."

Bob Marley

YEAR THREE

I hoped this was to be the start of a new era, or for loosely termed literary purposes, the start of a new chapter. A chapter full of positivity on the one hand, yet one peppered with many complications on the other. A scenario that can only be tantamount to the escapades of Gene Simmons, and more specifically his thousands of proverbially positive balls deep encounters, yet these erotic and envy inducing escapades were dampened and corrupted by a honeycomb of positive STIs. I mean it was a swing's and roundabouts kinda season. But nonetheless, this next stretch of my life was once again a paradoxical time frame, as oxymoronic as artificial grass, affordable housing, autopilot and anarchic governance.

You see this year started somewhat differently to its precursor, for I had left the lonely confides of my debauchery and lothario like exploits and leaving them at the wayside for the time being. For I had once again landed in a puddle of luck, landing a veraciously amazing and unbelievably tolerant girlfriend, known by many as Phoebe. She was the sort of fairer sex that was so enticingly stunning that her reflection could have alleviated arthritis. But more than this, she was pleasantly patient and undeniably loved me for the potential she saw in me. She was also the calming influence I needed and that voice of reason when it came to my formidable attitude that was desirous of everything and all at the same time.

However, there was one giant wedge that came between us that prevented true happiness, and that was quite simply the inauspicious alley cat I call me. You see, when you've suffered so much pain and lost the people you loved the most in this Milky Way of a Galaxy Bar, it becomes a naturally chemical reaction to close off, and that is exactly what I experienced. I buttoned up my emotional zipper because I was scared of being screwed again. In fact I was so perpetually panicked and terror-stricken at the thought of losing yet another person I was close to, that I found I couldn't fully commit to anyone anymore, thus I would involuntarily keep these wonderful peeps of mine at an extended arms length instead.

Fuck, I was so shaken and startled by the prospect of enunciating my emotions I thought my sphincter might shrivel up and die. This wasn't just the case with Phoebe though, for it was in fact a strongly similar scenario with regards to my mother and my brother, so much so I'm positive that no jury would have ever contemplated supporting my fluky and fickle behaviour or my astonishingly dicey antics. To put it frankly, I was in a bad place, and one that is as hard to explain now as it was back then.

I had lost more than enough family. We had all lost more than enough family. But what was eating away at me like some species of larder beetle, constantly keeping me on the back foot and sleeplessly worried, was my Mums unstable health. I was petrified and weak at the knees about her physical stature, and what's worse is that it always seemed as though I was being drip fed the most crucial information. It seemed as if everyone was hiding half the realities from my brother Oli and I. Maybe this was because our loved ones widely believed we had been through enough already, which is of course an outrageously understandable outlook. However, if anything, Oli and I were made stronger by such life lessons, and unlike the well-known saying, we were now only scared by what we didn't know.

This fear then sparked a back-against-the-wall type reaction, in which I was unintentionally pushing my family away, scared to have a close relationship for fear of having my heart ripped out, yet again. What's more, I had also accidently acquired an Independence Day / Star Trek type force field that proficiently protected my feelings from any 'attacker', with the only difference being my force field was characteristically uncool, adopting a similar personality to Screech from 'Saved by the Bell' as opposed to the bad ass Captain Kirk.

I had just been pounded and pounded by deaths direct punches ever since Dad died, and now death was also affecting my relationship with the living, and this was an entirely incongruous motility. I was petrified of losing my only parent, petrified of losing my magnificent mother who'd cared for me all my life, never forgetting the tender-hearted and rad hospitality she also showed me whilst I was kicking back in her wicked wonderful womb. I could only guess this fear was a natural response that I had no control over, as if I were a puppet controlled by an emotional puppeteer of unequivocal experience. I hated my attitude. In fact this was probably the least proud period of my longevity, and trust me, that's saying something, because like most kids, I've done plenty of ill-advised, puerile and senselessly moronic shit in my short time. You'd only have to ask my Dad for verification. Nevertheless, I never suspected nor intended such a yellow-bellied and spineless charisma to cradle me, but it was at roughly this stage I was taken hostage by a lily-livered rationale and snared in a hostage situation that was prolonged for far too long.

For anyone who has been through the whirlwind wank shaft of bereavement, or has been affected by it in anyway whatsoever will know first hand how unpredictable everything becomes! Death affects us in any and every way, and there is nought one can do to prepare for this ball bashing belittlement. In an attempt to win the understatement of the year, those of us who are living with the derangement of death have very little fucking control. Moreover, it is our behaviour that capriciously fluctuates like a knuckleball, obtaining a template more volatile than any revolving phantasmagorias.

I was aware that I was incredibly irritable, and that I was also being unapproachably short with the family I loved so very much, but I couldn't alter this besmirching realisation as much as I wanted to. It becomes a cacophony of feelings with no apparent prevention techniques. This notion is hard to understand and possibly straight up ridiculous to comprehend, for all our loved ones want to do is help us alleviate our trauma. They desperately want to discover a way to help you overcome this torture chamber that you're noticeably trapped in. Yet this is far from simple to swallow, for whenever my friends or family approached me about how they could assist in easing my pain or asked me what was wrong, they suddenly became the victims of a ferocious tongue slapping and some seriously ballistic backchat, but I couldn't help these outbursts.

Maybe I was just not ready to take the blame for my actions, thus palming it off, condemning external reasons instead. I'm sure we have all done it. I'm sure we have all placed accusations elsewhere and shifted the blame to the likes of our job, the broken spark plug in the car or the lack of sleep. I'm sure we have all shifted the blame onto the Internet being too slow, people asking too many question and there not being enough participation in stand up sixty-nines, or whatever crap excuse we decide to pluck out of this tombola of bullshit. We just can't artlessly accept that we've become the problem, finding it easier to blame the world instead, cursing up at the sky as if there is a God laughing it up amongst his angels, all of whom have an equally sick sense of humour. But that aint the case, mourning just takes time, and that can quickly transcend into a lot of overtime before we can make the adjustments that are needed, before we can accept that it is down to us as the individual to change. Thus, I am once again ensuring a climaxing crescendo that ends on the finger pointing and questioning notion of one's own attitude.

Anyway, I am sure I will visit that avenue again given the importance it demonstrates, but right now it seems I have left yet another busy high street topic as a result of repeated deviation. So, back to the unforgiving notion of what it is to be completely closed off to any love interest.

Maybe someone told me I was a bad guy somewhere along the way, and I took it to heart. Maybe I believed this observation because it was someone else's opinion. This is nonsensical because I know I'm not a bad guy, but then this opinion has been confused by the possibility that I am. It is an obscure orbit, but one that requires an answer, thus I have to state that I try and do what good guys would do in this picture. I try and prevent illicit love affairs from becoming too emotional because I know my past will only hurt them at some point, its only a matter of time. Yet in certain aspects of life I follow the idiosyncratic rules of engagement even though I may not be ready to. Maybe I conform in the social areas I believe I'm inept. Maybe I conform to tell myself I am a good chap. I don't know, but what I do know is, I confidently hate conforming. Maybe I'm not good or bad. Maybe I'm just a work in progress. Whatever the case I just want to find out who I am and be true to that person, that's the only way I'll make it out the other side of the utter confusion.

Maybe it's something to do with the lessons of history, and more definitively, the lessons of our own history. You see, to this day I wonder whether I'll ever be able to fall bowler hat over brogues in love with anyone. This is probably because after Dad I found it incredibly hard to even say 'I miss you' to people, and I won't dare say the life-changing trio of words 'I love you' to anyone either. I think this is simply because I know the true meaning of these words, for I truly miss the Dad I loved. It's not the easy way out by any means because its comically far from easy, in fact it's a fan-fucking-tastically foreign feeling to be scared of welcoming cupid's arrow by raising a very real shield, all of which enables the 'inability to completely commit' clause.

It is a discerning twist, and one where we are afraid, afraid that once the armour has been removed, there is nothing left to protect the now exposed and tender feelings we've tried so hard to defend. For once this occurs, we are exposed to the excruciating pain and exasperation that we would do anything to never experience again. Yet trying to spit these words out in such a way that allows their connotation and value to hold even a fraction of their meaningful depth is impervious and futile. I want to ensure some worded justice that could allow the listener to relate and understand, to help the caring family and the doting girlfriend understand, but how do I possibly do this. How are words possibly meant to do such deep rooted feelings any justice, for no matter how impressive ones plethora is, words begin to seem so unspeakably lame in comparison to the actual pain that I know so damn well.

Moving on in my experience though, I discovered this third year of trials, errors, attempts and endeavours, all of which were constructed as a means to cope with the mourning methods, were hands down more effective and more successful than its twelve month predecessor. I wasn't blindfolding myself with drug tinted glasses as much this year, or at least not as much as I had during as the previous three hundred and sixty five days, but I wasn't in any rush to accept my fate either. As formerly stated, I had just reconnected with my dedicated drive of yesteryears, not so much with regards to my college degree, but certainly with regards to choosing which vocation I wanted to fully dedicate myself to.

Now I'm astutely aware that I'm about to head off topic here, but I have a particularly parched thirst for knowledge, and one that walks hand in hand towards the sunset with my adoration for education, yet despite this appreciative hunger; I downright despise the methods and means of our Governing body and the way in which it enforces a curriculum on our schools, colleges and universities. Quite simply stated, our education system is heavily seasoned with flavourless flaws.

Where to start though… actually I know, lets start off with the concept of age and the fact we are obliged to choose which career path we'll cavort down at the blind age of fifteen, if not earlier. This is ludicrous, for it is an age where we are little more than overgrown babies, cute pups and walking talking embryos. Yet despite the immaturity that dominates us at this youthful age, we are made to choose our GCSE subjects, and what's more, if we choose to tackle the next step in education, the likelihood is we'll choose our A-Level topics based upon the results we receive in said GCSE subjects. The repetitive roll continues with regards to university, which for the majority of students, is little more than an extended gap year where everyone gets to make exceptional friends, drink disgustingly cheap wine, watered down beer, hangover-extending spirits, and if they're lucky, cocksure in their peacock based attention-seeking or living off Daddy's black AMEX card, then they may also get to participate in several short lived relationship, encouraging more and more notches to make their way onto their bedposts.

But despite all this distracting hoopla, this vicinity called University is still an establishment of education, supposedly. A place to expand our minds in a scholastic sense and I'm sure it fulfils this expectation on a daily basis, for some people. But irrespective of this, the degree topic you choose will either be chosen as a correlated result of your A-Level report card, or an outcome based around the gospel fact that no one knows what he or she wants to do in life, especially at fifteen, especially during this lost age of uncertainty.

However, it doesn't matter whether you left school at fifteen, sixteen or eighteen, or whether you decided to crack on with a docile degree in pet grooming or self-fellatio, for the whole point of this endless education process is one that is set to gear us towards a job, or god forbid, an actual career, at least that's the fostered paradigm in this modern day of doom and gloom. Yet what continues to shock me is the lack of real word understanding, for this entire track of tutelage is encouraged without delivering any knowledge of what our extensive options are, and without any mandatory industry experience being promoted or provided. You may or may not agree, but that doesn't detract from this entire hullabaloo remaining fantastically bizarre to me, especially as we're the next fucking generation and generation with very little experience, knowledge or understanding of life outside the cosy confines of the school walls.

But my woes, worries and tribulations don't cease there young firecracker, for in addition to my struggles of understanding this bullshit 'educational' system, I have miscomprehensions of the way in which the syllabus is taught, and the way in which we students are indoctrinated. I'm not referring to what the curriculum may be beefed up and deep-filled with in terms of content, but rather I'm referring to the way in which we pupils are taught so little, for there are essentially no more than five fuckwitted but fundamental 'building blocks' throughout each and every stage of the almost interminable education system. But why be so vague when I can proficiently spell out what five areas concern me the most, and these centre around the fact we are taught that:

1. Truth comes from authority instead of taking authority from the truth.
2. Intelligence is the ability to remember and repeat.
3. An accurate memory and repetition is rewarded.
4. Non-compliance is punished.

And

5. We must conform intellectually and socially.

What a load of fairy dust and bollocks. I mean, how many times have you remembered a couple of great arguments, or several meaningful points no more than three minutes after the exam moderator demanded you put your quill and ink down and stop writing, only to receive the dreaded results three weeks later and find out that you were two marks shy of an A, or one mark off a pass. Does that really mean you're less qualified for this career or that role? Does this really mean you are a failure in our society? Of course it fucking doesn't, for no one can tell you what you are worth except for you.

To put it into a more poetic syntax though, I'm going to have to use the lyrics of Suli Breaks, who expertly stated:

'Exams are society's methods of telling you what you are worth, but you can't let society tell you what you are. Because this is the same society that tells you that abortion is wrong, but then looks down on teenage parents. The same society that sells products to promote natural hair looks and smooth complexion, with the model on the box half photoshopped and has fake lashes and hair extensions. With pastors that preach charity but own private jets, Imams that preach against greed but are all fat. Parents that say they want 'educated kids' but constantly marvel at how rich Richard Branson is. Governments that preach peace but endorse war, that say they believe so much in the importance of higher education and further learning, but increase tuition fee's every single year.'

Now look, I am in no way trying to undermine the importance of education, nor would I ever want to put anyone off this crucial notion, for knowledge is power after all, and the pen is mightier than the sword. Instead all I am trying to point out and articulately argue are the reasons as to why I hated school but loved education.

To me, the education system ironically examines everyone under the same rules and the same means, ignoring the fact that each of us has "different abilities, thought processes, experiences and genres." It's like gathering a common carp, an Indian elephant, a rock hopper penguin, a golden jackal and a spider monkey and examining all of them under the same microscope. Examining all of them on their ability to climb a tree.

It's a wank concept that will continue to produce wank results, at least on the best part. It's not the way to further humanity but rather it remains depletive and detrimental to such progress. As Monsieur Carlin once splendidly spewed out with his majestic economy of words, 'we shouldn't just be teaching our children to read, we should be teaching them to question what they read, we should be teaching them to question everything.' It is for this reason I decided to put my higher education thingamajig on the backburner, and instead concentrate on getting into a business I am, for want of a better word, passionate about. I mean History and Politics was either going to guide me down a perverse political path, or encourage me to become a historian, librarian, or god forbid, a career's advisor.

I didn't know what I wanted to do when I was at middle school, sixth form or even University. In fact I still don't. I was guided by the generation that came before me, a generation that held steady jobs, but remains wholly unfamiliar with my perspective on what I want to do with my life. Then the education system failed to highlight my talents and passions. It underscored my English report by stating I was a piss-poor creative writer who lacked imagination, and instead promoted the idea of maths even though I can't spell *calculatar* and still have no idea what the value of 'X' is.

Teachers made comparisons that weren't theirs to make, judging my classmates through quota-tinted-glasses. However I was lucky, for something in me clicked not too long ago that said I didn't have to tow the line or spend my life trawling down a route that made me miserable, and that I could instead find a way out of the groove and into a position that suited me better. Who cares that I have no 'qualifications' in the sector where my joy lays. It's just about finding a passion and diving in head first, because if you really want to do something with your life that makes you smile, it just takes self-motivated motivation. It takes no more than safari or Google Chrome to grab hold of the free education we all crave and deserve. It takes a short bus ride to a library where the books actually want their spines to be bent and their pages to be pawed over and scrutinized.

I can't blame where I have ended up on anyone else and nor would I want to, for I love the path I am taking. I like my determination to do what I truly want to do. I can't blame my qualifications on the education system, my teachers or lecturers, even if the process is riddled with corruption, misrepresentation and perversion. I can't palm off my mistakes to those around me, even if this is the easiest option out there. I made the conscious decision to enjoy my work, sacrificing objects of luxury, and I have done so guilt free. At the end of play, I learned one thing, and once again it wasn't taught to me by an orange and grey overhead projector or a specific area on white board highlighted by the laser point of a laser pen. Instead Scroobius Pip decorated such wisdom to me, with the wise words in question being, "The system might fail you, but don't fail yourself."

Anyway, I think that's my rant about education over, primarily given that this entity is about the process of bereavement, but who knows. So lets get back on track.

So I had set my heart on the film industry, like a real life Colin Clarke as embodied by Eddie Redmayne in the motion picture 'My Week with Marilyn'. This decision allowed me to get my hands stuck into something, finally. Something that would allow me to progress with reckless regards to the education baffle, the mourning process and a desirable career. But despite all my efforts, this move still didn't help me come to terms with the demons that I had learned to painfully ignore, much in the same way I am able to walk past buskers and beggars, always wanting to help them but hating myself that I can't.

I was angry, which is one trait that I guilelessly couldn't shake. I'm cocksure it's a mutual distain amongst those of us on the bereavement bus, but I was angry that my Dad wasn't going to be there to see me graduate, I was angry that he wasn't going to be supporting me on the touchlines of a rugby pitch again or see me secure my place in a seductive career. I was angry that he wouldn't be present at my wedding, nor would he witness the birth of my kids, or see them grow up, and I was angry that he wouldn't be able to be the generous and amazing granddad I know he would have been. These realisations made me angry.

The sort of awful anger that we have deep in the pit of our stomach that is forever kindled, occasionally bubbly up and spilling onto the surface of our expressions and actions. The sort of anger that makes you grit your incisors and molars so hard you think all of your teeth may shatter, splinter and burst into an undisclosed amount of fragments. A mirror ball of enamel caused by antagonised ire, which isn't all bad. At least its not all bad if people can still dance the funky-chicken to your moving mirror ball of flying teeth I guess. But more to the original point, there was no career, hobby or repeated activity that was ever going to eradicate this incensed anger, the kind that dwelled within me as if I were a twenty-first century Gollum, only with a fuller head of hair and bigger desire to get my finger inside the ring. Anyway, I've divagated yet again.

So after three years I was still not ready to open up, annoyingly. It's an unpleasant spiral that digs it's own charming cesspit of a hole, for when something goes on for this long, not only do you begin to believe it'll never change, but it becomes that much harder to walk the proverbial plank. It becomes that much harder to take the plunge into the opaque water below, for the water's of opening up are so impervious they refuses to hint at anything that could be dwelling below the rippling surface. It's like randomly picking a Mark Wahlberg film, in the sense you have no idea whether it's going to be 'The Departed' or 'The Happening', or to put it into more direct dialect, you have no idea whether it's going to be greatly genius, or absolute shit-stuffed-ball-bags. But that's the nature of these circumstances.

However, as with everything in this world, there was a positive terminal on this heavily negative battery, for I was at least aware of my inability to confess to any grief, my incapability to open up and my impotence in allowing others to get close to me. This awareness didn't make it any easier of course, in fact this recognition became a tedious torment, but it was nonetheless a move that forced any 'running and hiding' into a check mate situation, forcing this gutless hand to make a move for the first time.

The fact I was open about not being able to be open was, and remains to be, a confusing concept, even though I always explained my reasons whenever I could. Ok, so this is a little white lie given it took me some time to get to this articulating stage, at least when I was sober, for I would sometimes pour my heart out to Phoebe when I was immensely inebriated on any number of cocktails. A release, sure, but it was probably more of a tricky-dickey-Dick-Dastardly release and one that accidentally caused more harm than good to my better half, for it had the presence of mind to suggest something that wasn't there. What I mean is, such a drunken confession could have only hinted at my potential, providing an argument against the belief that I couldn't open up, providing hope fuelled reasons for my Phoebe to believe otherwise.

It's hard to come to terms with the far from fun fact that my actions made me an downright dick, no ifs and buts about it, just a dick so substantially large that not even a Trojan pecker poncho or a Magnum condom would have been able to offer any form of protection. It's hard to realise that despite my best efforts to not be a dick in the conventional sense of cheating, beating or even mistreating, I instead became a dick on a more grandiose scale, on a more harmful scale. I look back now and understand that I was hurting a girl who was going above and beyond the call of duty to help my wounds heal, yet I couldn't prevent this anguish I was causing, for it was never intentional. But this sort of rectum ramming realisation is still enough to make me doubt my own morals, gangbanging me into accepting that I may instead be ethically unpredictable on a round the clock daily basis.

Looking back at it now, being in this state of mind where I was aware of my closure yet unable to Bruce Lee karate chop my way out of its harmful antics, was probably not a situation best served with Swazi Bush, booze or any other drugs. Who would have thunk it, hey. It's almost as if I wanted to be a paradoxical person and that exception to the rule. To some extent though, I believe I may have been, but that could just as easily be my extravagant ego jumping in here. I wanted to be productive and proactive despite the fact I was flying with Mexican airlines. The way that I saw it and still see it is that I wasn't a stoner, and I made sure of that.

I set my sights on the film industry as a way of proving something to myself, a means of testing my self-worth, for it was a career move that was able to partner up with me in my fight against the beer battered potato wedge that was sat so comfortably on my shoulder. But my romanticism with this business didn't stop there, because it was also an industry I had a relationship with. It was both a nightly escape from the terrors that overran my dreams, as much as it was a production-based career that I was erratically turned-on by. Not in a Lara Croft Womb Raider type pornographic way, but in a 'fuck this is an impressive and righteously rad business, oozing with glamour in the public eye, but far from glamorous in reality' type way. However, these weren't the sole reasons for my pursued interest. Oh no. I wanted to take on a career and a challenge that could only be credited as my own doing. I wanted a no-one-can-take-this-away-from-me sort of sentiment and the I-made-it-without-a-leg-up-from-anyone feeling. I wanted acclaim and glory for it was my blood, sweat, tears and stalker like persistence that secured my position here, thus recognition was all the kudos I sought.

I don't have a problem with anyone who is 'lucky' enough to receive help, nor do I hold issue with anyone who inherits a legacy. Fuck, you would be stupid to not use what you have and foolish to not use what you are given, I mean you live once right, so why not use the resources available to you, dude. I am also not trying to stand aloof on a stallion of a moral horse because that would be ridiculously bitter and an echo of my sixteen-year-old self. For me, it is now all about making my Dad proud, and as a tough taskmaster who had experienced his own fights;

this extreme method of mine is the only way of providing a truly pride filled and successful outcome, or at least that's what my irrational and imprudent outlook believes.

Moreover, and the last motive behind this challenging career choice of mine, is one of possibility, for I ultimately fell for the endless possibility that film offers. You see I am of the unadulterated opinion that film has power and influence that can be used to help people, enlighten an audience, make the viewers feel emotion, make the viewer laugh and cry, clap and jeer. Film can heal and hurt. It can offer a relative perspective that is special to you. It can be political or romantic, comical or fantasy, heart-warming or blasé, and it has the ability to word situations that can otherwise seem so inexplicable. Film is a means to reach out to the masses with an unadulterated perspective, able to tell stories that can intelligently inspire or prove a notion that can prevent corruption. Film is magic, forever political, yet non-stop magic. But cherry-popping-penis-shaft, I've once again managed to loosely adhere myself to self-appreciation. Thus I apologise, because who really gives a shit about why I got in to films. So lets head back to the previous cocky outlook that narrowly avoids the self-destructive wall path that I was preaching about before.

As I was saying, I felt as if I was the non-stoner of stoners, a King of the un-Kingly and back on the determined highway to contrivance and achievement. I was constantly raising two fingers to the joint in my hand, but in a you-can't-deter-me-from-success type of symbolism, as opposed to the 'V' that I used as a holster for this sunny stick of joy. I was focused, I worked, I socialised, I went out and I networked like a mother fucker, but I don't believe I was the sole exception to the rule, for this is what so many of us did during these time. Where I was going wrong is visible to me now though, for I was looking at all the things I was still able to do whilst a little up in the air. But what I should have been examining was the fact everything I was doing could easily have been executed with much more precision and much more focus.

Yeah I may have been able to play both football and foosball, socialise and sleep, network and work, but I wasn't addressing the feelings and hurt that hindered me so much. Instead I was still smoking most nights to ensure I was physically sleepy and emotional numb. I mean, every other night there was enough white smoke rising from my bedroom window to convince any intrigued outsiders that the Cardinal's had elected a new Pope. What's more, I think only the pulchritudinous Phoebe knew the reasons behind my literal smokescreen, but for her own relevant reasons she couldn't condone my habit and quite rightly so, for this was the year that I started sneaking out for a toke on the rolled up joke and in a sly secret service style manner. Not cool huh. In fact this bewildering behaviour completely removes any cool element that goes so uncouthly hand in hand with dope, the sort of cool image that Howard Marks inspired. However, my hard-hitting habit fundamentally began simply because I needed my sleeping pill, tis all. That's how steep and icy this slope can turn out to be.

Maybe this is the first step in overcoming the long process of bereavement, and the first step in overcoming this personal equivalent to the Hundred Years War. It just seems that if we're not ready to accept the direct impacts of this bitch of a sitch, or not ready to sit down with ourselves and discuss exactly what it is that's holding us up in the moving on process, then maybe we just need to initiate the proceedings by righting some of the other wrongs first. Step by step. Maybe becoming proactive and regaining those astray, bespattered and disorientated parts of us is the crucial stride in establishing order. Maybe fighting the relentless fight in order to reignite the determined hunger for success is the much-needed first step in which the rest of one's life will fall into place around, like life changing dominoes. But this is just simplistic speculation, because it's so hard to know what's beneficial and what's harmful, yet so easy to fall between the cracks and so easy to fall into the devil's attractive and curvaceous cleavage. This is something I can empathise with, for I was clouded by the distracting thought of boobs, foolishly forgetting that these were boobs that belonged to the female devil that dwelled deep within my emotional capacity.

Anyhoo, my bond with the educational extravaganza side of University life improved drastically during this third year of mine, although I can't go as far as saying we had become totes bezzie mates. I knew I had to come out with a degree of second-class honours, for fear of wasting a dear amount of dollar-dollar bills more than anything. But this was also because I despised the thought of receiving nought more than a single-letter being printed onto a piece of paper and a limp-wristed handshake as a consolation for completing three years of study, although this came second in the priority rankings.

Ok, I may have unfairly belittled higher education a little bit here, but screw it, for gaining a career that would make me smile and shine on a Monday morning was my primary objective at this time. Yeah, I'm sure I could have concentrated more on my studies, got a 'better' letter on that condescending certificate and maybe even fallen into a well paid office job that I would loath five days a week, 12 hours a day, and then remind myself how much I loathed it on the weekends too. But that just aint my bag, baby.

Now I'm not making any excuses here, but rather pointing out that no matter what stage of your life you are at, whether at school, university, an internship or a job, life after death becomes a life that is Fresh Prince of Bel Air-ed, for it is flip-turned-upside-down. What I mean is, life is not just made up of the normal responsibilities anymore, not after the death of a parent or someone close, for these responsibilities are now complicated by legal issues, financial worries, medical by-products such as insomnia, the wearing of a mask and mourning in private, and on top of this shit stack we also have to succeed with the comparably mundane tasks of a job, intern, uni or school.

When you lose someone your thought process is completely altered and it becomes a battle royal between what has been lost and how to adapt for survival, for you kind of get a grasp on what's important in life. I was no longer motivated by financial rewards and instead I wanted to do something that made me smile. I wanted to wake up and participate in something that gave me a tingle in my testes every morning and something that had the capability to help others, and guess what, I aint regretted this razzle-dazzle decision ever since.

Maybe my gritted-teeth-won't-take-no-for-an-answer type attitude I adopted in an attempt to get into this business was in fact just another way for me to ignore the internal combustion that was happening. But we all find ways to stay busy and ignore the dusty dramas of our being, right? So in a way, this persistent pursuit was just a legal numbing gel that enabled me to crack on. You see I concentrated on this daily grind to take my mind off the actual daily grind. It was my medicine when the sun was high in the sky, and the herb was my medicine when the sun went down each evening. However, whilst this progress was one to be celebrated and praised with my family, I found myself pushing them away more than ever, so trigger happy to criticize them on the phone. Even when I took the trip back home, without the girlfriend that is, it was clear that I was as bitter as the Doom Bar I sunk my sorrows in, but I still couldn't snap out of it. I was so focused on the fact they didn't know my pain, that I wouldn't let them in to understand it.

What's more, I was fudgetastically fickle, for when we were in the company of others, I was more than charming. In fact I was the epitome of chivalrous and in spite of all indication pointing towards the contrary, I was an old school gentleman, at least when we were out in public or chillaxing with my parent's friends and other family buddies. I was that son my Mum could show off again, the one she previously had the strong mother and child bond with, a son that people would praise and hawk over. But behind closed doors, I was a diabolical-and-wart-wrapped-dick, at least the majority of the time. I guess I was just too close to the memories I had blocked out, so much so it was as if I was standing on my own nerves, standing in a bucket and trying to lift it up by the handle. I just couldn't deal with it.

I hated being at home when I missed the road, for the road was more than just theoretical escapism. In hysterical hindsight, what I needed was someone to just grab a twenty-five pound ten ounce carp and slap some sense straight up into me. But admittedly, this option was never on the cards, for this approach would have only pushed me further away, for an intervention would have given me an excuse to be incensed and irate, encouraging me to beat my chest like a small enraged alopecia ridden King Kong. What's worse though, I know from well-rehearsed practice that this would have been the only outcome! I know this because my Mum tried. She didn't slap me with a large scaly sea creature, but she would try raising her voice and shouting, all in a much-needed attempt to get my attention and a tactical tirade to make me listen, but I still wouldn't. Or I couldn't. Or I wasn't ready to. I don't know the actualities behind why I wouldn't listen, but I do know that my alternative reaction was to sarcastically laugh, or raise my voice in retaliation, both of which were defence mechanisms up there with the best the US Armed Forces has to offer, especially the caustic chuckle.

When it came to friends though, I was again more open this year. Don't get me wrong, I would never initiate the tantalising topic of death, nor would I crash into a conversation with the opening gambit of, "My Dad died, who fancies a mint cornetto and what's sure to be a heavy chit chat." But patience young Skywalker, because to this day I'm still not wholly comfortable with initiating such a discussion piece. The awkwardness scares me more than the condition of the 'sloth' victim in the film 'Se7en'.

If this sensitive subject was approached by anyone else however, or if I thought I could use my past pain as a conversation case to help someone else that may be struggling, then I would jump in with both feet first, no hesitation. You see, I love talking about my Dad, it's just the timing and context I am wary of. I love gushing about his antics and his stories and I'd try and explain my ever-evolving perceptions on life that has changed as a result of his death. It was as if I was given permission to touch on the tabooed. I mean, chewing over such conversation whilst chowing down on chow mien somehow made me smile, but in so many ways, I was also immune to its effects as if I was the storyteller of little more than fiction and fable, for I never really believed the content to be fact.

Yeah, I'm sure such reflections should have affected me more than it did, but I shut off the hard fought meaning behind these strung together sentences, and instead transformed my expansive lexicon into nothing more than hollow proses. In fact I was so good at doing this that it would most probably be my talent on 'Take Me Out'. Well, it would at least be a toss up between this emotionless skill, and my ability to cut wrapping paper in a flawless gliding motion, never needing my fingers to move in a pincer movement. Anyway, the fact I was steadily opening up, even if only one drip at a time, proved I was making headway and it made me feel like the 'hey diddle-diddle' cow in the nursery rhyme, you know the one that jumped over the moon. What I mean is, talking to others and talking to friends was a remedy of a release, a seductively emotional hand job.

But to give this period of my life a worthy synopsis is extremely challenging, especially in hindsight, for whilst the pain can stick around for some time, exact feelings and emotional responses are just fads to the frontal lobe. This makes any inception into a past dream-like state quite precarious to say the least. However, it was indeed a time of progress in certain fields of play, but regression in others, as has been the story of my life so far, but I'm confident that this is a relatable reception. I was processing and progressing, regressing and digressing. I was being pushed and pulled as if a characteristic and lively replacement rope in the dick measuring sport of tug-o-war. I was confused. Actually, looking back at this time of confusion is even more confusing. In fact, watching 'Donnie Dark' on mute, whilst a miniature Minotaur clown performs a lucid lap dance on my big toe would arguably be less confusing than this attempted dissection of specific memories.

It's an unearthly headspace to find oneself in, but I've lead myself to believe it's a necessary learning curve, and one that needs to be carved whilst riding a metaphorical hover board. I can't disclose whether this very specific and very hard route to the holy land is a certainty, nor whether it is always a definite hurdle in the bereavement steeplechase, but my Mum used to tell me if it's hurting then its getting better. This is quite plausibly a placebo, but even if it is just some sort of bullshit masquerading as a cliché, so be it, for it was a predominantly awesome vehicle in my journey to enlightenment, and I canny hate on that now can I. This is the thing with healing, we are always learning, but once we accept this is the case, we are placed in great stead for the rest of our life. We become scholars in the sure fire school of sentience, a school that can be a real ball-bashing-clit-flicker at times, but increasingly helpful at others.

In other breaking news though, I have also come to accept that we should try harder to listen to the advice of others, for not only are these hoi polloi external to the fucked up whirlwind running a mock inside of us, but also because they can be rich in life experience. Much like moi, they most probably don't have all they answers, but they may have some, and at the end of the day I'm of the opinion it's better to have something than nothing, especially when it comes down to an opportunity of overcoming the hardships that hinder our experiences of eternal youth.

I've learned to listen to those wise old owls of the previous generation for they seem to have this jaw-dropping ability to respect others and know what sort of shit we're going through. They can sympathise with what we are struggling with, what we hate so much and I fear this has been lost amongst us youts. Now I usually hate people telling me what to do, and maybe that's because I get my boners from going about my to-do list in my own unique fashion. However, maybe that chip on my shoulder is what prevents me from accepting or wanting any help. Maybe its because throughout most of my fan-fucking-tastic childhood I seemed to be underperforming, at least when compared to the ludicrously high academic expectations of my family. But Shanghai-shit-sticks, any one of these reasons could be held accountable as to why I would get pissed off at being told what to do. Either way, it was a habit that may have encouraged my determination and strength of character, as well as my individuality, whilst it simultaneously hindered me in my hours or years of need. Sensationally stupid really, because I was fighting a battle unaccompanied, when reserve forces were readily available.

Anyway, what is crucial to remember as a former hide and seek world champion, is that our parents and their friends knew how to communicate, you know back in the day, during the Boer War or whatever. Shock horror, this complex communication thing used to actually be normal. Not anymore though, for we now have the Google Internet machine, texting, tweeting, Tinder, Facebook, BBM, WhatsApp, even fucking LinkedIn, all of which we cower behind like pussies. It's just not interaction like we should understand it, nor a communication the older generation knows. Now I'm not saying this cohort of oldies always spoke aloud when they were feeling down, but as an alternative means of expression, they probably wrote their pain down or sent letters that had honesty and heart.

We don't write anymore, we text and blog at best, with no sign of grammatical tidiness, whilst the use of punctuation has become as elusive as the great white amphibious Unicorn. We live in an age which is meant to be more wirelessly pertinent but it is in fact unaffiliated and disconnected. We are hermits, scared of reality and actual confrontation, dwelling in a globalised world where it seems isolation is now the norm.

We pseudo-communicate in a primal and ape like manner, using four letter words that are broken up by an equal amount of full stops. Its proto-language that renders itself discouraging, and in my opinion it's a step back. It's no wonder as to why I, and so many others, keep things bottled up in such a disheartening and harmful way. It's bullshit that provides a stronger argument to regression than it does to progression.

It is for this reason I have begun to really listen to what others can offer, not just parents and the over bloody fifties, but anyone who will give me the time of day. It's a step into the past that takes us forward. Getting our feelings, our worries and our concerns off our chests, expressing our stresses and allowing others to offer some contour of help to our suffocating emotions. So for those of you at the back in the cheap seats who have been unable to hear these far from revolutionary words already, listen up. I encourage face-to-face spaghetti western style showdowns, void of guns and loaded with words. There may be tears and blubbering, but this will ultimately help you, as well as helping those closest to you, irrelevant of whether this refers to friends or family. Communication will also release the aggro that friends and family would otherwise have no means of understanding, for not even the dream team of Watson and Sherlock would be able to decipher our inner feelings without the means of a hint.

Anyway, like Bruno Mars states it's time to move on, so let's move on to another of these incredulously important lessons I learned over the duration of this year, and that is compromise, for this is a characteristic I will keep hold of in the same way a fifteen-year-old lad keeps hold of his boyhood magic wand when the lights go off. You see, I enjoy being a nice guy, a good friend, a doting son, a loving brother and I hope a boyfriend to be proud of too, and I'm sure you revel in these certificate worthy festivities as well. But as we all know, compromise is the key to ensure all of this is maintained, for everyone of us gets pulled in every each way in a balancing act that is so impressive the Cirque du Soleil should come a knocking more often than it does.

To me, all of these people I momentarily aforementioned were involved, and all these chaps and dolls helped me get by in day-to-day life. Maybe not all of them knew the extent of my struggles, but they were aware that some degree of pain was present. But that defines kindness to me, for none of these beautiful specimens expected anything in return, they just wanted me to heal, and I am perpetually appreciative and a little bit aroused by such a gorgeous gesture.

Not to name names or anything, but the phenomenal Phoebe was something special during this time. She knew more about me than anyone, enjoying the highs of my triumphs and enduring the lows of my tortures. She was that one person we all have in these times of need, that one person that tips the scales of reliance and selflessly goes the extra mile. Phoebe was that person who can subconsciously tell when things are good and when things are bad, whether by the slightest glance, an invisible grimace, a shudder awake or the smallest change of octave in any response. What I'm trying to say is, this girl eased the pain in ways I will be so eternally grateful for. But I was lucky all round, with regards to everyone I surrounded myself with, it's just I never realised this at the time. It's only now I know what a harmonious balance I had and in so many respects, for my friends bring bucket loads to the table in the form of banter, sarcasm and profanity, whilst my family remain endlessly supportive, bizarrely. But all of these pimps and hoes, ladies and gents deserve recognition and my undivided attention. But despite this identification, it remains an uneasy balance to strike up, with all the people in our lives wanting to spend time with us, but that's just how it is, its just a learning curve and we learn how to reach equilibrium along the way, and so we should.

I only bring this up because I believe it's a pukka life lesson, however it is one that I only began to listen to once it was presented to me in a way I could relate to, for I was oblivious and ignorant to it before. Thus, without further ado I bring to you, a sensational short story I am completely certain you may have possibly heard before. But whether you have or you haven't is erroneous, for this poetic piece of scripture never ceases to strike a handsomely humorous cord with me each and every time it graces my grateful ears, much in the same way as Tim Minchin's politically correct song's do. So, on to the slightly spiced up and impeccably altered allegory:

"*A chiselled Professor stood before his intrigued class, displaying numerous pre-watershed items in front of him. When the class began, wordlessly he picked up a crystal clear pint glass and proceeded to fill it with your standard white golf balls. He then asked the students if the vessel was full, to which they unanimously agreed it was. The captivating Professor then picked up a mug full of pebbles and poured them into the golf ball filled chalice too. He shook this jar lightly, and of course, the pebbles rolled into the gaping spaces between the golf balls. He then daintily asked the students again if the fireless goblet was full. They once again agreed it was. The Professor charmingly chuckled, and proceeded to pick up a Tupperware box of sand, pouring its contents into the pint glass also. Naturally, the sand filled up the miniscule spaces that were left everywhere else in this glass container. So, he asked once more if this see through mug of education was full. The students responded with yet another undisputed and resounding yes. The Professor then produced a can of European beer from under the table, resisting the temptation of showing off his drinking ability in front such a packed auditorium, and instead pressed on with charismatically pouring the entire contents into the pint glass, effectively filling the empty space between the grains of sand. The students then ruptured into a riotous mix of laughter and applause, with the school boys jealous of this Profs irresistible coolness, and the girls seductively swooning.*

"Now," said the Professor, as the giggling and guffaw subsided, "I want you to recognise that this glass represents your life. You see, the golf balls are the important things: your family, your partner, your health, your children, your friends, your favoured passions, things that if everything else was lost and misplaced and only they remained, your life would still be complete & full to the brim. The pebbles are the other things that matter, like your wicked fun job, your humble house, your home sweet home, and your midnight black convertible girl magnet of a car, whilst the sand is everything else, the small stuff. "If you put the sand into the jar first," this good looking and titillating Prof continued, "there is no room for the pebbles or golf balls. The same goes for your life. If you spend all your time and energy on the small stuff, you will never have room for those things that are truly important to you. Pay attention to the things that are critical to your happiness. Enjoy the fruits of your family." Take your partner out salsa dancing, bungee jumping or shark cage diving. Ensure you are healthy like the glowing Gwyneth Paltrow. Fuck, given we have golf balls at our fingertips, why not play a round of eighteen and hit a seventy-six of the

front nine. "There will always be time to go to work, hoover the house, host a dinner party and take the rubbish out, so instead we must take care of the golf balls first, the things in our lives which really matter. Prioritise, for the rest is just sand." One of the students then raised her hand and inquired as to what the appetising hops and barley represented. A good question, to which the Professor flashed a flawless smile and confidently replied, "I'm glad you asked. The lager just goes to show that no matter how full your life may seem, there's always room in your life for a couple of beers, a bottle of vino and a few whiskey's on ice."

I admit this may just rub off on you as an extensive amount of worthless words, thrown together with a loose narrative. This story may also establish nothing more than recognition as an elongated cliché, and one that is nothing more than glitter doused horseshit, and who am I to tell you otherwise. However, this lengthy phraseology has helped me get my priorities in check, and after all, it was my priorities that were royally fucked up during this period.

Now, I had always put my brother and mother first, even if I hadn't been the most pleasant company at times, for they were and always will be my heartfelt priority, but this still didn't stop me from thinking I had it worse than everyone else, ostensibly riding a high horse of dismay. I then wrongly began to prioritise my nightly need for the chronic Aunt Mary Jane. Goddamn that lubricated water slide of drug addiction.

However, this bizarre and ill-advised plan free plan is similar too the way most of us tackle the thousand-bit puzzle of life after death. Piece-by-piece. Yeah, its Lexington Steele long, and a straight up lame and whack plan of attack, but it's a circumstance with no alternative. You see, whilst a jigsaw starts out looking like Mission Impossible Twelve, the more we string together the more we can see, and week-by-week, year-by-year, shit just starts to come together in a clusterfucking-cluedo type manner.

Mentalities and attitudes alter, and we learn from the trial and errors of our sorry situations. We teach ourselves how to enjoy the fruits of life, wary of our weaknesses but understanding of our strengths. Maybe you've relied on alcohol or leaned on narcotics, whether that be an escapists eighth of weed or a slaphappy slither of crack cocaine. Maybe you've continued to lock yourself a way to roll solo on this one or maybe you've resorted to self-harm as an immediate distraction, aiding one invisible and irresistible pain by moving to one that is more skin deep and abrupt. Each of us has our own method of dealing with shit, and in my eyes, all of these are valid reactions to our farcical fuck ups, fuck-ups that seem to have no moral issues when it comes to kicking us when we're grovelling in the gutter.

But, and this is one huge Kim Kardashian size but, there has to be an end game, or at least the arrival of punctuation, whether it comes in the form of a full stop or exclamation mark is almost irrelevant. We can't dwell on the past, because until Dr Emmett Brown's time travelling DeLorean is made available as a consumer product, there simply aint nought we can do about what's been and gone and happened. With this in mind, the only thing we have now is the future, and even better than that, the charade of the here and now. You see, your future is in your hopefully hairless palms, and the path you want to go down is a choice that's been handed to you and you only, it just requires Samson like strength.

We can learn a huge amount from our own personal hardships and struggles, but most pivotally, we can learn how to harness our strengths and exploit our resolve, making our gifts work in our favour. As the magnificently chivalric, celibate and far from curvaceous Ghandi once whispered to me in my time of need, "Strength does not come from physical capacity. It comes from an indomitable will."

I stated before that I hate comparisons, even at the best of times. I mean don't get me wrong, I love comparing Messi and Ronaldo as well as Jolie and Anniston, but that's a contradictory character flaw of mine, but one in which the aforementioned win on both accounts. I don't like comparison's elsewhere however. What I mean is, I don't believe we can look at someone else's life and compare it to our own, or wishfully think I'd rather be him or her or whatever, because even if you're the quirky and queer Professor Dumbledore, it's just not gonna happen.

We cannot try and be better than anyone else, and it is a wasted exertion to try, for it is a poignantly pointless endeavour. So instead of trying to be better than others, we should only try and be better than our previous selves, we must help each other to ensure this is the case wherever we can, and that is a challenge only we can put down and accept like some personal and proverbial pink slip. So I suggest you grab life by its marvellous manjigglies and wrestle with these impressively proud plums to the ground, and don't give up until we have succeeded in bashing the bishop into submission, for this is what is required, fighting the good fight, compromise, and the ability to enhance our selves. It just seems to me that getting knocked down is far from failing. Instead, one only fails when they decide not to get back up.

With this in mind, I am delighted to say I have no intention of letting the big dick of life throw me onto the bed and pin my legs behind my ears. I have no intention of letting life fuck me without any form of lubrication, not even a polite splodge of spit. I have no intention of letting life just ram its rigid rod home, whilst taking my pride and anal virginity in one foul swoop before cumming on my nipples and wiping its cock on my towel, leaving me to die in the sewer. No, I won't lie down and give up, for I would much prefer to take the lead in this fanciless foxtrot and invite this dick of bereavement back to my place, ensuring this Lucifer known as life is helplessly bent over my desk so that I can relentlessly show it whose boss, enjoying the wild ride it's certain to be. But that's the attitude I've learned to adopt the hard way, having endured back-to-back marathons during my time of running away from such a macho mentality. In the end I just got bored of being raped by life.

By the beautifully boyish features of Baron Beckham, things break, fracture and crack, they fall apart, and things can also get lost along the way. But fuckity-fuck-fuck, that's just part of the fun when it comes to this bitch of a teat we call existence, a teat in which we so solemnly suck on. You can't deny this, not even the amazing spider man can deny this. So, now that we've unanimously established this is the way in which the pin spins and the earth drops, surely we need to plan the next amendment of the craptastic constitution. For it's not about dwelling on how to change the past, but rather it's about what the fuck we are going to do next, what the fuck we are going to write when we turn the page and we see its blank, when we see that it's ours to pen and that it's ready to be written on.

I can accept that it may be impossible to create a completely barren and unmarked background, despite how hard we me try to convince ourselves otherwise, in which we occasionally adopt a J. Gatsby type obsession with the past, trying to forget the complex complications of what has gone before. I can accept it may be impossible for us to doodle exactly what we want across this canvas of ours, a canvas that still has faint stains much to our dismay. But I'm also not trying to suggest there is any alternative, and quite rightly so, for the past is who we are, and as tough as it was, it has laid the foundations for our strength of character, and this should not be neglected.

We can't alter what's happened nor can we can't tussle with it or change the events, but we can decide where we go from here. We can harness what we've been through and use it in our favour. Optimus Prime our ordeals. Transform the hardships we perceive to be negative, and alter these perceptions of weaknesses into solidified strengths. It's about what we decide to do now, in this moment, what we decide to adopt, what we want to kick and what we want to change and alter, for there is no time like the present, there is no time like now. You see it is what we decide to do in this very moment that matters, and what we decide to do in this twinkling second that changes our future, and allows us to do it on our terms. It's about the here and now, but then it's always been about the here and now, for that's all we have, the here and now. I just suggest you don't let yesterday take up too much of today.

Figure 1: My Dad with Baroness Margaret Thatcher

Figure 2: Dad in his beloved South Africa

Figure 3: Dad and Zack arriving at Cape Town in style

Figure 4: Dad in his beloved Mozambique

Figure 5: Dad with Mike Lima Delta (that's the plane)

Figure 6: Dad with his pilot Johan 'Rooikat' Wessels (middle)

"If you're going to kick authority in the teeth, you might as well use two feet."

Keith Richards

YEAR FOUR

Keeping up with the common theme of this schematic scribbling, this final year in office remained firmly planted on the regular fucking-free-for-all that is a gravy train of hitches. I continued to be caught in the metaphorical jaws of a Lake Placid Mega-Croc and thrown about like a burst beach ball in distress. However, this became more erratic in numerous ways.

In a sense this was the year I started to stroll down a destructive wall path almost taking on the role of Marv from Sin City, only less scarred and backlit. I was tearing down the emotionally erosive walls inside and beginning to actually accept my situation for the first time and fighting back with intention, for I was pulverising and pounding the belly of the beast. This was by no means a period without its recurring speed bumps and hiccups, or hiccups while going over speed bumps, but then no one said this was going to be doddle in Dorchester. However, it was a year where I was able to get more in touch with myself. Of course my emotions and me were still not the kind of mates that call each other day in and day out, but I was now at least at a sort of pen pal stage with my faint feelings.

Immaturely, I was still clinging on to the university lifestyle, having to partake in an additional semester in the extensive confines of this palatial City of Dreaming Spires. However, this was almost entirely due to the fact I missed out on my initial semester way back in first year, refusing to defer my course gracefully because of this goddamn pride thing. However, this wasn't the sole participant in the blame game line up, for it was also fractionally due to my second year adoption of a George Best inspired philosophy, for I spent a lot of time with booze, birds and creaky longboards, with the rest of my time being squandered.

Anyway, this extended stay in the sunny capital of traditional values, Kings English and punts full of cun-ahem-cute-couples, was commonly described by the rest of this fourth year club as a way of avoiding the 'deep end of real life'. Unfortunately, and I assume much like yourself, this expression slapped me in the face like a Santa sack of solid silver shit and rusty nails, for the day I lost my Dad was what I would call 'the deep end'. I mean, this sort of crucifixion is what real life is, or at least it is in my wise Gandalf the Ginger type opinion. But once again, this is a comparison that cannot be made, for 'real life' means different things to different mortals.

This outlook is truer now than ever before, for we now exist in an age of first world problems, weeping because McDonald's doesn't deliver its food, having tantrums because t-internet on our phones doesn't work on the tube and wailing over the fact our iPhones only come in black or white. Anyhow, as per usual I enjoyed this year as much as always, how could I not when it was full of sun, sea, surf, studies and long skins, albeit tainted by obvious struggles and strife of course, but it was nonetheless partial to straight up progress too. I wanted to make substantial strides, I wanted to hit the ball busting bereavement nail bang on the head, and this was encouraged and supported by my girlfriend, Phoebe. (Insert Jack Black singing voice here) 'Cos that's fucking teamwork.'

I had become aware of the need to deal with such a showdown, for I had been called out of the Silver Dollar Saloon before. But instead of kicking open the batwing doors and squaring up to my issues, I had always found it easier to just slip out the back like an unprepared and lily-livered coward. But not now, because this time I was ready to finish my drink in one foul swoop, whilst propped up against the tavern bar, before slamming the tankard down and waltzing out into the main street, for the first time showing face even if I wasn't at the full fighting stage just yet.

You see, I was finally getting back in touch with my emotions, occasionally relinquishing some eye juice in the form of glistening teardrops, albeit these were at spectacularly sporadic intervals. It was as if I was beginning to feel human again. Now this may well sound seriously fucked up in some sort of sci-fi fantasy way, like a real life starry eyed Gigolo Joe straight out of A.I. It may even sound like an extract of hyperbolic and exaggerated malarkey. Either way, one hand rests upon the Old Testament and the other against my heart, for this is the bible truth and nothing but chapter and verse. Actually, given my atheistic optique, this statement of intent falls a little flat on its fanny, thus I change the items on which my hands rest, from that of my heart and a bible, to that of a copy of Jack Kerouac's 'On The Road' and my calm and undisturbed dick.

Anyway, I'm not sure if I made this decision to locate my balls on my own, or whether it was subtly prompted by my then partner, either way it was an ambiguous decision that had a dubious response. I wanted to make progress. I wanted to understand my emotions. I wanted to know where the hurt was coming from and what was at the core of my inability to move on, but it was a steady process that could only gain as much traction as one would allow, like a pump-trolley-hand-car-Kalamazoo-thingamajig.

It's possible that I found headway after my Inca trail type search, or more specifically as a result of finally achieving some sort of balance in my existence. It is also possible this balance could have held one of the keys that allowed space for any emotional furore of mine, in which this usually bubbled up when this said balance was interrupted. You see I was performing a high-wire-tight-rope-balancing act with studies and ambition-fuelled work at one end, and celebratory cheer and copulation at the other, whilst simultaneously balancing a cannon ball shaped emotional weight on my nose as if I were some sort of performing seal too. But I saw these as the building blocks of my concentration and focus, although I have over complicated their 'official' names with my need for opulence and allure.

However, this situation was like an office desk pendulum type contraption, for once one of these building blocks frustrated my occasionally short irritability, I would use it as a means of release. Now I don't know what your specific emancipation techniques are, but I would cry uncontrollably whilst trying to gather my composure, grabbing the closest object that I inherently knew to be breakable, and then simply proving that fact of physics. If this option weren't unavailable though, I would alternatively embody Chuck 'The Iceman' Liddell and take the ground and pound to my defenceless mattress, observing the memory foam become the victim of an unruly assault, getting angrier at the fact this memory substance would gather itself and slip back into its original state.

However, this doesn't herald the notion that I had changed from a Terminator type specimen into that of skin and flesh with feelings and heart, for anyone can give in and release their aggravating anger. There was a discreet difference though, the cognisance that I was now welcoming these emotional outbursts, realising their efficacious effects, whilst I hid the negativity inside until a vehement explosion of commotion would erupt, welcoming the semi-perpetual positive outlook that would wash over me as a result. Quite simply put, I could finally see the benefits, see the amelioration and profit that I had previously refused to accept, and I weigh these against the con's that had clearly been so cancerous and cutthroat. Yet despite all this, I was still being held back by one gorgeously gargantuan fucking leash, and that was the golden leaf of the Green Goddess, Marijuana, as well as other numbing narcotics, all of which I consciously hated, despite the glamorous following such a lifestyle has with British rockstar's.

I was still hooked on anti-reality. I was still reliant upon the peaceful powers of the plant, albeit there had been a scantily clad break in this humble habit of mine. I was now only getting the itch when I was sleeping on my lonesome, you know, unaccompanied with no one to wrap up in my arms, no one to hold and no one to fuck like there is no tomorrow. I was instead only dabbling in illegals when left on my tod with just my prick in my palm, for when I was with my significant other, I was lucky enough to have someone who knew my troubles and struggles, someone who acknowledged why I smoked and acted upon it.

Phoebe had that magic touch, that awesome ability to send me off into the dreamland of imagination, floating up, up and away to the castle in the sky, and at her own expense too, for she would selflessly lay awake just to ensure I was able to drift off with ease. However, when these optional extras were not available, I willingly fell straight back into the loopy life that this portable and rolled-up la la land always offered. Of course it was fun and it even encouraged TV shows about bridge building or Antarctica's Next Top Model to suddenly become BAFTA worthy. But, it also meant I was deadening my nerve endings yet again, for I was pounding my emotional capacity like it was Candice Swanepoel lying beneath me, bum pressed against my crotch and bedroom eyes staring intensely back at me.

Nevertheless, I am thankful that I wasn't doing it in secret so much anymore, as I was cotching and blazing with friends or smoking in bed, but I'm still not sure if I deserve a medal and the complimentary but unwanted bouquet of flowers that always accompany such a trophy. What I can't deny though, is that I was hiding my habit from Phoebe as much as I possibly could. Yeah, of course I enjoyed relaxing with friends and witnessing the wacky baccy make the wacky chitchat escalate into boundaries well beyond the extraordinary, just enjoying the small things in life. But when you smoke by yourself, you become partial to a very different euphoria, a very different high, and unfortunately I became reliant on this dark side of the hoon.

Anyway, when I finally finished my gleeful Uni days, I almost immediately got my first break as a location scout, my first full time and paid role on a film set, Closed Circuit. There are a very little amount of occasions that can instil such ecstasy as that first job. I mean I had 10 weeks of living my ambition and I was arguably too close to the 'I could piss myself' sort of hysteria. I was working eighteen hours a day. I was getting my hands dirty and my feet stuck in, but it still wasn't enough to take my mind away from the death of my Dad, and subsequently my Godfathers demise and my Mother's unstable health.

It didn't matter how long my day on set was or how tired I had become from such extreme exertion, I would consistently get back to which ever sofa I was inconsistently surfing on that night and, um, light up. I mean for fuck's sake boy, even when I was being non-sexually abused by three weeks of night filming and returning home from work well after sunrise each and every morning, I would still roll up an L-plate, chuck on an episode of Suits, or whatever heart-warming principal photography I would decide on, and smugly smoke away. It seemed to be an ultimatum of a stupidly superfluous spliff or a night of little to no sleep. Still, I accept the blame and refuse to object, for this was too much of a Snoop Dogg & Wiz Khalifa influenced attitude to adopt when you're about as far from a famously large-lunged rapper.

In fact this was an especially crazy and cockamamie concept given one was in fact a hard working chap who was contracted to more than double the working hours required by most nine to five's of regular occurrence. Anyway, looking back on it now is what has made me aware of the possibility that my antics may have had a detrimental effect on my ability. Yeah, this was probably more blatant than multiple flashing neon bar lights silently shouting 'Strippers' in the dead of night, but I would just pretend my puffing away wasn't affecting me, or I would weigh up said conclusions of the purple haze against those of my insomnia, and pronounce weed the obvious winner for it favoured my needs. In hindsight, these were not the two ideal options to be given. In fact this was a scenario that felt a lot like my nuts were being squeezed from every which way, with no sign of a gentle female's hand in sight, thus absolving any chance of a silver lining on this occasion.

God-fucking-damn-it, I just couldn't break this obsessive obsession. I couldn't leave this friend that so kindly eased the pain. I couldn't rupture this habit and nor did I want to. Shock horror, this was a worry for my girlfriend, but then of course it was. As I previously confessed, I didn't rely upon weed during the day. I didn't wake up and hit back-to-back bongs or walk down the stairs in the morning and have a coffee and some chronic, no, I would simply have that top up toke before naptime.

I just hated the recurrent nightmares as much as the irresistibly rough reality, and the nightmares highlighted the reality, which left me bouncing of the woebegone walls in one far from desirable cycle. However, my forlorn friendship with this flower fuel was never an addiction in my mind, well not until I went home to visit my Mum and my family for a week or two at a time, a journey which became part of my coastal bed hopping between Norfolk and Plymouth. Anyway, it was when I had my feet up at home and hanging loose with my family, that I found myself sneaking off for a smoke, and that is when I should have realised immediately that this gaudy green goblin was stopping me from healing, but instead it took me some serious rotations of the clock to realise this obvious fact.

How could I have not realised what was happening instantaneously? I mean I had become a youthful curmudgeon. I was angry, unapproachable and always trying to turn the blame around on others or point a crooked finger elsewhere. I was stroppy, sensitive and always ready to flee, although this reference is as literal as theoretical, for I would fecklessly jump in my torpid one point one litre vehicle and just take off. I would head to a friends abode or peg it to Oxford, fuck I would occasionally pull up in a quiet spot, like an abandoned Little Chef, and just sleep in my car, with the outcome of these options simply depending upon my madcap mood at the time. You see, sometimes I'd be aware of what I needed to do, and I'd pluck up the courage to visit the sombre graveyard where Dad lies, trying to bring some honesty and questions to a place where I would be forced to answer them in the way Dad would have wanted, as if his much welcomed scrutiny had wrapped me up in a mackintosh of morality. In fact, this was exactly what I should have done from the get-go and something I should have continued to do throughout, for this was a release, but one that was proactive, connecting and a resounding reminder, and possibly the addiction I needed.

This sort of positive reminder was a pleasant realisation. A realisation that allowed such astonishingly awesome actions to become more frequent, thank fuck, and what's more, I was beginning to take an interest in actually addressing the underlining issues that pecked away at me all too often. However, after four years of following the five rules of the ADAA (American Dodgeball Association of America) by dodging, dipping, diving, ducking and dodging my poignant responsibilities, I found myself isolated and in a rut of repudiation, not too far away from the ditch of despair. You see, I had haphazardly caused Phoebe an insufferable amount of pain, all of which had stemmed from the limitations I had set my emotional capacity. However, it didn't stop there, for I had also become unable to fully commit or outright open up, even to the one person who had given her all to me and this was utterly soul destroying.

I had been brought up to be a gentleman, caring, kind, altruistic, propitious, obliging, bounteous and if I dare say myself, crazy fucking awesome. But, despite all of this, I wasn't allowing Phoebe to be herself, not with regards to expression anyway, for all she wanted was comfort in being able to tell me how much she loved me, how in love she was with me, and to hear those almighty words said back to her. But that was just it. I wasn't able to say the very words she wanted to hear, for that part of me didn't exist anymore, it had been wiped out with the dinosaurs and dodo's, thus I was only able to offer her a look of lies and an 'Alfie' awkward response of, 'Thanks babe.' I just couldn't lie, and the truth was, I had become so furious and so hurt by all those that had fortuitously ripped out my heart by dying on me that I had shut off my deep emotional recoil. I was unable to say 'I'm in love with you' because the words meant nothing to me anymore, they were empty and hollow, powerful words of powerless meaning, but that's just what my series of pain did to me. I loved her, of course I did, but I had been limited by the combination of helpless loss and my own self-destruction.

In my opinion it can go numerous ways, but only one option seemed to clearly stand out as the alpha male to me, like that governing individual in a sault of lions, like Simba or Mufasa, looking out over the Pride lands, dominant amongst all the other options available. So, lets take a look at what's behind this illuminating, enticing and handsome door; a real life piss creak without a paddle and the route I was forced down. It was a divergence which I was unable to commit to, scared of losing yet another loved one, riddled with fear and forced to ride this turbulence alone, almost absent from any statutory seatbelt. Now I'm not one to preach about the toxic turmoil this choice creates, for that is the point, it was a choice and I chose it as my way of dealing with said dealings. I guess it just seemed the right thing to do. However, it wasn't. Of course this may be disputable, but the results spoke their own viscous volumes, for all this decision turned out to be was the fanny-tastical-piss-easy and recreant way out. In hindsight, I wish I hadn't chosen such a response. I wish I had left my pride at the pillared entrance, plucked up some courage and grown a sizeable pair of bollocks, bollocks big enough to make the rockstar-cum-amateur-porn-dabbler Tommy Lee a very satisfied and proud drum-kit hero.

Yet it rescinds me to know that this selfish act of mine was evidently poisonous to both my girlfriend and I. I just wish I could have opened up. I wish I could have let someone in to help ease the pain and allowed someone to comfort me, someone I could have shared my grand-canyon-deep-feelings with. Instead I was forcing everyone to tread carefully, hypothetically forcing them to establish some sort of self-centred sixth sense that allowed them to guess when I was having a rough old time. That's not the right thing to do, not for them or me, for this unwise tact produces an uneven seesaw of soul sucking fucked up shit.

It forces those around you to be understanding of something they can't understand, and open to the pragmatism of something you refuse to be open about. This expectation requires an obscene level of patience and trust. A waiting game based on hope and potential that is wholly wrong, for no one should have to deal with this, and yes, looking back at it now, honesty should be the only way, and this observation should have been my ritual from the unforeseen and bitter inauguration. Look, I know it hurts to delve in too deeply and share, for so many reasons, but it aint exactly smooth sailing when we bottle it all up and let it bubble away either. Trust me.

My advice is a promotion of honesty and the need for it to prevail over solitude. I say run your emotions up the forever-feared flagpole and see who salute's, and trust me, someone will. It will probably be those people who are crazy close to us, our families and partners and bosom buddies. Those people who will do anything for us, the people who want to help us through to the other side and hold our hands on the jumpy journey to the greener pastures, which we are constantly assured are on the horizon. But this is a task of impossibly tall proportions, for these wonderful wanderers can't help us get better, not on their own, not without that all important and vital ingredient. I'm not talking about cumin, paprika, thyme or five spice, I'm talking about us, I'm talking about you, for no one can help us unless we let them. No one can help you if you refuse to let such help have a platform. But more damagingly than this, no one can possibly help if we refuse to help ourselves. They say you can lead a horse to water but ye canny make it drink. I say, fuck that, for there was less than a handful of times I let anyone lead me anywhere close to water, never mind make me douse my gullet in the tasteless clear liquid. I just ostensibly refused to think I was thirsty.

However, what I found to be the hardest thing to accept in my change of character was also the hardest thing for my family to understand. It had been four years since my Dad was killed, and yet I was still Clint

Eastwood angry, minus the cucumber cool factor that is. I was angry at my core, and this rage rose like simmering hot air, coursing through my nervous system as much as my circulation structure and emotional recourse.

Maybe I hadn't given myself the chance to mourn? Maybe I was so used to keeping my pain and struggle away from the surface, the prying eyes and the media that such anger was the only resulting end game? However, it could well be that this riposte is the natural response after receiving such a direct punt to one's godly gonads. Now I accept that this bereavement battle was lengthy and that four years is possibly a touch too long, but I was unaware of any expiry date to such seething embitterment. Nonetheless, this is where the powerful influence of film stepped up to the mark yet again, expressively enunciating the way I was feeling and lucidly vocalising what I was unable to say, what I was unable to identify.

"Not a lot of people know what it feels like to be angry, angry in your bones. I mean, they understand, family, friends, everybody understands – for a while. Then they want the angry little kid to do something he knows he cannot do; move on. So after a while they stop understanding. The angry kid is forced to shut himself a way, constantly fighting the anger inside him. You eventually learn to hide this rage and you practise smiling in the mirror. It's like putting on a mask."

John Blake

The Dark Knight Rises

(Slightly adapted by me, apologies)

193

I went to see this film with Phoebe on the opening Friday, early enough in the morning for there to still be sleep induced rheum in the corner of my eyes and spare seats dotted about this popular cinema screen. I remember the scene in which these words were spoken so sonorously though. I remember Joseph Gordon-Levitt vocalising these words. I remember trying to fight back the tears as this quote cut me down without hesitation or cautionary warning. I remember tears rolling down my face as my girlfriend squeezed my hand, as if she instinctively acknowledged how relevant such a portrayal of pain was to me. I didn't sniff, croak, choke or make the tiniest smidgen of a sound. Instead, I just listened to the words, soaking them up in the same way my cheeks were soaking up the emotional raindrops that my eyes were balling out.

This quote quite simply changed me, in fact it humanised me in a way. It told the story of how I was feeling. The story I embodied but hadn't fully accepted. It also articulated this powerful story in a way that I could never have told it, using just a few words and a scarce number of sentences, whilst ensuring the heartfelt meaning and the morals weren't short changed, by holding onto it's blunt honesty and delivering this narration with an accuracy so significant that it would have put Robin Hood of Sherwood Forest to shame. For this notorious Prince of Thieves may have split an arrow, but this John Blake quote struck a cord so deep within my heart that I wasn't even aware it existed. Now that is meticulous mastery.

Given my short synopsis of JBs quote, it's needless to say this powerful and perplexing prose jump-started me awake and managed to get the ball rolling, with regards to my ability to portray my feelings anyway. It was just a quote that explained so much in so few letters, and allowed me to understand what was feeding my determination and fuelling my anger. Sometimes I hid behind these words, and at other periods I thrived off such a haiku. But no matter how I decided to use such a directive, whether as a sword or a shield, it was a major step in my emotional advances and it created a renewed need for me to think about my troubles. But more than this, it gave me the drive to finally act upon my struggles.

The first time we completely concede to the internal commotion and hullabaloo of our veracities is one of aggressive rousing. It's that leap in to the unknown and a split second that has the ability to change us, if we let it. In my experience of this, it was barely any more than three shakes of a spider's tail before I had baptised myself in the bare truth, and only minutes after the Dark Knight's closing credits that I remember being sat on Phoebe's bed, fully clothed shockingly, as we both sat there in tears, both shaking as I tried to articulate a spurred on and sincere sequence of words that had never before escaped my lips or left the confines of my mouth.

You see, it was the first time I had ever braved such a heavy and complicated topic, so as you can imagine, it was far from eloquent. It was instead a blotchy, bumbling and expansive use of basic words, a style of articulation more similar to the language of cavemen than what we were taught at school, but still, this lexicon seemed to exemplify the pain and freedom in one billowing wave. This gurgling of thought and feeling wasn't a quick fix by any means, but this wasn't to be expected. I mean it wasn't one of those conversations that flew by in the autumn wind, collecting a mix of rose petals and tulips in its wake, as if symbolically ensuring everything was rosy again in no less than two hops of a kangaroo cub. It wasn't like someone had simply taken away the black and white backlit lighting and released beams of instagram-filtered dye and unsaturated colour in a timid attempt to hide the true darkness of this insolent scene. No. It was a conversation that gave Phoebe the truth, using a poorly constructed composition and badly blabbered proses, with the only interruptions coming in the form of those infamous crying fuelled hiccups that are so unique to each of us.

But it was also a two-birds-with-one-crazy-fucking-helpful-stone sort of situation. You see it was the first time I had ever allowed someone else to see that deep into me, without me bending over and spreading my cheeks anyway, whilst it was also the first time I had ever delved that far into the depths of my own unfathomable arcane too. It's no lie that I hated what I was doing to others simply because I couldn't face my self-deprecating pain, and this made me feel so unselfishly selfish. However, this began to change when the wonderful Phoebe spurred me on, when this caring girl gave me courage and gave me a reason to man the fuck up and grow a pair of cracking cracker jacks. It's like my Great-Great Grandma used to always say, 'No woman is gonna want to see your dick if you've got no balls.' Strangely it was this prompted realisation that gave me something to think about, taking my mind of the usual fluttering combination of sex, drugs, rock n roll, for I was now focussing on the next legitimate steps in my recovering. Whoa, a self-remitted pat on the back for this one huh. I mean, where is my well-deserved medal, Malteser milkshake and meek and merciful manhandling.

Anyway, and as I keep saying, this wasn't a flawless path of begonia's and blowjobs. Actually, thinking about it, this was the kind of path that came disguised in the form of a miraculous scissor kick to my prized ornaments. You see, this deep and meaningful was also the prizewinning chat that forced Phoebe and I to take a break. Admittedly, this arbitration had no chirping sun or shining birds from the get-go, but we're all used to the outcome of a 'break' casting a dampening light over all positivity now aren't we. However, it was a move for the greater good or some shit, for it was an attempt to get me back on the straight and narrow arrow. It was a way to cuckold me into facing the dogged demons of mine, ensuring an undivided and exclusive mentality was enforced and drilled into me. I just needed to stop being so fucking angry with those who loved me, I needed to stop running away like the legend-maker that is Mo Farah, and I needed to stop hiding like the hungry gamer that is Katniss Everdeen.

So now was the time to change. Now was the time for me to lace up my gloves, call myself Cassius Clay, address who I was and ensure I Ali-shuffled past the strangleholds of bereavement. Now was the time to perfect the endurance encouraging rope-a-dope, and fight back with heart, energy and effervescent charisma, and with this in mind, I drove the fanny-fucking-tastic four-hour journey back home that night. No music, no company, no chat, no nothing. I was left as physically alone as

I had been emotionally, for all I had with me on this long ride was undisturbed reflection, relying solely upon my need to sort out my painful problems.

I remember being in floods of tears for the entire journey, watching the foot wells of this four-wheeled and rusty skip slowly fill up with reclusively rare eye juice. I would start hitting the steering wheel at desultory and erratic moments, finding myself unable to contain the anguish anymore, testing the condition of the horn as much as the patience of the airbag. I would just start shouting endless curse words that were so ghastly no amount of Hail Mary's could have forgiven my repetitive verbal sinning. I was getting it all out, everything that had hurt me and hurt others, everything that had been antagonising my headspace, and everything that had progressively built up inside me. I just couldn't stop crying all the way home, feeling so incredibly low, yet with no one to talk to. What was so hard to accept though, was the knowledge that I was completely alone, and so soon after I had finally opened up to someone after so long.

Anyway, this drawn out and verbose free drive finally came to a stop after a marquee load of minutes, thank fuck. I arrived home having not warned anyone I would be arriving, but once again and despite my enlightenment, I could only muster up a sheepish greeting and salutation upon entering the front door and seeing my glorious Mum, for I was still as tetchy and ill-humoured with her as ever, slipping up to my room and sweeping the door shut with the grace of an acid fuelled rhino. She burst into my boudoir blazing! However, this is probably not the 'blazing' terminology that you're thinking, for there was no long-skin joint dangling from her mouth. Instead, my Mum was loading round upon round into numerous theoretical Smith & Wesson's whilst letting off dynamite as she erupted into my room fuming, in a blonde, female, Caucasian and mask free Antonio Banderas type fashion, slicing J's everywhere she could.

In short, she had quite rightly had enough of my behaviour. She sat me down like I was a pre-school kid again and questioned me as if she were Jeremy Paxman, with a tone not dissimilar to how I imagine a drill sergeant barks orders. This approach forced my quick-wit to step-up to the mark, with my response arriving in the form of an absolute break down, relaying the breaking news that I'd just broken up with Phoebe. "Why? Why? Why?" Were the expansive set of interrogation queries I was met with, and that is when the astonishing happened. An event so overwhelming even a rim job from the Tooth Fairy sounds shit.

This astounding, miraculous, stupendous and startling occurrence I speak of is as follows. I was open with my Mum for the first time in modern history, for the first time in years, for the first time since my Dad was killed. I told her I was still not able to cope with the loss of my Dad. I told her I was still angry because he had been taken from me. I told her I was still fucking fragile, despite my Teenage Mutant Ninja Turtle type exterior, in which I am undoubtedly the bad man Raphael. I told her I hadn't been able to come to terms with it all and that I hadn't been ready to either, with these true confessions of revolutionary hype marked a new dawn. It was the step I needed in terms of recovering, recouping, convalescing and straight up mourning. But, it was also a huge moment for my Mum and I, because for the first time, I opened my mouth and out came my heart, landing straight onto my Primark sweater sleeve and then leaping into my Mum's ears. To her it was a completely rad concoction of achievements and a combination of all things great. You name it and it was there, synthesising a slam-dunk, touchdown, goal, ace, try, bull's-eye and a hole in one. It was a victory lap on the same scale as Charlie Sheen's 'I'm still alive' celebratory dance that I imagine he does every morning upon realising he's still alive despite the tiger's blood and cocaine cocktail of a lifestyle he loves.

Anyway despite the beauty of it all, this mother and son honesty was a weird moment, for coming clean about my worries to Mum ensured an intimate audience indeed. I find it odd to say that this honesty was abnormal, but it was, for I had not wanted to worry her with my worries, especially given her recent spells in the six-by-three cell of her hospital room. I had just always thought that sharing my issues with my Ma would be an added worry for her and a selfish decision by me. However, what I realise now is, by leaving her in the dark and keeping her out of the loopy loop that was my mentality at the time was très harmful. In fact, this decision would have incited more worry than if I had just given her some honest info all along, giving her something to digest and offer help on, instead of letting her speculate throughout numerous sleepless nights. The reason I can accept this as gospel now however, is because I hated it when she withheld vital information from me, and thus it almost became a plimsoll on the other hoof sort of reality check.

I guess we're both to blame for our contradictory behaviour, for we both encouraged silence when spoken word was needed. It was piss poor timing basically. But no matter how we slice this cake with the knife of hindsight, we're past it now, and when I look back I just smile at this revolutionary scenario, our chance to talk, the moment we were open and that moment we hugged and cried. I am just happy to know we are Mother and son again, how we used to be, how we should be.

I will never again neglect this relationship as anything but something special, for that is exactly what this bond we have with our parents is. Unfortunately though, I had taken it for granted. I forgot what I had, instead only concentrating on what I had lost, foolishly concentrating on what I couldn't change instead of what I could. This must have been horribly hard for both my Mum and my brother, for they had to deal with me when I was in this cold, confused and shivery state of mind, a time when I had really lost my shit. The thought of my Mum losing that bond with her son is simply soul crushing. The idea of not sharing ludicrous laughs and farcical stories, at least not as much as either of us would have liked to, must have been truly torturing for her. Yeah we loved each other an immeasurable amount, for that was unspoken. But fuck, this immeasurable and unspoken love is far better when it is placed in the 'spoken about' column too.

You see, we have no idea when we are going to pop our clogs and cease dancing away this unforgettable night in a Saturday-Night-Fever-

Travolta type testament, so lets revel in the now, for that's all we have. We all seem to enjoy this touristy perspective of life and conform to what we believe we should do with our time, and that's tiptop because that's what this party is all about. But, what I've come to take on board is the understanding that life is also as much about the little things too. The things that are normal to us and our families and weird to others, for this is what makes life so serenely special, for this is what makes us who we are, even if that is a kooky modern day metrosexual who wears non-prescribed glasses and concealer whilst listening to Mika. I'm kidding, I'm kidding... I don't listen to Mika.

Anyway, to put some much-needed proof into the pudding, I am now bonding with my Mum in a way I was scared would never be possible again. I am no longer waiting for the bi-annual blue moon to take position in the night sky before I speak to her on the phone, for we now speak almost everyday and I cherish these moments, no matter how trivial the drivel may be. I know I will never be able to talk to my Dad again, and yes that upsets me no end, but what am I meant to do about it, kick myself every morning and bite my nails every night?

I have a mother and a brother who I love more than anything, and I am not going to let this moment slip away simply because I'm too busy living in the past and trying to reverse the irreversible. Now I'm not saying I suddenly have a spotless relationship with my family, because it isn't, but it is at least an honest one, and that's far more important than a relationship that's squeaky clean and full of bullshit answers to poignant questions. I guess I have learned to be who I am with my Mum and she is learning to accept that, which is not an easy task given our paradoxical upbringings. She had a plush upbringing, a three-line whip regimental discipline and the need to conform for one reason or another, and one that I presume to be wholly part of her generation. But with this in mind, it is at least easier to understand how hard this acceptance task must be for her, for I am as far fetchingly far from that.

I am far from easy to command, whilst I also have too much flare and pizazz to live in any way other than the way I plan it. Stubborn? Maybe. However it could just as easily be that I prefer recognition and the freedom to think on my own accord, and that is what we call distinction. Nonetheless, my mother, brother and I all understand there are bigger things to sweat over than condemning differences, and that's the evanescent focal point right?! Of course we downright disagree and categorically clash on certain topics, but as I said, we are from different generations and from the same family after all. But I am myself now, and I have my own perception on what this brutal bitch called life is about. Thus if I were to try my best to give you one more slice of humble guidance, and some exhortation to assist you through the ravenous dark, then let it be this:

Be yourself, move forward at your own pace and be honest to who you are no matter what others may think. We may know what we have to do or we may not, either way, we all have our own way of doing what's right, and what compliments this more than anything, is the fact we can do what's right without being scared and without conforming to the mostly mundane norm. We are who we are, period, and being unique is something that should be celebrated, not belittled! So when it comes to the perceptions of others, just remember, those that mind don't matter, and those that matter don't mind, which is bang tidy because love, pals and eternal dudeship is all about quality not quantity, despite how muddied this belief has become since the rise of myface.com or whatever. However, it seems I have yet again acted in a similar, albeit less brave, fashion to Christopher McCandless and drifted acres off topic.

So, having finally relinquished all guardianship over my worries and released them into the open meadows for my mother to cast her entitled aspersion, we came to the unanimous and slightly strange decision to visit a recommended cognitive therapist named Madam Merlin. Ok, so this person wasn't called Merlin, but that doesn't mean this stylish sobriquet isn't one that is more than deftly deserved, especially given Madam Merlin's attire and office. What's more though, this abrupt and personal decision to visit a senile psychic wasn't the only decision I suddenly made in an attempt to level the monsters within, no, for also I said goodbye to Puff the Magic Dragon, waved a fond farewell to the wizard, removed myself from the rodeo and straight up stopped smoking weed and dabbling in drugs that very night, rash but right.

As you may be able to close your eyes and imagine, I was shit scared to sleep alone on that first night, especially given my evidently emotional day. However I must clarify what is meant when I say alone, for what I mean is free from all alcohol and all inhalation of the cushy Kush that I was so stupidly reliant upon. Of course this may sound slightly trivial to you, but I was scared to face the dreams and torture of previous experiences, especially because I knew exactly how lucid and vivid one's dreams can be in those first days of spliff and skunk sobriety. But, as far as I was concerned, I owed this overhaul to too many beautifully important people. Now I wasn't being valiant, courageous, lionhearted, gallant, resolute or even gutsy by unpretentiously braving these treacherous waters of realisation. No, instead I was a coward for not doing it sooner.

I was indebted to the admirable patience and strength of others. I owed this abstinence to those closest to me. I owed it to my Mum, for both my irrational behaviour and disgraceful conduct over the years. I owed it to my brother for not letting our friendship suffer at times. I owed it to my ex-girlfriend, for I promised her I would finally look my devastating demons in the eye, give this fight everything I had and try to actually overcome my fears and torment. I owed it to my Dad, because he would have been confounded by the fact I had struggled as much as I had, he would have hated the fact this event had hindered my progress socially and academically, and he would have slapped me silly for not cracking on with my ludicrous life and instead failing to always fight the good fight.

However, I also owed it to myself. I needed to be myself again. I hated being lost. I hated being angry. I hated being afraid, timorous, rattled and aghast. I hated feeling distanced, desolate, estranged, lonely, and renounced, and I hate feeling like a timid troglodyte. I was bored of being worried, on edge, fretful, tormented and perturbed. But I also passionately fucking despised the constant fatigue and fragility, I fucking hated being unreadable and short-tempered, and more than anything, it was fucking abhorrent to know all this affected others, whether this be a direct reaction from me or as a direct result of the eggshells that surrounded me. The bottom line is, this had to change, I needed this to change and I wanted this to change.

Unfortunately, I think my fairy Godmother was away on sabbatical at this time because nothing dramatically altered after the first 40 odd winks. Shame really, because it makes me believe fairy tales are all smoke and no fire, and as such, I must now assume the majority of my childhood is as much a fraud as the life of Charles Ponzi. But I mustn't fret over this tit-for-tat trifling, for that's yesterday's bullshit and I had too much going on today. Thus moving swiftly on to more relevant pastures, I'm of the factually supported belief that every vivacious voyage and exhilarating expedition starts with a single step, no matter how long the journey may be. So I packed the essentials and got ready for the long haul, searching in every draw and every nook and cranny until I found the courage to do so.

This first step is T-Rex terrifying, and I know you may be too scared to make this move right now, and quite rightly so, but an expansive exchange must always remain on the cards, no matter how faint this glimmer is. I mean, we all know this sort of journey is not one that can be rushed and we all know that we can't simply shut our eyes and hope all our strife just passes. God knows I've tried. Instead we just have to ride these tenacious tsunamis, fight back where we can, get back up on our feet where we have to, swallow our pride where possible and look for help where plausible, for we cannot attempt this journey alone. But to ensure we accomplish our vagrant adventure and make it to the proverbial shores of our pacific blue lagoon of harmony, well then we must want to better ourselves, we must strive to succeed and we must excel in our ability to endure.

So, after a week of staring down the barrel of my internal enemies' sawn off, I was already feeling extensively enriched, for I hadn't gazed at a grinder, collided with cannabis, opened a baggy, rolled up a twenty-pound note or even licked a vapid long skin. Yeah my dreams were more lucid and vivid than the graphics on 'Skyrim', and more ominous, curious and weirdly kinky than those dreams that occur as a result of a post-cheese-and-wine night. But I felt good, and moreover, I was beginning to live Pinocchio's dream of becoming a real boy, one who could feel an almighty spectrum of emotion, only comparable to Dulux's sprawling paint range. But to ensure a pat on the back remained a possibility, I made sure this wasn't the only step I made in securing a future even brighter than the one Orange incessantly advertises. No. For I was also voluntarily forced to make the trip to see that cognitive therapist I aforementioned, and trust me, this sort of fantasy preaching stuff is very much against what I believe in at a cellular level. I mean there's just too much emphasis placed on spirit and faith and not enough science and facts for me. However, I was at a stage where I would try almost anything, for I wanted to progress no matter which route to the finish line I took. Oh, and I wanted to please my Mum, who loves horoscopes, palm reading, tea leaf guess work and all sorts of Jedi mind tricks and fantastical fables. Chalk and cheese her and me, chalk and cheese.

Nevertheless, the ride there was somewhat sombre, especially in the sense that there wasn't much chin-wagging between Mum and I. However, I would have rubbed a bakers dozen lamps and used each of these chances to wish for some degree of chitter chatter, not least because the long silences of this car journey were in fact filled with the dull murmur and pathetic excuse for music that persistently plagues today's radio. However, I can't shift the blame of this taciturnity onto mother, for after a week of commitment to the cause and literal voyage towards self-improvement, I still hadn't managed to completely shake the cobwebs. I can only assume this was because I was still to proud to accept any help, biting my lip a bit, probably still scared to open up to this Old Dear of mine due to my inherent fear of getting close to others. Mum seemed to understand this though, but that didn't make it much easier in all honesty. Yet looking back at this scene now, I can willingly put on the dunce cap, sit in the corner of the crèche and loudly verify that I was a colossal cock for my behaviour, but I accept this and I refuse to make any excuses, whether lame, valid or otherwise. Anyway, lets move on to the actual mastery of this Madam Merlin, or more specifically, this new cognitive therapist of mine.

So, upon arrival I sheepishly stormed into her building with as much of an open mind as possible. I can admit my mentality was not quite located in the middle ground, but it was slightly more open to the unexplainable than that of the walking talking Stephen Hawking, Professor Brian Cox, and a touch more sceptical than that of Ricky

Gervais. No doubt this psychic she-male knew this though, for she was probably reading my every thought from the birth of time and was thus able to hear my taunts of, 'try your best, I dare you to impress me, I am unbreakable.' For this is all I was thinking about upon my incline up the rickety stairs towards the room where 'the magic happens' so to speak. Well that and the full-frontal naked pictures of Kelly Brook that my mind constantly conjures up.

After an hour with this sexy and delusional wizard though, I was childishly gobsmacked and decidedly dumbfounded. Now don't get me wrong, Dynamo is incredible. I mean, tittie-twisting-nipples-of-Christ, he walked across the River Thames. Then there is David Blaine who is also somewhat impressive. He was buried alive for seven days at Trump Place for fucks sake, and of course there is Derren Brown, who is exceptionally extraordinary, for he has somehow convinced the world that the name Derren is legitimate. But, and with a colossal Paul McCartney divorce settlement type objection, I must sign off from brown nosing this list of magicians by saying, 'I have seen something even more astonishing.'

You see, this newly acquainted and spiritual woman of mine, who I made sure knew nothing about me for the want of a level playing field, told me stuff that only I could have known. I mean by the Penis of Poseidon, her opening gambit told me that my life was drastically altered when something fell out of the sky. C'mon dude! That shit is freaky Friday, especially as I don't watch psychological horror films ever, even when our solar source is at it's highest point on a long summer's day, so as you can imagine, I had no intention on participating in such an event for real, steering well clear of Ouija boards and people who can see dead people.

Nonetheless, I remained sceptical throughout this shady rendezvous, keeping my cards locked in a box and close to my chest, so much so that the entirety of this first meet and greet, and for the full sixty minutes of this hour-long seminar, I didn't say a word to this master of the mind, this spiritual sorcerer or world-class guesstimator, instead I simply nodded my head where appropriate and listened to what she had to say.

Don't get too excited though, because I'm not going to repeat what this wonderful witch-like woman said to me, professional courtesy and all, so just keep taking deep calming breaths. What I will say however is that she was awesomely accurate, and even if she was nothing more than an excellent fraud who had unbelievable Cluedo type tekkers, she was a humungous helping hand, not literally though, because that would be weird and possibly inappropriate to some people.

This experience just wasn't like any other therapists I had seen, where they say nothing, you say everything and then you come out thinking, fuck yeah you sweet child o'mine, I feel as light as feather, for that was a huge burden off my shoulders. Nah, this was a complete role reversal. This was almost as good as the role-playing sodomy of bedroom antics that I'm more used to, but not quite. I wasn't shepherded into a corner by a heterogeneous herd of collie dogs this time, forced to speak my mind as best as possible for fear of an extensively awkward silence worthy of any 'Made in Chelsea' episode. No, this time I sat there as this perplexing person explained to me what I was feeling, telling me the depth of my emotion, telling me what was going on in my head and heart, and explaining it with the clarity of the 'Cullinan Diamond'.

I was relating to things I had no way of explaining, coming to terms with stuff I had no way of identifying, not without her help anyway. But what was most impressive was the impact this therapy had upon me in the hours, days and weeks after this blind date, because instead of leaving this humble ladies home with the same feeling as I was previously used to after such an engagement, where I simply felt relieved that I had spoken to someone and relieved of an invisible pressure, I was left to actually ponder what she had said and this was a world exclusive for me. I was left with questions to ask myself, ambition to live up to and a refuelled determination that seemed to fill me up by the bucket load. This was a sentiment as foreign to me as a love child of Colonel Gaddafi, Christopher Walken or Casper the Friendly Ghost.

As I've discussed, I had been to counselling before and it was super-duper helpful, even rad at times. But it also became predictable. It was just someone external to address with my hurt, someone to have a little cry in front of and then momentarily move on, temporarily deciding to live my life as if were dandy and problem free. There was never any dwelling, never any questioning and never any pondering, just the need for the tears to dry, my voice to sound confident and my happily masked face to be flawlessly reapplied. Not this time though, not with

Merlin's magic making a deep impact. The librettos of Merlin were just too accurate to ignore, almost forced to listen as her spiel hit resonating notes, so very personal and yet so very far from the words that would I could have mustered up and let leave my mouth. Instead these were words from the gob of a lovely lady I had never met before, and that impacted upon my listening abilities.

Such precisions made me pause, think, breathe and assess everything that had been spoken about in a modus of complete consideration, and this was unerringly what I needed. I needed to interact with myself, ask questions and seek answers, and this is exactly what cognitive therapy did for me. The entire journey back home from this eclectic office was spent in a way eerily similar to the journey there. Silences filled with the crap music of some talentless youths from some direction and restless radio hosts provided minutely updates on what Katie Perry's favourite flavour jellybean is or some shit like that. But it wasn't a tense ride home; rather it was just thoughtful, quite literally full of thought.

I can't tell you therapy will be the same for you. I can't tell you which techniques will be used by each counsellor or each cognitive therapist and I can't tell you what effect it will have on your recovery, in the same way I can't tell you what advice to expect from a priest, rabbi, bishop, monk, nun, abbot, cardinal, acolyte, lama or deacon. What I can say about counselling though, is no matter what form this advocate surfaced, it was beneficially breathe-taking, but how could it not be, for it was human help that was both interactive and proactive. It was a hustle and bustle that helped restore my faith in me.

What's more, and I know this may be a bitch to hear, but if you can't concede to the bullshit aura that clouds such services, especially in a time of such scientific dominance, you must try and accept it for what it is, and that's a helping hand to lead you away from your previous self-subjugation of yesteryear. It seems to me that society is now a greater community, and with the arrival of this change we now care too much about what other people think of us, and thus the idea of counselling comes with unscrupulous scrutiny, for we are afraid people will judge us for such participation. Well, that notion can fall backwards into a wheelie bin and suck itself off, because if you want to overcome the horribly fucked up situation that you are in, then who gives a fuck what the ignorant eyes of others think.

I was bullied by people for being 'messed up' enough to need counselling, bullies who didn't know anything about me, bullies who had it easy all their lives and were popular for no other reason than the flawed fact they shouted louder than others and belittled those around them, and this was just to help them feel like their dick was far bigger than the realities of their nakedness. I quickly learned not to let this get under my skin with one elementary school question… "If bullies are so fucking perfect, how come they lose at life so god damn always."

You see, we should be aspiring to better ourselves, never doubting this concept nor disparaging it, and we should most certainly never feel inferior for trying to do so either. Because no matter what situation this is applied, whether it be a healing process for close personal loss, intelligence, sporting ability, music, finger-banging, cunnilingus or whatever, we will now forever stand in good stead throughout the good times as much as the troubled. I sought help and you can be crazy certain that I'm godly-glad I did, especially as I found the outcome of this service to be on the same lustful level of help as 'Milka dime bars' and bi-hourly blozza's.

So I swallowed my pride where I had to in order to better myself as much as it was to simply get better, so to speak. I'm not embarrassed, in fact I'm using the pages of this book as a metaphorical mountaintop to scream, 'Fuck yeah, I threw caution to the wind and sought the assistance of professionals, lovely people who are skilled, aloof and contemptuous enough to have certificates of merit peppered across their walls of pride, and I would encourage anyone else who is suffering from a life pounding lesson to at least give counselling a chance, an open mind, a kiss on the cheek and a cheeky fondle of its sexual organs.' Counselling can do wonders.

However, the desire to be happy and to better myself wasn't the only reason behind my decision, for I also sought out the help and support of professional others, somewhat due to the fact I was swinging and missing without it, or not swinging the bat at all. I hated the fact people just presumed the pain would disappear with time and that things would get better naturally. Well from my experience I can say with throat clearing clarity that this myth is, ahem, bollocks. I know it took me a while to recover, and I hold my hands up to those who say it maybe took too long, but I was tired of people thinking of this as a 'just get over it' situation. In fact, I want to say to those naïve-nit-clits out there, go and find a phallic shaped object, make sure it's quantifiably large and then sit and swivel. Sure time is the greatest healer, but you don't know the struggles that accompany that and the strength that needs to be mustered to allow time to help. Those who have never suffered have no idea what's going on in my head. They have no idea how hard it is to get over something so disabling it will never be 'gotten over'. It just doesn't work like that. Fuck, I was even aware of this in a third person sort of way, aware of how terribly très tired I was of not being able to get over this slippery situation myself.

It is for both these reasons, the combination of fatigue and the fact I couldn't 'just get over it', that I did what I had to do in my adapt or die fashion. I sought help, and guess what, it was a miraculous decision void of any true definition of miracle. It was a human decision, where one human simply sought help from other humans, taking a humane journey only to find the lost meaning of humanity.

Yeah, this should have been an easy decision to make, especially as it has a difficulty rating of half a star when put on paper, but it wasn't, and nor was it a situation that was played out on paper. Hell on high, it wasn't even slightly seasoned with a sprinkle of easy. It was an existence plagued by an attack of a thousand razor blades. However, I've always believed this burdening image and painful practise was heightened because our generation suffers from presumption, pride and the belief each individual doesn't need help because his or her problems are his or her problems and no one else's. It's a mentality that suggests seeking help is akin to showing weakness. Behave. You do not have to deal with anything on your own, and nor are you expected to.

Counselling is complicated, frowned upon by others and perceptually a pussy move. Well that uninformed presumption can holla a cab and fuck off outta here. Counselling is one hell of a service, and it comes in so many different forms and layouts, some of which will suit your needs, whilst others may just waste your time. But surely it's better to try and possibly fail than to not try at all and remain a lost pup. You may want to wait, putting it off and then putting it off again, but try not to because life is about this very moment we're in right now. We can't press pause on the old dusty life button. We can't hope time will take a breather or wish the hourglass sand will ignore the rules of gravity and cease falling, because it won't happen. Period.

Life doesn't stop its whirlwind journey, it doesn't go on vacation and, whether you find it desirable or not, the world will keep spinning on its axis despite how many lamps your rub, prayers you make and clovers you collect. So I advise you to seize the opportunity that is each day (except hangover days) and to do your absolute upmost to make the best out of what is no doubt one messy pile of fucked up circumstances. But do it for you, above all else, do it for you, because on the odd chance that you're not an immortal Greek God like Apollo or Artemis, and thus accepting the argument that you're probably not going to live forever and ever, why don't you just throw caution to the typhoon and take a shot at being happy now. After all, nothing ventured, nothing gained.

Anyway, what appeared next on the menu of my understanding was this notion of clarity and sobriety, which seemingly walked hand in hand down the aisle of recovery, and I achieved a lot once I accepted this and took responsibility for my actions. However this wasn't the walk in the park I had contemplated, for my teetotalism only lasted three weeks, max. Maybe this was because I was only able to kick such temptations to the curb due to my being at home, and thus I subsequently had the time to focus and concentrate on reaching my goal and succeeding with my much needed objective. Maybe it was helpful that I was in the place I was brought up, closer to the memories, closer to the source, closer to my family and settled in a galaxy far far away from distraction and the usually accessible possibility of running, maybe.

You see I had managed to take a step forward in the film industry, at least a step in the direction I wanted to head. I was moving away from the freelance world and the world in which I was proverbially whoring myself out from film to film, with work forever sporadic and never set in stone, and instead moving into a fulltime position within a production and distribution company. Thank you for your applause, kind words, tittie photos and sexy letters. Now I am of course aware that this means less than nought to you, but in my hard fought desire to climb the ranks, this was a step toward my ambitious ambition of becoming a promising producer. However, with this power came great responsibility, I mean, with this job came the permanent move to the smoggy metropolis of bright lights and overpopulated streets that we love to call London, and with London comes temptation, and we know what Oscar Wilde's accurate thoughts were on temptation. Keeping this in mind, it doesn't take a NASA rocket engineer to understand exactly why my sobriety faltered so furiously, for I could not resist the 'on tap' lifestyle of London Town and the chance to have a dealer on each and every speed dial option.

This move itself couldn't have worked out any sweeter though, well logistically and socially speaking, for a room just seamlessly popped itself into the available column, presented itself on my radar via the form of a lovely voicemail and offered itself to me like a racy gentlewoman on a raunchy rebound at exactly the right time. What's more, this room happened to be within a house that was occupied by five great mates of mine. However, there was an immediate downside, for this fortunate godsend of a house did mean I could no longer purchase any lottery tickets, for I lucked out on this erection stimulating house-share in West Hampstead.

Anyway, despite the obvious and alluring temptations that came with such an illustrious move, I was determined to stay focussed on what I had accomplished in my three weeks of application and abstinence, but clearly this wasn't to be as easy as I had presumed. Now look, I didn't completely fall off the wagon, but I didn't exactly stay seated either, although this is sorta hard to explain to those who have managed to stay on the path of moral integrity and proper conduct, or more specifically those of you who have never been tempted by a dabble in what are essentially mood altering narcotics, but I will try to explain in any case.

So, I had stopped smoking weed, grass, skunk, high grade and herb, and thus stronger stuff too. High five. However, I simply substituted this ingredient with the super-sub known as 'hash' and a party far less often than my body was used to. Now this may sound like a ridiculous statement, and I am inclined to agree with you, as it's a lot like saying I've swapped Coca-Cola for Pepsi. But, the difference between weed and hash is huge. Hash is mellow, it's not disabling, it's far from the same extreme of weed, it's not as powerful, you don't get as high and you don't suffer dire drowsiness the next day, or as we call it in the business, a 'stoneover'. Now I'm not looking for a congressional medal of honour, a knighthood or even a penny sweet as congratulatory praise, but I am pleased I managed to keep to this new rule of thumb, the one that read, 'Hash only'.

Looking back at this decision making process now, or lack there of, I understand why I relapsed so spectacularly like Aldous Snow, who, and I quote, 'was famously sober and now is famously not sober' and the reason for this is, I was a pussy-o-bitch, or to be more polite about it, I was all aghast and scared. I was moving in with five friends, some of them I was best buddies with, some of them I didn't know exceptionally well, but all of whom I was not ready to share my emotions with.

I was under the impression that I wasn't close enough to these handsome housemates of mine to share or show my torture, but now I realise that I wasn't close enough to anyone when it came to this sharing

219

hogwash, at least I wasn't in my panic-stricken and personal perspective. I simply wasn't ready to show this side of me yet, and so in my startled and cold feet state, I decided to run back into the sanctity of my private cave, where I tripped and fell, helplessly witnessing my puckered lips land perfectly on a smouldering spliff. I know it makes absolutely zero sense, but I felt numb again.

This wasn't the right thing to do, and in all honesty, it was just another instalment of the 'What the fuck was I thinking' show. I had finally made some progress, progress that was both necessary and desired, progress that I had evaded for so many months and years in some stealthy Metal Gear Solid 'Snake' type fashion. So why did I then theoretically whip out my dick, carefully take aim, and just piss all over this heroic headway. It was a completely unnecessary roll of the dice and one where I wasn't trying to fill the cool and edgy quota of previous stints. I guess I was simply running scared, unwilling to take any more grenades whilst laying in the trenches, and thus I sought comfort in the knowledge that I was dumbing down and killing off my emotional capacity, yet again. This reaction showed me how easy it is for growth and development to deteriorate, flip-flop, retrogress and transpose, for I actually watched my indulgence recrudesce.

Luckily this relapse wasn't as bad as before though, with my dexterous desire to dumbfound such a disastrous set of circumstances in that three weeks, possibly aiding my long term perspective. Maybe I was just on hiatus, but this is a topic up for debate. However, what I do know for definite is that I was steadily becoming more accepting of what was required, understanding the fact I had to start sharing what was under the surface, and what's more, I began to appreciate what my housemates were offering. I began to understand that they were there for me in this transitional time of need. This attempt at clarity was another trial and error ball ache though, albeit one that had to be attempted, and so I shamefacedly began to open my wardrobe full of skeletons.

I was open with these guys and gals about my situation and thus the need that came with it, the need for weed, or more correctly hash and any numbing narcotic that coerced confidence and ridiculed reminiscence. I was honest about why I smoked the herb and why I rolled up notes. I was honest about what I was struggling with, and occasionally I was even honest about my perception of life after such tragedy, like a modern day member of the biblical magi. However, when I say I was finally opening up after all this time, I should specify that each one of these topics were only touched upon at immensely infrequent and seriously seldom moments. But even with this in the forefront of your mind, there must be kudos where kudos is due, for these cherubs I was bunking with had the patience and understanding of any practising Buddhist.

Talking of kudos though, I must footnote the fantastic foundations I had forgotten during my time at University, the foundations of organisation that comes with a 'steady' job. It was just nice to have some sort of structure in my life again, removing some of the belief that I was Peter Pan sort of lost, a familiar feeling in this rite of passage I'm sure. Anyway, it was just nice to know that Monday to Friday I would be working and giving it my all, exercising each morning and every evening in an attempt to relieve any unwanted stress, and then playing to my hearts content at the weekends. It was this heartfelt knowledge that I found so welcoming, so grounding and so new, especially after my years of wandering around the wilderness, completely absent.

London, and the subsequent work that came with this conurbation, just gave me the structure I had otherwise been lacking and a structure that I have found so important during the healing process. It encouraged me to look at the bigger picture in question. This help doesn't just fall into place because of the arrival of some structure and we're not instantly healed because we've not got something else to concentrate on in day-to-day living, no. But it does mean we can start putting our lives back in order, willing on the different segments of our being to fall into place around this new found and fundamental framework.

You see, before I had this format glued into place, I was bouncing around like an irate Jack-in-the-box, for when I wasn't working I would get provoked, piqued and plainly put, pissed off. I would try and fill the monotonous boredom with something, fucking anything, for I was frightened of what pondering periods could do to my instability. Sometimes I would find myself using this unemployed status as an excuse to explain why I was convulsed, poorly hiding the fact it was because I had too much time to think and thus a chance to get riled up by the loss of my Dad. However, this was flip-reversed and completely contrasted when I was working on set. Don't get me wrong, I would occasionally get upset, despondent and vexed by my schedule, realising I hadn't had even a moment to think about this endearing old man of mine and this was like hot coals on my heart strings. In a sense, it was a balance I had never thought to question, but a balance that I so desperately needed.

Once I realised and accepted how effective lifestyle equilibrium is to the healing process though, I seriously started to work out how this philosophical outlook of mine could be made into one of my strengths. I began to work the angles and take on projects that would allow me to hit three squirrels with one brick, restoring my damaged confidence and self-assurance, whilst proving I still had that tenacious fight in me. But let me explain what I mean by 'projects' that I touched on so briefly... I foolishly said 'yes' to an offer, an offer to participate in a fight night. I stupidly said, yeah I'll get in the ring as an amateur boxer or as I prefer to be called, a biffer, allowing my imagination to get involved so that it could trick me into believing that I was in fact a fighter from the 1906 Olympics.

Anyway, the reason I said yes to this ridiculing event had nothing to do with my eccentric ego, the 50/50 chance of winning or even the result. Heckle a hen; I didn't even care about my opponent. Instead I saw it in tunnel vision, for it was just another example of the much needed and highly addictive structure that my life got its fix from these days. It was a task that demanded discipline and heart, and it was the opportunity to try and restore what I had previously lost during the battering blizzards of bereavement. However, I can't deny I also saw it through sordid-tinted-glasses, for this was the greatest chance to get laid amongst a bevvy of beauties I had ever been faced with. The centre of attention, all ripped and manly. Hell yeah.

I trained hard, I ate well, I focused and I built up an anger just to see if I could control it, all of which I found extremely challenging. Nonetheless there was one thing I still couldn't overcome or fight off, and that was my addiction to feeling nothing. I still couldn't stop ending my day with a joint or dabbling in more, and this proves how strong its grip on me was, latching on to me like a wild vine from Jumanji. I found this so hard to understand, for I had stopped smoking cigarettes, stopped glugging down all devil juice and stopped myself from indulging in any sexual deviance, whether that be a ménage-et-trois or a scenario that was two members short of a threesome. Basically, I showed self-constraint in every part of my being, but I was still too scared to face my emotions. I was enthused by the chance to step through the ropes and into the ring, but terrified of my feelings, and thus I refused to provide any opportunity for such emotions to creep out into the public domain.

I proved a lot to myself in this period. I learned what was possible and what was a struggle. I learned a huge deal about my character and myself, and it is this lesson that has had a long-lasting effect. However, it wasn't all optimism, Haribo and champagne, for I took a bit of a knock during this eight-week preparation period. Not the kind of set back boxers are conventionally used to, for I'm not referring to that of a physical wound, nor any pathetic injury to my pinkie-toe or whatever David Haye blames his weak-no-show performances on. Nah. Instead, what happened next was probably the one thing that had the ability to make me or break me, help me move on or take me back to square one and that hammer blow arrived via the news that one of my Dads oldest and best friends, Reg, had succumbed to the evil that is cancer.

Now it wasn't so much that Reg and I had grown exceptionally close, as is the case with the other losses in my life. In fact it was quite the opposite, for if anything we had grown apart. The fact was, this man had done more for me than I could have ever appreciated at the time and more than he knew he had done, but painfully I never got to thank him. You see, my Dad wanted me to go into a profession that he perceived as an old school professional, pushing me in the direction of politician, army officer, lawyer or anyone of those types of jobs that would have most definitely enforced a round peg square hole type of outcome, and as always, I found myself going along with these requests of his.

That is until the magnificent man, Reg, saw something different in me, changing the direction and course of my life outright. Reg quite simply highlighted my creative side and pushed me towards this colourful route of ever changing vitality, selling the colourful conspiracies of a spontaneous lifestyle with enthusiasm, a choice I had always been fascinated by, but never had the backing to commit too. As you can probably imagine, even from this short synopsis, this was an awe-inspiring man who saw the best in people. He was a pacifist, a man who loved fashion, cars, jazz and eccentric company, always surrounding himself with people who would challenge him to grow, and he was the man who inspired me to follow my own love for what are essentially 'the arts' in the same way he inspired so many others, and, I have never looked back since.

The news that Reg had been taken from us absolutely devastated me, hitting my suddenly glass jaw with the force of a wrecking ball. But despite how scared I was by yet another crushing loss, I was subconsciously aware of what my options were and took control of what route to take. I mean, I got the news on the way back from work, as I made my way through the pouring rain, undeniably depicting a Baz Luhrmann inspired backdrop, when my Mum phoned me and delivered the damning news. Oddly enough though, I stayed completely composed, calm and collected, like an emotional Johnny Wilkinson in front of the posts at Twickenham, although this didn't last too long.

Nevertheless, I remember the moments after this phone call more than the phone call itself. I remember walking at a picked up pace down the high street, opening the front door to our West Hampstead home with a level of rushed intention, striding into my shared house, through the kitchen, past my housemates without saying a word to anyone of them, picking up my skipping rope, walking back through this communal area and finally into my ground floor bedroom and as soon as that bedroom door of mine clicked shut, I just broke down. Without any hesitation whatsoever, I just clenched my fist and punched a gaping hole in my bedroom door, much to the distress of my helpless right hand. However, I was so overwhelmed by emotion, I didn't even have time to respond to this sudden shock of strength and not even a moment to think, 'Am I a Power Ranger, and if so, which one am I?' I was nothing but completely distraught and overridden by the transpiration of another great loss.

Having gone all Thor on the door, I guess it's no surprise that my friends rushed in to check what the loud noised commotion was all about, bursting in simply to find me cowering on the bedroom floor in hysterical waterworks. This moment then revolutionised something within me, for my housemates were so comforting, so caring and so kind. They were true friends and I tip my metaphorical sombrero to them for this was a new dawn of realisation for me, helping me understand that I wasn't alone in this struggle, alas this was the first time I had felt such uplifting optimism.

However, despite all the positivity peering through, I was now faced with yet another mindboggling set of major crossroads in my life, for I knew Reg's death had the irresistible capacity to send me off on one, again. I knew this because I'd already been down that unruly path. I knew what it was to be lost and afraid. I knew what it was like to intentionally lose myself amongst a flurry of white powders, credit cards and rolled up notes. I knew the only way to avoid binge drinking was to make my drinking constant. I knew what it was like to chase emptiness.

I had learned from the past though. Luckily I had learned from the past. This time round though, I was reminded of an old school trait of mine, one that gave me a reminiscent and slightly egotistical semi-boner. What I am referring to is my reaction, for instead of hiding at the bottom of a bottle of Bombay Sapphire, I chose to use this emotional power-up for the power of good. This was a fantastic first, searching for that tiny silver slither amongst the cirrus clouds above. I used this emotion and the memories I had collected of all those charismatic characters that were so full of love and used them in my favour, using these recollections to fuel me and to fuel my drive, allowing me to take on this lion's den of a hurdle, rather than retreating like I would have previously done, at least that's what my personal records and internal history book suggest.

I focussed my anger and took out my emotion in a very obvious fashion given the timing of everything. I took my pain and anguish out in training, whether running, rowing, skipping, weights, punch-bags, searching my right nostril for ready to pick bogies, dutch-ruddering or whatever the activity may have been, but I also made sure I kept myself calm and that's where this project became so beneficial. Essentially this boxing task of mine became a godsend, for it gave me something to focus on. It provided me with a heroic hands-on challenge that demanded I better myself, training before work and at the days close too. It gave me six weeks to prove something to myself, and it was a trial period to get me back on the boulevard of integrity and purpose.

However, I hadn't really thought about the most pivotal part of this training, for not once did I come to terms with the fact there was to be an expiry date. Not once did I accept that I would actually get inside the ring in front of nine hundred bloodthirsty spectators and face off with an opponent who was intentionally trained to take me down inside three rounds.

Now I was somewhat haphazard with most musical instruments at school, thus sport was my chosen time filler when it came to the extra curriculum of modern day schooling. I guess I had speed on my side and a slightly above average hand eye coordination, but then again, what teenage boy isn't good at handling balls. So this was my scene to excel, referencing sport that is, thus it made a fair amount of sense for me to take up an endeavour, an activity and a distraction that would contest my sporting ability whilst challenging me in every way. I was contested mentally, emotionally and of course physically, and that's exactly what brawling envelopes and without any bubble wrapping whatsoever.

It was an experience and an avenue that was second to none, and if boxing were running for electoral office in the 'how to treat tribulation' primaries of New Hampshire, it would without a doubt get my vote. Well maybe not boxing per se, but any 'extra-curricular activity' that requires the participant to better him or herself. Don't get me wrong, I mean fuck I wish I were offered the opportunity to learn the electric guitar in a pressured environment that required me to top the string skills of Jimi Hendrix in less than seventy-two hours, but alas, I drew the short straw in becoming a human punch bag instead.

I did manage to learn numerous valuable values when pursuing this interest however, and that was all I could ask for. You see, the great thing about taking up an interest is that it tries and tests you, it sets you a challenge with set goals to achieve and fuels you with the confidence and assurance you may have thought to be lost. It gives you a purpose and fills you with reason. It takes the life lessons you've learned in the harshest of manners and forces you to apply them to something almost measurable, and by doing this you can find the positives in what is so impressively negative. It's a chance to demonstrate your strength of character, your thick skin and your ability to pick yourself up, all of which are influential, extraordinary, imposing, majestic, noble and remarkable traits.

What you must understand is what you have gained through the shit you've been served, instead of focusing on the opposite. Yes, we've been knocked down too many fucking times, but we've gotten back on to our feet on each occasion, sometimes due to an unknowingly natural instinct, whilst other times we've fought fang and claw for this stance. We have proven that we can take the hits over and over again, but more than this, we've proven that we can keep going despite its implacability. We stiffen our upper lip, take it on the chin and we plough on like humanoid shire horses and this is something to be proud of. Now these qualities may feel as alien to you as R2D2, E.T, Wall-E and Lady Gaga, but it's crazy fucking normal for these truly incredible abilities of ours to often fly under our own radar for one reason or another. Maybe this is because our confidence has been smashed down time and again, or maybe the application of these unbelievable traits tended to be applied in wholly foreign, avant-garde and unconventional circumstances. Thus, when we decide to take on a challenge and exert ourselves in a means that is more obvious and orthodox, we remind ourselves of our innate ability to survive, and from this we can build.

I lost the boxing match, but fuck I loved every moment I had in that four-sided arena of blood and doom. I hadn't stepped in a ring before and I was oblivious to the nine hundred live spectators, including those friends of mine who came along, the ones bellowing their unrelenting support and galvanising applause. Yes, I was battered, bruised, bleeding, and hardly able to stand by the end, but I still enjoyed it, literally an excruciating amount. It is a promising punishment that tests your physicality almost as much as your mentality and heart, but that was just it, that was what sparked something inside me. I didn't care about the result, and I like to think I was humble in defeat to an opponent who was a better boxer than me. But, I had achieved something monumental that night and something far greater than my opposition's victory, at least as far as I am aware.

I had proven to myself that I had the endurance against the odds. I had proven to myself that I was mentally sturdy and cerebrally heavy-duty, a sexy camouflage-free tank on seriously spindly legs. I had proven to myself that my heart and spirit was unbreakable, even when I was grazed, wounded, cut and covered in claret. I am unreservedly proud that I never backed down, that I never gave up the fight, and that I held my own, keeping on the front foot as much as my opponent in what was a true spectacle. I didn't care if the spectators were aware of my internal battle or my private pride, because that is the ferocious fight that is void of all spectators. You see the boxing event and the build up to it gave me the self-esteem, encouragement and faith I needed. It literally beat me to my senses and allowed me a platform where I could prove something important to myself. A platform where I could prove I still had quality attributes and an unrivalled tenacity. I learned the importance of self-perception, and I learned that I didn't need to prove anything to anyone else, for it was my fight and my pain, so what does the null and void discernment of others matter?

The only thing that matters is your own perception of you, for this realisation allows you to revel in the beautifully beaming confidence that you have every right to revel in. We are not here to please others, nor do we need to seek the approval of others within this chaotic culture of conformity. We only need to be happy with who we are, ignoring the fear of what others may think. As Cypher Raige stated in After Earth, 'fear is not authentic or real, it is in fact a product of thoughts that you generate and invent, and more importantly, it is a choice.'

Accept this for what it is, understand it and use it to push beyond the pissed-up perceptions of other peoples and persons. Now I'm not saying we should all take up boxing, in fact fuck that, I'd rather do my best to deter you from such a dramatic marvel. Instead I urge you to throw yourself at an enjoyable endeavour of your own selection. Of course this could well be boxing. However, it could just as easily be kayaking, hiking, the jazz flute, inverted saxophone or the electric violin. Not all of which will get you laid on a nightly basis as I've learned, but will at the very least help you recover.

It could be marathon training, a focus on weight loss or weight gain, starting a fashion line or even battling on with a business plan. Fuck, it could be the kind of abstract painting where you use nothing but your webbed-foot to hold the brush. It could even be standing at the oche wearing a blindfold simply as a means of refining your spidey-senses, in which you will definitely get some serious action in your slam van of a vehicle, although this is very dependent upon success I would imagine. Heck, you could even start writing. Whatever you choose though, set yourself a target no matter how ridiculous it is. In fact make it as ridiculous as possible, because even if we aim for the moon and only get half way, its better than giving into the man by refusing to try.

Whatever you choose and whatever you decide, trust me it will be rad, and I give you every assurance I possibly can that it will be breathtakingly beneficial, horrifyingly helpful and fucking fantastic, for you will learn more about yourself from this dedication than you thought possible from any flippant 'fad'. These sort of challenge's remind us of who we are and what we can achieve, they remind us that we are stronger than those around us and they are complimented by our nurtured ability to endure. They cement the life lessons we've soaked up, and they display them in an illuminating light so unavoidably auroral, you'd think you're walking past the window displays at Harrods in the depths of a winter's night.

To have that level of input and that degree of self-motivated understanding of what it is to be dedicated to something again was preciously priceless. It made me think long and hard, it took away the fear that I had hidden from for so long, the fear that was nothing more than my own projections of what I thought I should be scared of. But what I have come to realise now, I had nothing to be scared of. I had already been through the worst and was now journeying out of the dense woodland, stronger and wiser than ever before, and heading to a place where the grass is greener and full of genuine happiness, self-confidence, re-assurance and horny co-eds.

I had taken the big blows and experienced the devastating pain that life has a tendency to throw at us, and this pain scared me shitless. But I was beginning to prove to myself that my jaw wasn't made of single-glazed glass and that I wasn't going to get knocked down and simply stay down anymore. No. I had seen the worst of it, I had endured a fast and furious flurry of infliction, and yet I was still here, coming round to what I had achieved and coming round to the fact I had worn my invisible opponent down to the ground. Realising this, now was the time to fight back and show this ducking and diving devil what I had left in the tank, show him that I was just getting started and ready to hit him with enough power, supremacy, clout and authority I'm sure I would have made the tenacious Tyson proud of my efforts.

I was scared of something that I had constructed in my mind because that was what I was aware of. I thought life had got the better of me and I wasn't willing to accept anything other than this. That was when I realised I needed something to restore my confidence, cockiness and self-assurance, and that is exactly what happened, that is precisely what this dedication provided and this is exactly why I am blabbering on about this natural phenomenon in the same way that the legendary Sir David Attenborough goes off on one about the bird-of-paradise.

In any case, I began to appreciate where my faults were and accepting which vices were tying me down. Now I know there isn't much practicality in acceptance alone, but from my perspicacity, the first step in solving any problem is quite simply recognising there is one. Thus I quite sensibly started with my smoking habit, realising that I had originally adopted this proclivity as a sleeping aid, only to watch this fixation transpire over the past six months to a year, and that this routine inclination had somehow adopted the absolute reverse effect, for this medicinal marijuana had suddenly ceased obeying it's primary principle in sending me off to dreamlessly sleep. Yeah it had previously eradicated all chances of my subconscious entering a bad dream, but it had now defected to the bad side altogether, having decided to adopt a newly negative stance and one that very much involved keeping me awake. This Judas of a notion could literally bore off, or at least it should have. But like I said, I had finally acknowledged the devilish dominances of cannabis and hopefully I could find a way to open the door, unlock a window and watch this strain of vegetation do one, or to use more appropriate English, find a way for me to finally reject this damning dependency.

Anyway, it was at this exact time that my Mum was also back and forth between intensive care and the high priority ward at a hospital in my home county, a stay that was caused by a combination of misdiagnosis and the unavoidable aftermath of Crohn's disease. Now I'm not talking some short-stay-long-weekend type situation where the hospital visits were succinct sojourns. No. I'm talking a straight three-and-a-half months in this undersized and unpretentious vicinity of a room, the sort that showed no signs of growing any more expansive no matter how much miracle grow I sprinkled around the bacteria free floor. But despite this further pain and suffering and the harrowing thought that I was about to lose my Mum too, we did have some good news arrive and brighten our faces. Good news which came in the knowledge that Mum would make a miraculous recovery and may even make it out for the day on the 25th December, which I must say was completely rad and by far the best Christmas present I could have hoped to receive. I was even more excited and animated about Mum's arrival than I was about receiving the Hungry Caterpillar book and the saucy Supercar Scalextrix set I had picked out of the Argos Bible. That's how totally thrilled I was by the transformation, and just to clarify, yes I am a 24 year-old child.

However, even with this tip-top-heel-clicking-and-theme-tune-whistling good news, it was one of the toughest experiences I had ever come across, and that is saying a little something. You see, I was working in London trying my best to make an impact on the world, and thus unable to hop back and see Mum as much as I desperately wanted, what with issues involving business schedules, travel expenses and all shades of mucilaginous malarkey. But this was a viscous reality, for I was stuck in no-mans-land, having to helplessly stand by as I received sporadic updates about my Mum's condition, her worsening fragility, her pitiful physicality, her unanswered health and her devastating deterioration. Similar to the outlook of her doctors, I don't know how she did it, but her strength of character never faltered, whilst mine did. I was petrified I was going to lose her, desecrated by the profane prospect and the far from favouring odds, constantly wondering how many times she could keep fighting back with such strength. She was unbelievable, astonishing and incredible, whilst I was a complete coward in need of her strength, for this encounter left me thinking, 'I'd really appreciate some weak narcotics and strong liquor right about now.' What's worse, I conceded to this notion if you consider its loose terminology, for I resorted to a heightened amount of afghan black throughout this holiday period, left all alone and worried, and thus warranting any form of distraction.

As you may be able to close your eyes and imagine, it was a relatively tough Christmas, as Christmas' always are in the wake of wank-shaft wretchedness. You know, no Dad around to ensure a laugh, a story and discussion on how to change the world, and on top of that, we had a Mum who we weren't sure was going to be out of hospital in time, or ever, and yet this is a festive period when we are supposed to think about God and the birth of his son and all the good they have done as a colossal couple. Well guess what, I was thinking about my Dad, his son's, my Mum and the rest of my family, instead of the fictional bullshit that conformation has tried forcing me into accepting, trying to make me a believer of the unbelievable. I mean atheism, or at least the idea of being a humbly heroic heathen, became more attractive to me due to both a combination of scientific advancements and the fact I cannot just accept the norm because it is the norm, but rather I was predisposed to question the ridiculous in the same way people question me. However, atheism was also an encouraged route for me to go down due to the sorry set of circumstances that I had been dealt, in which I've fought off the negativity and finally embraced the wonderful power of happiness, and guess what, I've done it without any conceivable help from the almighty Father and son due on high. I mean, Jesus Christ, and of course God, please go fuck your self-righteous pedestal and your absurdly blissful ignorance, the one that encourages you to think you're better than everyone else. Oh and here's a suggestion, how about you dabble in the completely insane and ridiculous, and by that I mean actually helping people who need it instead of just chilling out on your chaise longue with you calypso coffee and cocaine, thinking you've had a long and stress-filled day. I would say 'God knows people need your help' but it's clear that bearded man of ancient times aint got a clue.

Now don't get me wrong, I have absolutely no problem with religious individuals in the same way I hope they have no problem with me, because after all I am a fan of whatever helps us become better people, and I'm definitely not here to judge. It's just this religious route hasn't helped me, but that doesn't mean I'm not happy and inspired if you bow down to God, Allah, Horan or Zeus, and please don't hesitate to do so if this has helped you beat back your bereavement, provided you with an inner strength and engaged you in a positive healing process. Heck, if it's beneficial, I don't care whether you pray to the abtastic and awesomely chiselled Christ of Nazareth, or if you bow down to a top heavy Dolly Parton lookalike at the local 'Boobie Bungalow' or whatever strip club you choose to frequent. All I'm saying is, I lost faith when I was given the polar opposite reason to believe in something that refuses to show his or her face, because if that someone up there really does love me, he or she has a horribly horrendous way of showing it. However, I've taken yet another diversion off topic, and for that I apologise.

So, what was so surprisingly splendid about this particular Christmas Day, beside mother's day pass, was that fact my brother and I visited my Dads grave, as brothers. We went there to support each other, to say our piece in silence and together. We went there to remember everything Dad taught us, and reflect on the numerous stories that made us chuckle. It was a way for us to be close to him, whilst embracing the significance of such a day. We got to spend time with him in the sense that he was dominating our thoughts and memories, before we left to spend time with the rest of our family. Yeah, it's not an ideal situation, nor is it one that is conventionally normal on this holiest of family days, but it is an example of us making the best of a bad situation, it's a system of love that works for us in our own way, for it's love and devotion as it will eternally be, and it is never superficial even if it is physically far from pragmatic. It is a way to remember my roots, a way to stay focussed and a way for me to keep control of what direction I want to take.

Now I'm aware I haven't spoken about or even mentioned Ayesha and my beautiful little brother Zack since the chapter titled 'Year One', but that's not out of neglect, instead its more due to the complications shrouding this important sub-title. It's a sore topic I guess. I can't help but choke up at the thought of Z and his absence, and I struggle to get any words out when it comes to this utterly sad story. You see, just after Christmas we found out Ayesha was moving back to South Africa, sure enough she was taking a lot of my family's possessions, heirlooms and items that were clearly not hers, but then again they are only possessions. It was the fact she was taking Zack away from that I still can't handle, and all of this was with about four days warning and thus no chance for my would-have-been-hysterical goodbye. I think I struggle with it still simply because I care about Zack so much and the situation he is in. I just want to be there for him like a father, like our father, and I want him to know who his father was.

I want him to know the Dad I knew from my childhood, the one who got stuck into homework with us, supported us on the side lines no matter what and ensured an adventure would take place on bi-daily basis. I want to paint a perfect picture for Zack from my nineteen years experience with Dad, as well as bring him back to life through Dads best friends, who all survive him as much as Olive and I, and not just from the three years that Ayesha was with him. I miss Z almost everyday, which is maybe not helped by the fact I still have a passport photo of him when he was six months old decorating the interior window of my wallet, or the fact he is my screensaver and wallpaper on my high-definition phone, but I can't imagine not seeing the face of purity every day. I know one day he'll have questions and that he'll want to make his own decisions and chill with his brothers, but a decade is a long time for me to wait and even longer for him to ponder on the what-ifs of his Dad's death, especially at such a young age. But like I said, I struggle with articulating the complexities of our modern family, I just didn't want the story of Zack and Ayesha to fall away as if they're unimportant, not when the truth lands so far from this perception. I just can't find the words to do Z justice, and my silence on the topic is founded entirely on my inability to cope with what I can only call another loss, for I am unable to see him and speak to him, cuddle him, kiss him, tease him and teach him all I know both about life, school, work, girls and snowboarding. But one day we'll get to do it all, and then he can teach me about life, school, work and girls I hope, but never snowboarding.

Anyway, I'm sorry to be the bearer of anything other than optimism, but

I found this year just as hard as the years that had come before it, not in the sense that the pain was as raw, but because the situation had become harder for other people to understand. What I mean is, it had been four years and yet I was still obviously suffering, and what's more, I had arguably become more distanced from my family than ever before. I was isolated from any tolerance and acceptance, reaching peaks where I was more livid than ever, incensed by my family's lack of understanding and my inability to explain. I was outraged by my own behaviour, privy to its presence and unable to alter its vengeance, which had outbursts far worse than Christian Bale's infamous rant based relationship with the sound guy. I hated the fact I was still wallowing and suffering, and that this complication wasn't anyone else's fault other than mine, and that was what I really struggled to accept in the first half of this fourth year. You see the fact is, it had been four years in everyone else's mind and there is no arguing with this reality, but shock horror, there is no guide-lining template, nor is there a countdown style stopwatch that allows you to snap out of this mourning when the correct amount of time has flown past. Time will let it get easier to accept, but maybe not easier to understand. Instead, the pain will continue and the hurt will not subside until we decide we want it to and I believe that is the bottom dollar. But the good news doesn't cease there, for it is also an acceptance that can be ushered by no one else except for us. It is a challenge that no one else can take part in, for it is a self-inspired desire, need and want that makes us overcome such strife, and this is as horribly solo as the harsh premise regarding the Hunger-Games-battle-of-the-districts-tournament.

What I learned most from this fifty-two week cycle of elongated frustration and family torment however, was the importance in no longer being a colossal fanny-pack-wearing-Ping-Pong-poontang-type-coward and to instead take responsibility for how you want the next chapter in your life to play out. As always, the journey to this realisation is an absolute mother of all bitches. Maybe you'll resolutely stumble upon this mucho-needed conclusion by pure chance. Maybe you'll listen to those around you and decide to end this once and for all as the result of such a divine intervention. Maybe you'll seek the refuge and help of a counsellor or cognitive therapist, see what the underlying issues are and become hyped about the reasons to fight for change. Maybe you'll reach this supposition due to the equally direct and indirect result of a motivational kick-start, harnessing the confidence arouser, self-assuring instigator and dogged determination that are provoked as derivative side effects of an event or activity. Whatever the means of realisation, act on it and use this momentum to go forward, for there isn't enough time for one to mope around brooding over the shit storm that was sent your way. You can't remain ominous, menacing and frettingly ruminant as you go about each day. You mustn't walk down the same streets with the same fake smile, unfazed by the changing seasons, disregarding the colours of the trees as they fade from green to gold, ignorant to the sun fading and snow falling. For despite all of these obvious time passing indications, I know what it is like to remain unaware and oblivious to the fact time is passing you by, believing time has stopped simply because you're stuck in the past. Well your time keeping is wrong, for this private perception is both a ridiculous trust and a scientific impossibility, because by the combined power of Lion-O and Panthro, time don't stay still for anyone, not even King Canute the Great.

However, I am pleased to announce that this wasn't the only ontological speculation I learned, for I opened my eyes to what I can only describe as a new philosophical axiom. I learned the need to swallow my ever disgustingly distasteful pride, because much like modesty, this proud virtue has the capability to be a vice. But despite this clear understanding, it seems that a majority of us misfortunate martyrs have caught the non-sexually transmitted disease commonly known as pride. We may be aware of its presence, we may hide behind the meaning of this word, and sometimes we may not even be aware that we are suffering under its wrath. But this is more than understandable, for it comes in so many forms, sneaking up on us unsuspectingly and dragging us further down the rabbit hole of discontent, difficulty and distress.

I mean I can hold my hand up and say that I consciously allowed my conceited arrogance to hinder me, because for a long time I thought I was too awesome to let my pride slip and slide away from my controlling grasp. However, this has begun to change, and thank Captain Fantastic it has. The reason I say this is because I used to keep all my thoughts inside, only rarely letting my feelings out, only rarely letting my story make peep-hole-peek-a-boo sort of cameo appearances, and even then my releases would be aimed at strangers or entry-level acquaintances, and more often than not, they would only surface when I was intoxicated. That latter part of the paragraph was not an innuendo you sexy-minded beauty you.

You see, for everyone else, and more accurately those that I was significantly close to, I chose to raise my protecting pale of pride, biting my lip and letting the proverbial cat into my mouth, allowing this metaphorical feline to get my tongue. Nonetheless, the reasons as to why we do this are subtly understandable, commonly based around the contrite notion that our problems are our problems and what not. But, fuck, when conditions, situations, circumstances, postures and ballgames blatantly show no signs of improvement, even though we have witnessed spring, summer, autumn and winter come and go time and time again, and our attitude and mentality still remains as sour as the old 'Toxic Waste' sweets, then surely we should consciously try and open our arms and our mouths, even if just to our nearest and dearest. For if this expansive timespan does in fact show little change, then maybe we do need to do our loved ones a favour, open our gobs and let the painstakingly problematic words croak out, whilst simultaneously letting our biggest fans in.

I mean, I was pre-eminently pissed off, but because I never spoke about my trials and tensions to those I was pissed off around, they had absolutely no chance of understanding what was going on, and as such they could only make outlandish speculations, hazard a guess and throw their weakly fathomed perceptions towards me all in an attempt to see what comes back, and all in the vain attempt to help. I mean, talk about a needle in a haystack based likelihood.

So my suggest is you swallow your ego, perform an elegant swan dive and just go for gold when it comes to this open honesty shindig, whether it's instigated as a means to alleviate the pain you may have been causing your family, or whether it's a way to help your own incessant irritation and injury, just open up. I mean the truth surely can't make things any worse right, especially when you look at the alternate option, the life I chose. For this route leads you down a path of sequestration, and the longer you roam this desolate land like a nomad, the more it becomes second nature and thus the harder it becomes to snap out of this temperament. Time passes you by against your will and still you're the same silently suffering shadow, caught in a stance that suggested the wind had changed direction. Yeah, this may present a horrible picture, but it is also an accurate one, and if I had time-shares in any time machine, I would Mos Def go back and change my egotistical embrace of solitude instantly. But I can't and neither can you, so why not kick this hindering dark side of vanity and futility square in the family jewels, and just get on with the healing process, now. Right now.

Nonetheless, I am pleased to welcome to the stage the part of the story that takes a turn towards positivity, the period that exposes a little ray of sunshine and is arguably the most significant day of optimism I've had since the days I was able to kick it with my dear old Pop. Yeah, of course I've had days filled with laughter and smiles, moments run by escalation and occasional breakthroughs with regards to hard fought achievements. I have beaten the drum in exultation on numerous birthdays, copious Christmas' and a multitude of old-fashioned knees up events. I have celebrated and consecrated my first job within the film industry, enjoyed my workplace promotions and frolicked at my graduation ceremony. But, with every one of these miraculous exaltations I was sure to be in a frame of mind that ensured a dark cloud would adumbrate the occasion. I would feel sombre despite success and more often that not I'd have to take a minute, or an hour, just me, myself and I reflecting on the hollowness that engulfed whatever the milestone or occasion was in question. Now this is no doubt another example of attitude, in which there are times where I just think, 'give a fuck', because instead of thinking positively and searching for a break in the clouds, I would simply succumb to the saddening truth that my Dad was unable to be here for me, and be here with me. I understand that this is normal behaviour, but that doesn't make it any fucking easier, for this fruitful knowledge doesn't make me sing and dance, or even whistle a medley of theme tunes from some jolly TV shows of yesteryear, like the Wombles mixed with Catweazle and the Magic Roundabout.

However, this mentality has now begun to shift like the tectonic plates, seeking a positively stronger mentality and a much more Mr Brightside outlook. This new focus and responsibility is one that is helping me use my twenty-twenty vision to see the sun through the clouds, it is a mentality that stops me dwelling on the inevitable and encourages me to concentrate on changing what is possible. Of course this is not an overnight manoeuvre, but it's been far quicker and far more successful than I ever thought to be conceivably achievable, and all it took was focussed fortitude, the steadfast will to succeed once n for all, and a candid conviction to be a 'greater fool'.

"Welcome every morning with a smile. Look on the new day as another special gift from your creator, another golden opportunity to complete what you were unable to finish yesterday. Be a self-starter. Let your first hour set the theme of success and positive action that is certain to echo through your entire day. Today will never happen again. Don't waste it with a false start or no start at all. You were not born to fail."

Og Mandino

YEAR FIVE

So, without hesitation, lets move on to the upside of the downward spiral, focus on the buoyancy amongst the wallowing waves and engross ourselves in the sanguineness that lays within these stringent sucker punches to the oesophagus, all of which have been on going for too many harvests. In other words, let me crack on with deciphering what I meant by 'arguably the most significant day of optimism' that I harked on about no longer than a finger full of moments ago.

So, January 3rd 2013 is my distinguished day of conviviality, a newly founded but personal bank holiday, superior to that of St Georges, and more meaningful than that of May Day. For this day is so overwhelming to me, the pinnacle representative of my persistence against the tyranny of tragedy, so much so that it deserves the stage name of 'Admiral Awesome's Astronomical Day of Awesomeness'. Don't get me wrong, this date has deservedly obtained private and cloistered recognition, but of course it has. For this decision of shattering significance wasn't one that could easily fly under the radar and go unnoticed to me, not when you scrutinise it in the grand scheme of everything I'd been through and everything that led up to this point. I mean, it wasn't as if I woke up one morning to the songs of multiple lyre birds accompanying a Slash solo riff, arousing my ears before I opened my curtains to a spectacle of sunshine, white smoke waterfalls and an abundance of voluptuous woman all modelling different styles of pubic hair, a daybreak vision so stunning that I was stiffer than a zombie's arm. No, this was 'the day' I made the meticulous and predetermined decision to become a Tekken copycat, adopting the combined fighting styles of King, Marshall Law, Devil Jin and Yoshimitsu, vigilantly taking the fight to the this bereavement bitch once and for all.

Now don't get me wrong, I would love to say I was gonna go down swinging, but in all honesty, I had no intention of letting my back hit the mat or any intention of even going down at all, not this time round, not again, not ever. For this time was different, this time I had no impulsion to pick myself up and dust myself off, for I was instead spurred on by Sun Tzu's 'Art of War' notion that it isn't about winning battles, it is strictly about victory in war. I had fought these demons too many times, sometimes I lost gracefully, sometimes I accepted defeat and sometimes I got back up and kept on as if positively persuading my own self-opinion in this private Tet Offensive of mine. But no matter what the direct outcome of these battles had been in the past, I had always learned from them, and this time round I felt more prepared and more dogged than I had ever been, for I was more prepped for this examination period than any other I'd previously partaken in.

I don't know why I chose to draw swords on this particularly random day, but I can assure you that no tombola's were involved, as much as my spontaneous and informal adjudication points to the contrary. Maybe I hated the idea of New Years resolutions and the inevitable failures that accompany such decrees hand in hand, thus I simply decided upon a date that was no more than a stone's throw away from January 1st. Maybe I knew I couldn't resist temptation on the almighty hangover that is always the first day of the new year. Maybe it was destiny, fate or the power of my subconscious that safeguarded this date as all accommodating to my most revered of numbers, thirteen. And even if this double-digit number wasn't acutely lucky before the wheels were set in motion, I can rest assured that 'thirteen' will now be my certified answer whenever the question 'what's your lucky number' is directed towards me on any future first dates.

Anyway, like I said, I scrupulously cannot tell you what made me choose to take a course of action on this diurnal course. However, I can instead probably tell you why I conclusively removed my manpon, threw it to the hard shoulder, looked in the rear-view mirror and told myself to cease being a scared-of-the-dark-limp-dick-pussy-hole-pimp-slapped pooch, instead telling myself to get on with my life in the way that these people that I had lost, especially Dad, would have wanted me to. I was so over bereavement. I was so bored and spiritless from this tiring process of sorrow. I was sick and tired of having humongous and husky highs followed by lonesome and lulling lows. I was jaded by the thought of people having to tread on eggshells around me, forced to by fussy in confab, gossip and even my colloquial fucking favourite, pillow talk. I abhorred the idea of ever being aggravated, annoyed and even worse abraded, especially within the proximity of my beloved family, and I was disgusted at myself when I vented this frustration upon them. I was irked by my constant effort to be a conscripted 'nice guy' following the unwritten rules of morality in this principality of the unknown. I detested the need to consciously remember this old man I loved to such an extent that it is the majority shareholder of my deliberations, considerations and decisions. But, as shit as this seems, this is the only way society will let me reminisce, remember and cope. I was disinterested by my desire for doobie's, now fervently reluctant to smoke again, fucked off with my fucked up habit, ready to kick it to the long grass (excuse the pun) and instead ready take on reality with a clear mind, balanced behaviour and the kind of confidence that will allow my irresistibly horny and aroused mentality to stop being scared of commitment.

So I knew I had to take the first step immediately upon waking up on that fine winters morning, and highlighting that first step was obvious to me: quit smoking any form of mood altering plant or vegetation. To me this was the obvious next level in this video game of reality. After all, I'd started this fact filled dissertation with a preach about my new found clarity, and strangely enough, taking hits from a bong isn't the best way of securing such mindful transparency. Nonetheless, my decision to remove the spliff from between my fingers, leaving just an appropriate and symbolic 'V' sign wasn't put in place only to beat back my bereaving, but also because I was bored off getting high, and bored of my dependency upon it. What's more, this verdict to quit has become especially relevant since realising its healing power had become nothing more than a painful placebo, causing nothing but slurred speech, sleepless slumbers, red eyes and an increased inability to perform simple actions, such as reciting the phonetic alphabet, or even just the standard alphabet.

Of course my close friends supported this notion, understanding my reasons ever since I had started to open up with them more and more, whilst a lot of people warned me of the downsides to my decision, enlightening me to what the effects would be. I can't deny that this was mucho benevolent of them, but I can confidently state that most of these fantastic fables are bullshit, and seem to only be encompassed by stoners as a means to keep on stoning. You see, this decision to be smart, switched on and back to my quick-witted self should not come with a warning, it should come with a ballistic bunch of helium balloons, preferably in a display of different shapes, complicated, magical and inclusive of more colours than the entire spectrum of the rainbow. However, this is simply my experience, albeit an experience that discovered the combination of running away from the loss of my Dad, whilst hiding from my natural emotional response and then chucking a nocturnal reliance on cannabis into the mixing bowl, wasn't the most educated of cocktails.

Now I'm not presuming you have some sort of reliance on the unreliable, or even suggesting that you have some form of reliance at all. In fact, I sincerely hope you have avoided such pitfalls and gateway inoculations, whilst I also hope you have absconded any friendship with this drug called Lucy, whether she is in the sky with diamonds or dancing through strawberry fields. You see, what I am trying to get to with this painted picture is the need for prominent purity, for I oppose any opaque and closed mindset. I prefer to act as a hypothetical club promoter, again endorsing this new venue in town called 'Clarity'. You've most probably heard about this party from me before; in fact I've probably been clogging up your metaphorical Facebook newsfeed with my ceaseless notifications of support and advocacy with regards to this 'Clarity' domicile, but that's because it is severely underrated and requires some serious exploiting.

Nevertheless, it is of course entirely possible that you have already found clarity, and if that is the case, I'm sending you a six-step-street-style handshake via the means of this book. (Slap, slap, fist pound, rollercoaster thumb bump, backhand, shibby!!!) However, a sophisticated guess would suggest you might not have stubbed your toe on overt perspicuity, and thus I feel the need to act like some sort of Angel Gabriel, albeit minus the wings and trumpet of course. But no matter how you view my role in all of this, I will always remain armed with a basket full of platitudes all of which are ready to be piled into sentences at a moments notice. I just want to try and guide you as much as I can, to give you an end zone, a target or at least a sort of pencil drawn satnav, commonly known as a map, simply to try my best in ensuring there is some sort of path for you to possibly follow.

Thus, with the unconvincing powers I have pretended to invest in myself, like the modest megalomaniac I am, I feel I have to touch on the troubles that may lie ahead, and thus try my hardest to warn you a way from the exponentially marvellous lives of a rockstar. So drugs. Oh and booze, for this is arguably a gateway drug masquerading in a liquid guise. Now don't get me wrong, sometimes these can be passages and turnstiles to some fairly fun festivities, and this is usually the case. I mean, no great story ever started with, 'This one time, I had an avocado'. However, when Canned Heat, ethanol, moonshine, rotgut, pills, dope, narcotics or drugs are mixed with tumultuous turmoil, the chances of one ending up trapped in an unwise combination significantly increases. In fact I should warn you that such a lifestyle will only invite deepened despair, poverty, hastened harm, inverted penises, fourth and fifth nipples and even lactating man boobs.

So, if you want my opinion, stay away from drugs, if you can, because what could start off as passive playtime could easily turn into a spiralling whirlpool of addiction. Getting high gets boring, getting drunk never does. Drugs can really suck. It doesn't matter whether your guilty pleasure habit reaches an extreme such an addiction, or whether it doesn't become relied upon. Drugs manage to have an impact from the get go. Drugs dampen the emotional capacity better than anything, depleting the users availability to reality. Drugs essentially drag out the confusing commotion of one's havoc, and all for what, a few cheap laughs and mediocre moments? I wish, because if this were the clause free contract then I'd be signing up almost bi-weekly. Yet this isn't the whole truth, for drugs are, now brace yourself, addictive (shock horror) and the cheap-thrills, good time chuckles and all night raves that were so arousing and attractive at the start become a thing of the past, overruled by the desperate need to find that next ugly hit. However, in my more than apparent style of authoring, I have meandered off topic, ahem, yet again, so I do apologise.

So, within a matter of days after I made the drastic and executive decision to quit smoking, I felt an immeasurable difference, as if the fears of inadequacy, worry and my previously reprehensible lack of confidence were beginning to subside. Unfortunately I was forced to use the word immeasurable, which is fair given the results, but if I had to measure it, I would adopt an X-Factor influenced phrase and go with, 'I felt one-hundred and fifty seven million eight hundred and ninety four thousand per cent more enthused and improved.' Fucking X-Factor and its mathematical bollocks. Woosah.

This clear head posed such a phenomenon it challenges my very ability to scribble sentences, without offering any compensation or equity. I mean it was a freaky extra terrestrial sort of feeling, completely alien from anything I could remember and it had me running scared but, for the first time, not running away. It was unpredictable, but this clear mind arrived accompanied by anxiousness, butterflies and dismay, all of which were complemented by a startling elucidation and illumination. But what became instantly apparent, was my ability to identify which banana skins had forced me to unwillingly participate in an impressive Michael Bublé style lengthy skid, although my slip n slide was with out due care, purpose or style. I realised where I had to accept the blame, realising there are just some things that can't be blamed on family, friends, the government or even the economic climate, unfortunately. So the first step, and this required a hand reaching into the platitude pail and plucking out some worn out words of wisdom, revolved around the need for me to change my disposition, mindset, inclination and behaviour. You'd be right in saying this isn't an easy task, not on the whole anyway, but I was aware of this when I reached base camp on January 3rd. But I didn't just wake up one pleasant morning and spontaneously decide to take on Everest. No. I had been preparing for this mountainous assault since the day my Dad was killed, learning with each step of this disheartening and formidable climb, and it is a climb that we all have to embark on ourselves.

I made sure I was aware of what was at stake and I made sure I had a focus, an objective, an end game, and a desired outcome. This was crucial in my invisibly brainstormed awareness, because with this sort of fire, much like battling the flames at the gates of hell, it is impossible to plan the journey. The hurdles tend to be disguised; imperceptible and challenging, descending from all directions like the boobie-traps Indiana Jones had to face. (Ignoring the last instalment of this franchise, which was so fucking lame! Aliens. Seriously.)

So the to do list:

- Alter my behaviour with regards to my adoring familia.
- Focus on overcoming the loss of my Dad so it doesn't affect my day-to-day life negatively.
- Don't get bogged down in the trivial bullshit that life throws up but instead understand this is our only shot at happiness, so be exactly that, happy.
- Wake up each dawn and remember, today is a good day to have a good day.

So first up in my mission to claw back the worry free me of childhood photos, was to make amends with my Mum. I make it sound as though we had fallen out in some scenario from Josh Schwartz 'The O.C.' which is far from the case. It was instead just another area of my existence that had become dominated by fear, pain and uncertainty, petrified of getting close to her, scared of losing her and terrified of yet more tangible torment. What's more, and I brushed upon this earlier, I was pissed off and foolishly concentrating on those I had lost instead of enjoying those I still had, unable to love the uncertainty of what lied ahead.

Anyway, what was most surprising to me, and more so to my Mum, was my ability to change this shadowy side to me with almost immediate effect, for this was something that seemingly happened overnight. I'm not a stubborn alley cat, well most of the time I'm not, and I can happily admit when I'm wrong, once again most of the time. But this wasn't the dominating factor in these new transformations. Instead I knew I had to take responsibility and act like a family man should, thus I left all my self-destructive panda-shit at the front entrance, recognised my wrongdoings and dabbled in what is, for some ridiculous reason, so incomprehensibly, inexplicably and notoriously hard… I apologised. You see in addition to this huge leap and bound was my much needed desire to open up to this mother of mine again, to let her know what I was feeling, or to at least let her know I was determined to make things better. Fuck, I'm even jotting away on a daily basis in the form of this rambling notepad, all of which she knows about, and all of which has been a blessing with regards to breaking down these walls of silence between my mother and I.

This openness and this new relationship I have with my family is based on honesty, and thrives off an understanding of each other that wasn't there previously. But more than this, we are all affable and able to laugh at the past now. Its as if we're comforted by some bizarre but secure knowledge that nothing should be taken too seriously, and I guess that's somewhat gospel, after all none of us are going to live forever. We are similar, but also very different. Maybe it's the different generations, eras, mentalities, upbringings or god forbid, star signs. Whatever it is, we have begun to understand each other's perspectives, and learned how to appease each other instead of being confrontational.

I hate being told what to and my Mum hates being answered back to. This sort of realisation is a good start. It's a relationship that's tough to piece together, yet one that everyone presumes would automatically strengthen in the event of family tragedy, and who can blame them for such an assumption, for that's exactly what I would have thought too. But it isn't. Complications arise, the blame game is thrown about in one-way or another, and distances begin surface. But if you allow it, you can also grow closer to one another, closer than you were before, sharing your feelings and able to understand the worries and concerns of others, unifying as a family, no matter how dysfunctional you may be.

Yeah, I'm still a little scared. Scared about Mums health, scared about knowing the whole truth, scared about certain legitimates and scared of the Zeitgeist conspiracies, but I am far more willing to fight for harmony and fight for a feeling that says we are a family now. I understand my Mum, her points of view and ultimately what they are based on, and more miraculously than this, I think she is starting to understand me. She understands that I'm different from the other members of my family, far more free-spirited and open-minded. A transient vagabond searching for who he is and wanting nothing more than to be comfortable in whatever he finds. I try not to be serious where I can help it, and I won't ever conform to a direction that will ensure my unhappiness. For instance, I would rather be in a career that I love and can make a difference in, than to be in a job because it will reward me with millions of dollar, dollar bills yeah.

I am a world away from the background my Mum grew up in, strict, conservative, dogmatic and the type that tends to follow the rules of a gentleman's handbook, although she has her moments. Thus it must be hard for her to simply accept me, especially as these changes of mine have occurred in the wake of Dads death. I wear dangly earrings, question mark rings on my wedding finger and Spike Lee glasses. I dabble in Mohawks and other alternative headdresses, whilst trying out different shades of dark brown hair and bleach blonde locks, and its been going on for too many years for it to be called a 'phase'. I put my own twist on what should be worn, whether it's a casual combo or a three-piece suit and tie. I am I, and I push this concept as far as possible because I'm comfortable in it. In some ways I have pushed the boundaries even further since Dad died, in other ways I have reeled myself in, maturing with age. Maybe he would hate my extravagance as much as he did when he was around, or maybe he would encourage it knowing how short life is for the first time, which is especially true given he was previously as close to indestructible as humanly possible.

My family come from careers in politics and business, and thus there is a predisposed benchmark set, a way to do things and an inherent enthusiasm of what they perceive as proper. However, I think they are coming round to the idea of what I am trying to do. I don't work in the city dealing with credit. I work in the film industry where expression is currency. I work in an industry that can change the world, for the worse of course, but more often than not, it's for the better. It has the ability to inform and inspire, to unite people in the fight for good, and the search for moral aptitude, ensuring what is right is highlighted. Too many people are into big businesses and corporate destruction, with nought on their mind but personal money gains, even at the expense of others. I, however, take more of a David Orr and George Carlin stimulated approach, understanding now more than ever what they mean.

"This planet doesn't need more 'successful' people, but it does desperately need more peacemakers, healers, restorers, storytellers and lovers of every kind. It needs people who will live well in their places. It needs people of morale courage willing to join the fight to make the world habitual and humane. Yet, all these needs have very little to do with success as we have come to define It. "– David Orr

Understanding this myself has been as valuable as my mother

understanding it. Understanding what I want to do by using something I am passionate about, not only as a career or art form or technique, but also as a medium to invite humane alterations. A proverbial mountaintop for me to shout off, a way to construct change, and a means to enlighten those in the dark, hopefully much like this book. It is hard for some people to see this as my reason, but to me, this is how to achieve success in the battle to be a greater fool, or more specifically, a person with the perfect mélange of self-delusion and ego, someone who thinks that he can succeed where others have failed. For this, to me, is of prioritised importance, because without greater fools, we have no innovation, no progress, and thus no distinctive mould-breaking success. It is a way to impact the world with moral magnitude, and it is the way of thinking I seem to have enhanced, certainly since my Dad was killed, but even more so since I decided to get out of the negative and dark mind frame I was in, taking action, ensuring I wasn't just all smoke and no fire.

Keeping on the topic of changes and what stemmed in the days of aftermath subsequent to my judgement day of January 3rd decision, my relationship with close friends was also notably altered. I am still at the learning stages of this manoeuvre, thus my ability to report on this in a top journalistic consuetude is somewhat limited, so don't expect a Gay Talese form of accuracy, although I encourage you to remain hopeful nonetheless. You see, it is nigh unimaginable to talk to friends about this sorta thing because it is a pretty heavy conversation piece, one that is hard to sugar coat, and one that understandably arrives surrounded in a certain stigma, like when Rolf Harris now walks into a garden party holding his didgeridoo. It's a conversation that has a dark undertone as if Mike Oldfield's 'Tubular Bells' is all anyone can hear once this tête-a-tête has been breached. There is this awkwardness that shrouds the room, inviting the proverbial pink elephant in to perform its heavy footed circus tricks, whilst everyone tries to ensure their stance, tone and choice of words is both politically correct and socially acceptable. It's a constant and conscious battle for balance, but of course it is, for no one wants to harm the feelings of the person in question, and the person in question doesn't want to bring everyone else down or place them in an awkward and klutzy position of no retreat, even if he or she is in dire need of support.

It seems that such a conversation has to be perfectly harmonised, and that makes it even harder to bring up or broach. For example, whenever I suddenly grow a pair and spontaneously feel brave enough to approach the subject of my Dads death, I always feel I have to do it in a way that requires a light tone and a distracting smile, as if this will somehow bring about a more honest reaction from the other participants. I mean for fuck sake, even the fact I had to mention bravery seems corrupt, because I love talking about my Dad, remembering him and laughing about the past as I convey his stories. But I still can't overcome the feeling that others would not be so comfortable, with the thought of such discomfiture sending a wintery chill right through my softly shrinking scrotum. It's a vicious cycle that is smothered in an uncertain etiquette, one that requires each person involved to be his or her own raconteur judge.

Taking a leaf out of Russell Howard's book though, its not all doom and gloom, for this openness has now started to get caught up in a healthy avalanche of agape acceptance. I am now tentatively talking about my Dad, my explosive experiences and my many methods of dealing with its distasteful aftershock, or at least I'm hinting at this topic more so than before. I'm boldly bringing it up with friends and enjoying the fragile free chitter-chatter of confabulations, whilst I am determined to learn how to deal with the inevitably preordained look of compassion, because after all, there's no malice involved, it's simply a riposte that is meant as a warm gesture, so why not take it as that and nothing more. Yeah yeah, I know it's one of those Run DMC 'Tricky' powder kegs that are immaculately hard to approach, never mind defuse, but it needs to be mollified sooner rather than later, no? I'm talking about both the understated requirement of talking to your unholy band of brothers, as much as I am referring to your need to accept the commiserative and forbearing looks these people accidentally throw your way, not knowing any different, not knowing what to say, not knowing what presses your buttons.

So let's shake things up, resist tedium and take on the latter of these addresses first, a feeling I'm sure you understand. I refuse to think of myself as a charity, and any suggestion of this acted as an invisible clapper-like-switch setting me off on a vendetta of vengeance much like a very toned down 'Creasy' in Man on Fire, although I hid my fury behind closed doors instead of taking it to the man and wreaking uncontrollable havoc. It's just so infuriating when people seem to take pity on you, especially when you don't pity yourself. It hurts so much when people cast that look of 'I'm sorry' towards you, with the customary side dish of an obvious 'slow blink', the kind that makes you sink into further anger fuelled despair, replying to their look with one of your own, one that says 'Swivel on it you condescending cock-fuck!' Now it doesn't take a member of Mensa to understand why these sorts of look hurt and why their tone of voice always fuels your rage and causes you to be sick in your mouth without hesitation, even if we know they mean no harm whatsoever. Then there are their carefully chosen words that simply highlight those words that are missing, the words they have elected not to use for fear of cracking the eggshell flooring that surrounds us.

All of these avoidance methods killed me a little more inside, pushed me closer to the batman cave I was trying to escape, but breathe, and breathe again, and then try to understand that we mustn't take these mistaken and ignorantly oblivious gestures so god damn personally. These people are in the toughest of situations, which may sound rich coming from where you find yourself, but just remember that you don't know what they are going through as much as they don't know our thoughts either. They can set us off with a look, a glace and a sentence. They can infuriate us with what they say and what they don't say. They are in a fucked up cage of harmful mystery, and I don't envy that. These people want to help, but they are completely unaware of how to do so, in fact that's why they ask 'is there anything I can do to help', because they don't have the telepathic skills to know what will ease our pain. They just want to support you, and it would be kinda obtuse if they were laughing, smiling and pulling lame gag after lame gag in an attempt to help us heal, even if that is what would be more pragmatically productive. To them, trying to show they understand and that they really fucking care are hidden arts located deep within unknown territory, just behind Middle Earth and just before Mordor.

It makes logical sense for them to show compassion, compunction, benevolence and humaneness via the means of a glance, elongated look or a few stuttered and softly mumbled words, even if this ultimately makes us feel worse. I'm just trying to say that we shouldn't take the actual results of these gesticulations to heart, for we should simply respond to the gesture itself. We should welcome their wishes to offer some protection from the punches, and we should realise these are moments that should be gratefully appreciated with open arms and fondness, not rejected with fiery eyes and an unwelcomed retort. C'mon dude, I know it's tough, I know we feel downtrodden and believe we've been fucked harder and more times than Pamela Anderson, but dusty sperm sack, fuck being sour, stop perching on an emotional pedestal of hardship and let your friends make their mistake ridden but warm hearted and generous gestures. Let them show you that they truly care, and let them do so without the worry of any form of backlash. After all these peeps are willing to tread unknown ground in order to be there for you, aware that there are numerous landmines dotted around in the form of saying the wrong thing, but still they saddle up anyway. That is the definition of courage.

Now that I've covered that bitching field of business, it's seems somewhat timely for me to proposition you with the reasons why it's grotesquely fantastic for you to use what your pain-healing-listeners known as friends, buddies and pals offer in being themselves. First things first though, you have just gotta ignore the belief that this topic of bereavement is tabooed, and just saying 'fuck it' I'm here to engulf the bravery sauce and put on enough courageous chub that I break the mother-clucking ice, because I'm going to talk to my friends about those that I have lost and the successive sub-headings that occurred as a result. I promise you its somewhat ground breaking when this moment is grabbed by the horns, tackling the proverbial bull with one hand whilst the other hand raises its middle finger to the sky, blocking out the sun in some socially and emotionally maverick operated eclipse. You see it makes very little sense to not talk to these caring individuals that surround you like a ring of kindred spirits, especially given they have their own super-powers that somehow alert them when something is up, letting them know that you are feeling down even if you cross your fingers, control the growth of your Pinocchio nose, blatantly lie through gritted teeth and stupidly tell them otherwise.

It's no chamber of secrets that girlfriends, blood bro's and close pals have this awesome ability to see through the bullshit Batman masks we put on, somehow knowing when something is up, as if reacting to the silent arm that signals their spidey senses. Yet, whilst it remains undeniable that this is an almightily impressive superpower to behold, your friends still can't grasp any true understanding without your consent. They can't help you without you letting them do so, which requires you to vocalise your feelings, requires you to use the medium of words or, Minerva forbid, participate in a deep and meaningful.

Now I learned the difficulties of this during the era of my losing process, but I've come to understand its importance far more now. You see those people that I hassled to read my rough copies during this writing procedure have had almost identical responses, all of them. This response is some remix of:

"I wish I had known what you were going through back then. I just wish I could have been there for you!"

This response proved to me humans are inherently good, thus you can be god damn sure that your friends are fucking godsends, especially throughout tortuous moments like these. You must learn to trust them, let them be there for you, let them try and help, for not only will you feel better for it, but your friendships will be tighter. The comradery on the banter balloon will be even better, the persiflage Prius and the ribbing railroad will be incessantly superior than you have come to accept it and your feeling of being alone, misunderstood and lost will slip away in favour of friendship.

However, this is not the sole candidate out canvassing during this theoretical election, bidding for reasons as to why we should share our thoughts with our friends, whether these thoughts are cerebral, intuitive or just a way to wear one's heart on their sleeve, for there is more. I mean when I uncork the topic of sharing thoughts with friends, I'm not just alluding to a portrayal of feelings, but instead I'm all encompassing. I'm referring to past times, stories, adventures and problems, whilst never forgetting the importance of context. I'm referring to our coping mechanisms, our survival techniques and our methods of madness when it comes to overcoming the loss of our inspiring people. It's a way of casting a conversational spotlight upon what is truly at stake when we talk of overcoming the machete inflicted mourning ache. Fuck no it's not easy, in fact, winning a royal rumble against the likes of Mankind, Dude Love, Mick Foley and Cactus Jack seems more comprehendible and legitimate, despite the obvious impossibility of this scenario.

I don't know how long you may have been keeping your private life a separate entity from your public one, or whether you decided to even pop down this imperfect path of plentiful potholes. What I do know however, is it aint easy to talk to your friends. It aint easy to risk the hard fought perception that you have learned to control. It aint easy to been seen as 'that guy' or 'that girl', you know the one with the broken wing. It aint easy overcoming that look of pity on other peoples faces, despite this being the right thing to do. 'The less people know the better off I am' was my credence. But this piss poor paradigm isn't one to pursue for I was far from correct in adopting such a stance. Quietly suffering becomes an outlook that reinforces loneliness. It stops us from being able to live an unrestricted life and it emphasises a life that is closer to simply existing, than one of actually living.

I'm not trying to hark on, like a herald of angels or harem of women, about the need for us to dive deep and blabber openly to our entire social circle or send out a private message to everyone we have ever come in contact with via the soul destroying organ of Facebook. No. I am instead standing on my upturned egg box and promoting the bright idea of talking to someone. It could be your longest standing friend, and

I'm talking about duration not dick size, you know the person you've know since primary school or fifth grade or something. It could be those you've grown close to since the glorious university days or someone you met at work that has had similar strife. It could be a soul mate that you met by pure chance when you rented out the spare room in your newly built house. It could be a councillor or someone completely external of your life, someone who won't be able to judge if that's a worry for you. It could be the elderly lady you take the bins out for or that fall-back booty call you sometimes go down on (I must mention that this could lead to much more than beneficial friends though). This individual is so relevant and yet almost irrelevant, for what really matter's is that you open up to someone, maybe not pouring it all out at once, for it could well be a drip feed situation. Whatever you decide though dude, it is enigmatically effectual.

Talking breaks down the walls of stalemate, you know that common feeling where you feel down, upset, distraught, horny or whatever, for your friends and family can always sense when something is up, ignoring the erection pun. You know they know something's wrong, but it's a footing too fragile for either party to boldly break, scared of the ice they tread. This inescapable deadlock, standoff and catch twenty-two is, however, quite one sided. You see, and trust me on this one, it is far easier for you to initiate any bereavement burbling than it is for someone else to jump in to the deep and see if they can swim, or at least hold their breath. My best mate, George, knows when something is not quite right with me, and occasionally he might brazenly pipe up or send a text, but for this to occur requires some serious risk management on his part. Usually I want to talk about it but don't know how to show weakness and ask him for help, other times I don't want to talk but he knows it's best. He has to pick his moments and approach perfectly, and for that I tip my fedora to him. This is the same with the other cheeky chappies I have become proverbially joined at the hip with since the educational days. So instead of letting your buddies divulge in what is a far from peril-free gamble, why not help them out by letting them be the ear and the shoulder that they have so desirably requested to be on numerous occasions.

I have just started to open up to these people of similarly common interests, kick-starting the daunting discussion in question with numerous friends. I mean George has always been there pour moi, which is super sound as I can talk to him willy-nilly whilst throwing about my possibly-too-soon sense of humour or boiled up rage without scrutiny or due care, and I don't take this loyalty for granted. Additionally, my old flat-mates became new listening targets of mine, witnessing myself become more and more confident in talking to them as the days went by. However, they often seem out of their depth, understandably so, whilst one of them managed to master the stare of solace, which lends itself as good practice, testing my 'can I ignore this look of pity and see it as an act of warmth'. Tricky but necessary I thought. Then I have those playmates and consorts who I have become suspiciously close to during my time in the ever optimistic and opulent Oxford. The kind of friends that will always be there for me, which is an enjoyable understanding, and one that has proved to be a precious learning curve. Then there are those I have become so close since moving to London, those who have similar stories, different ways of coping and advice from what they have found in the aftermath of bereavement. Judgement free and caring people that I will treasure knowing.

I was Hans Solo for so many light-years, attempting to hide from others and keeping the truth away from one's skin surface unsure of the alternatives. A bad conclusion, for this wank-worrying choice only meant that friends didn't tend to know how to shuck and jive around such a sombre topic, for it's hard for them to judge how they should act for fear of how I would react. Now I've always focussed on making these heavy talkfests as light-hearted and far from lengthy as possible, aiming for a model that resembles a repartee more than anything deadpan and solemn. However, I guess this is because I don't want others to feel awkward, complementing the fact I simply don't enjoy being serious. This suggests a route that will best serve my friends and me, thus presenting itself as a two wood pigeon's with one rock sort of ordeal, or a winner-winner-chicken-dinner type development that I can regally rub-one out over knowing everyone's a victor in this sexy storyboard of underlying panic. But I believe we adapt to our surroundings and play to our strengths where we can, especially in these situations of life and death, situations where we are forced to use our strengths and toughen our weaknesses.

What I love about this though, and no I'm not talking about rubbing one out, is the amount of positive progress that is suddenly available as a direct result of such distinctive dialogue. Now don't get me wrong, there was a downside like always, but these were comparably limited when put next to the sweet nectar of available positivity. Of course there were always going to be optimistic outcomes, but I never realistically thought the rewards would be this bountiful.

However, before we hit the constructive causes of chitter-chatter, and for the sake of a Hollywood happy ending to this paragraph, lets crack on with the limited bad news first, dissecting the downsides and the worst-case scenarios with regards to opening up to one's mates. A scenario that is only limited to your willingness, at least that's what I found. You see, as I have repeated throughout this memoir of mine, nothing is easy, despite the often-apparent contrary when such catastrophes are placed on paper, and this is no different. So, as simple as it seems to chat to friends, and reap in the valuable crops that will be on offer afterwards, there is this intimidating and unnerving leap of faith that must be made first, an alarming jump that will see you become transparent to these people, and what's more transparent for the very first time in a very long time.

I'm not saying this previous opaqueness will disappear instantly, but in order to progress further and further, you must be willing to put yourself on display with no holds barred. You must be willing to accept there will be questions thrown at you that are far tougher than those you get asked when signing up for match.com or something sordidly similar. In a way it is a loss of control, but more than that, it is losing control of this most delectable and subdued of subjects, letting it fend for itself under the microscope of opinions. Now, I controlled this aspect of me for what I believe to be far too long, choosing what I thought others would want to hear, know and understand, ultimately controlling as much of the perceived as plausible. But, talking about your journey or struggles, your pain or memories, whether deep discussions or shallow spiels, is a sure fire advancement of massive magnitudes and arguably of equal importance to any world topic, equipollent to that of ocean desalination, or Robert Downey Junior's successful sobriety.

In all honesty, and with as much seriousness as I can portray, this deed was an apprehension as unnerving as the first stages of male puberty. Discussing one's feelings is one of the obvious anxieties, but this is cruelly complimented by the loss of regulation, the fear of outside sentiments and the knowledge that there is to be no turning back, naming just a few of the worries available. This is all outrageously overwhelming, but it is also an act of bravery that needs to be acted upon, for this type of scrupulousness and honesty, on such a real level, is imperative to the installation of intelligibility and clarity. Being able to express concern or joke about the past with friends is weight lifting freedom like you've never experienced. It draws you away from the days of bedroom door slamming, furniture breaking, pillow pounding and the explosion of unyielding whimpers. But that's because these aggro days of forcefully hibernating your emotional stress will be substituted with a new desire to discuss any disquiet with those around you, seeking advice, letting people in and preventing any distress from building up in silence and becoming as devastating as Darth Vader.

We are required to spill the beans as a way to help ourselves, and a way to help others, whether that's by enlightening those who haven't experienced such fraught, or whether it's by offering your knowledge of

273

imperiousness as a means to help others, especially those who may have recently become subjugated victims. It aint easy, as I scribbled above, but it aint all a Rolling Stones curriculum vitae of 'Doom & Gloom' and balderdash bollocks either. For there is a shimmer of hope and a shimmy-shimmy yeah of buoyant confidence, with rewards to be reaped and positivity to be pillaged, akin to those of a Viking tirade. You see once you do decide to wander past the imposing gates of candidness that have strong-armed any of your previous attempts at openness, you will begin to lap up the liberties you'd lost, you'll feel liberated, unfettered and free-wheeling. People will understand you, but more than this, they will understand where you're coming from, what stage you're at in the healing process and what your perspective is, instead of relying upon there own uniformed wank-wave of a guess. Jokes will be shared and merry monarchy of jovialness and insouciance will rule once again. Happy Mondays.

Unfortunately I was dependant upon desolation, but I had to be in order to wear that miraculous mask of yesteryear. However, by wearing such a disguise, I was preventing the pieces of progress from fitting into place, thwarting my attempts to see the bigger picture, and arrogantly blocking my view of the storyboard. I had to hide my thoughts, scared of using words and frightened of friends knowing my feelings, and by holding onto this insidious idea for so long I convinced myself it was the only option available to me. Well it fucking well is not, or more powerfully:

That. Period. Notion. Period. Is. Period. Bullshit. Period.

But I only began to accept this frightened philosophy of mine as dick-flavoured-dishonesty once I accepted the need for unadulterated action on January 3rd 2013.

Casting my eye over the setting as it stands now, I insentiently concentrated on making headway with my friends first, as opposed to my family. This is not a reflection of my priorities by any means, at least not in a conventional face value sense, and nor does it mean I have shirked my lineage. Like I said, it was an automatic move and one I am able to bring up because my family are all in a wholesome, happy and affable place now, celebrating the fact it is a work in progress instead of ignoring such a creed. Nonetheless, the reasons for me wrestling this school of subtle sea lions (friends) first has proven sensible, I think. You see, this approach allowed for a little wiggle room, a bounteous bumper that tolerates a tad more trial and error. Sensible in theory, because it will mean I am at my totally tip top transcendence when it comes to exhibiting my experiences, pain and feelings to my cherished blood-clan.

This decision to approach friends first has helped me recover my self-assurance and confidence, but even more than this, it has progressively eradicated that mass produced and technologically induced STI that pressures us to please others and care about their opinions first and foremost. The kind of insecurity that is projected directly into our faces on a daily dictum via the means of beauty magazines, newspapers and adverts, mind-fucking the timidities of everyone as if they are physically plastered onto the devils cock. Then you combine this accented attack with the personal hardships that are already in place, and it becomes a David and Goliath battle yet again, prioritising the happiness and acceptance of others as a heightened significance instead of placing ourselves at the top of this internal totem pole atop of seventh heaven.

However, this is exactly the changes I have made, for I am now focussing on what makes me a happy human and a cheeky chappy. Focussing on what drives my determination, which little things make me content, what clothes put a sparkle in my eye and a beaming grin across my frontal features. I am now a priority, and with each day that passes, I'm giving less of a fuck about what others may think of me for I am just trying to be a better me, something myself and Bruce Wayne have in common. Maybe it's because for so many years, or more accurately since Dad was killed, I was worried about how people would perceive me, how I would be welcomed or approached. How I would be judged on last imprints as much as first impressions, conscientious about the codex cover and the content, worried about everything, trying to fit in with society or some bullshit. Walking in to a crowd and wondering 'will they like me' instead of looking around and thinking 'will I like them'?

This idea of forgetting the opinions of others, going against the tide of modern day commercialisation and hoping to secure the permanent signature of happiness in the upcoming transfer window was not part of the quota I had in mind. I had never circled this out in a thick red marker pen like I do when I'm flicking through the back pages of local newspapers. No, instead it was just one of those Tetris pieces that fell into place without me hysterically tapping away on the cursor keys. It was just a natural by-product and a realisation that became apparent with time, maybe a result of the contagious word that is clarity. This has worked ideally with regards to opening up to my friends, and one that has sent back a supportive response to my bemusement.

You see, being happy in who you are not only sounds like the clichéd crap that even my five year old brother, Zack, would respond to with a pitiful laugh, but is also one of those bonus points that you collect along the invigorating footpath of tribulation, much like when Mario gets hold of a magic mushroom in his journey for greater good. It's the variety of happiness that is incited and urged on by frankness. By being open with your friends and family, or even your dog or teddy bear, your opening up to yourself too, realising what you've achieved in your struggles as well as sharing your memories. It is one of those things that allow you to be honest, which in turn builds your confidence in a wonderful way. As a wise man once told me:

"Expressing honesty is the maturing of an individual, for sharing is demonstration that you are willing to bare your soul to the wider world in order to better understand yourself, your reaction to life's tragedies and a readjustment to positively use those deep aches, a means to evolve into a better person."

I willingly respect my ability to reflect, for using an astute cognisance allows us to rise from turmoil and strive for the betterment of oneself as well as those around us, and maybe even further.

In bereavement, what is pertinent is that you grow from the emulation of the one's we hold most dear, a missive that proves you have matured into your own person. Acknowledging and sharing such strife, memories and stories is a courageous step, stepping out of the role of 'victim of life' and into the positive light of fashioning your own future. It proves you have freed yourself and are now able to help others in the way that I am attempting to, making a difference to those who need it, whether people close to you or not, by sharing your strength and insight whilst ultimately shaping your life and your own destiny in the light of your own shadow. Your own determination and will allows you to free yourself from the pain and suffering of previous times, ensuring you are free to make your own path and deal with the kaleidoscope changes that life will ultimately throw your way.

Taking that leap was inspired by my decision to open up to others, share with them and ultimately overcome the fears of transparency that had a stranglehold over me like some sort of serpent schlong. But once that front handspring in tuck layout had been made into the astonishing abyss, the rest just seemed to follow. I was no longer scared of the theoretical boogieman, and upon ignoring his pathetic torment I began to feel free. I felt stronger and more assured of my abilities and capability, I was ready to choose my own path and be my own person, and sure enough loneliness, sadness, isolation and presentiment all subsided to gaiety, mirth, joviality and reverie, in what seemed to be a far more serene and completely covert version of Gandalf's arrival to

Helm's Deep with the Rohirrim.

What I had come to realise was, running away is the selfish way out. It's a misguided attempt at escapism that is downright void of right or wrong, for it instead plays on that common concept that I keep banging on about, the moral propensity and intuition that states the only outcome that truly matters is the consequence of our actions. I mean instead of trying to bury yourself in a gutless manner much like I, try thinking about how your decisions may hurt others, how those close to you will be affected and how it will effect you in the knowledge that running doesn't encourage or ensure immunity, and nor does it make what has happened disappear or go away.

These problems don't just vanish. They will be there waiting at your door through hail stones and thunderstorms, just lingering, waiting for you to deal with them, forcing you to contemplate a means to deal with the incessant methods of your troubles. In fact, all running really achieves is harm to others, intensifying and prolonging your own burdening grief in the process. This is unless you are in fact the high-flying-always-smiling-anorexic-Mr-Muscle, my hero and the crowds favourite, King Farah, in which case, don't stop running and go for gold you sexy man puma Mo. But if you are in fact not Mo, then try looking back at old photos of the bewitching boner begetter that was Marilyn Monroe. Watch her flirt with the camera and smirk at the sight of her buxom bosoms, all whilst listening to her always-astonishing words, "Keep smiling, because life is a beautiful thing, and there is so much to smile about."

These are all concepts that I am currently trying to exemplify in my day-to-day swagger and night to night saunter, and one that I am slowly bringing to the family living room, although my gasconade in this setting is not as intrepid as it is outside of these homely four walls. I guess I just don't know how to approach the subject with them. Maybe I am the counties most convincing and courageous contradiction, struggling to open up to them because I don't want to cause offence, oblivious to their fragility. Maybe I am unable to completely commit, shitting actual bricks at the thought they may not be able to understand the reasons behind my sordid past, and as a result, I'm uncontrollably afraid that I've brought disgrace to the family, so much so the style and flare in which this disgrace was demonstrated is truly erroneous. Maybe, I am overly concerned about the confiscating context, hoping to bare my soul on to the page first, like an all inclusive holiday or buffet, offering my experiences, reasoning, debauchery and frolics to the wider audience, allowing my family to delve into it once I've crossed the i's and dotted the t's, and once there is no turning back.

I want to open up, and for want of a hugely more appropriate turn of phrase, come clean, and I am cockily confident that I will do so. I'm not one to believe in happy endings, unless we're talking about a Thai massage parlour based in Paul Raymond's Soho, but certainly not the kind of sugar-glossed-bull-fuck happy endings that see chirpy couples and united families walk hand-in-hand into the glorious sunset at the end of distorted Disney films.

However, I am peculiarly puffed up, convinced and upbeat that this poorly constructed and loosely phrased work of written dexterity will serve as a medium of enlightenment, and will throw this family train back on the right tracks. I see myself as an optimist, and despite the fact I've been peppered with enough pessimistic condiments and left in the oven at one-hundred and eighty degrees over the last few years, I am still a hopeless romantic and more than hopeful that we will become even closer and tighter than ever. Who knows, maybe we'll even participate in an emotional group hug, embracing over a large bucket that has been strategically placed to collect our non-stop tears. Nonetheless its more than likely we'll just trifle about with a magnum of Lambrini and cherry bakewells, whilst throwing around solid high fives and universally recognised fist pounds.

Unfortunately I can't give you a heads up on this one just yet, but by using the progress of this learning curve, reading between the lines, filling in the blankety-blanks and improving my Roy Walker inspired 'Catchphrase' ability, I have a pretty fucking sweet idea that opening up to the members of mi casa is a primary positive flex. The process has already begun, and the progress has been far superior than I could have hoped to imagine, and that's saying something given I have a pretty healthy and seriously sexy imagination. Metaphorically, I've already started on this round of golf, and even if I've hit a seventy-six on the front 9, I'm just proud I'm able to finally make my way round the course, refusing to give up and invariably making my way towards the 18th.

Of course I am a fan of the phrase, 'focus on the journey, not the destination' because it's a fair perspective, highlighting that joy is found in the participation of an activity, not the completion. However, in my humbly fucked up way, I tend to believe it's about the journey, and the destination. I mean, you got to stay focussed on something, have a reason to not give in and to keep on trucking, and lets not forget, no one gets on a plane, train, boat or wagon just for the love of the journey, instead it's the vision of touching down in Panama, the Riviera, Mumbai or even Saturn's god damn moon 'Titan' that gets us all wet and horny.

I've begun my journey and I've already begun to eradicate the metaphorical slice of Edam that managed to wedged itself between my family and I, although it must be noted that I take the all the blame for bringing this slice of Edam into play in the first place. I mean my brother and I are closer than we have been in many a werewolf-amplifying-full-moon. We've become the kind of friends that brothers should be. I would do anything for him. I'd go anywhere if he needed me. I'd do my limited best to stop anyone who would try to harm him. I aim to be a guardian in every sense of the word. But we've surpassed this instinctive brotherly bond, for we've become crazy close as of late, we've become bona fide buddies, understanding each other without saying anything, yet able to voice our verses too.

Then there is the only other member of my immediate family left, for my ever-motherly mother and I are throwing our differences to the wayside bit by bit. Of course there are moments where I just smile and nod my head as if demonstrating utter agreement, whilst actually biting my lip on some opinion based topic that I completely disagree with, but that's because I understand her better now. You may have lost your Mum, or your Dad, your brother or sister, cousin or niece, or indeed someone else who had a huge impact on your life, and as a result you understandably became troubled, like I had, taking it out on your next of kin. It's an intrinsic verdict that you decide upon simply because this is the only person who will always be there for you, the only person who you can drop your guard for safe in the knowledge that they won't judge you. This doesn't validate these action of aggro and nor does it make right, of course it doesn't, but it is still a natural reaction as fucked up as it may be.

These conflicts however, whether minor or not, can be limited by understanding this next piece of graffiti that's scrawled across this page in computerised and parallel lines. You see, our parents make a promise to their offspring, an unwritten promise that can never be broken. But despite the invisibility cloak that this promise parades around in, unseen to their progenies, it is an unconditional promise that very much exists. They are your parents, and for as long as these real life Wonder Women or Supermen live they will always be your parent first and your friend second, but that's because of how much they care. They will stalk you, flip out on you, lecture you, drive you insane, be your worst nightmare and hunt you down like an amphibious crossbreed of bloodhound and tiger shark when they have to, but that's because they love you and when you understand that, they will know you've become a responsible adult. That's just how our loving seniors work. But it's not all pointless negativity and suffocating bullshit though, for you will never find anyone else in your life that loves, cares and worries about you so unconditionally as they do, and if you don't mutter under your breath, 'I hate you', or whisper obscene curses like a young Fred Durst at least once in your life, then they are not doing their parental job properly.

They seriously care about you dude. I mean yeah parents have an unrivalled ability to get under our fucking skin like a battery of scarab beetles, able to embarrass us purposefully on a daily basis whilst playing dumb and acting ignorant. But we are all the prized possessions of our parents, even if they do harness the unrivalled flair to silence us at a bloody moments notice with the simple yet excruciatingly effective and dreaded combo of words, 'stop showing off in front of your mates Billy-big-and-barren-bollocks.' But that's just part and parcel of the plus side to parenting and can you blame them.

What you must come to terms with though is the chapter and verse fact that these aren't the only talents they have acquired. They also have this unsurpassed superpower of always being at the end of the phone, an ability to make us properly laugh when we're real with them and this aura that never whimpers and never stops caring for us. They are there for us like a beacon of shining awesomeness, waiting and ready to do absolutely anything they can for us. It's this that has pushed me to start pumping the theoretical hand-car-pump-trolley mechanism towards the tumbleweed free town of 'How It Should Be' and encouraged me to start enjoying the fruits of my fantastically crazy modern family. Well that and my desire to be Will Smith in the tumbleweed free film 'Wild Wild West' no matter what how bizarre the backdrop may be, or how distinctly average a film may end up.

I'm sure I am similar to most people, at least in the sense that I have my days where I am on top of the world. A princely chatterbox, able to make even the most sombre of fellows smile in all their glory, able to make my family cachinnate, chortle, roll around in the aisle's of any reputable supermarket and howl hysterically, and I love these days. However, I also have those days where I am far from that. Not depressed per se, but those days where I keep myself to myself, just focussed on what has to be done, sometimes a little low and possibly a tad unpleasant to be hanging around. But it is this side of me that I'm not great friends with, in fact he's kind of a dick, the kind of guy who causes unnecessary stresses to those close to me. I am amusing and bemusing, and that must be a right puzzlement for others to try and get their heads around. I'm serious yet affable, spontaneous yet structured, ambitious and determined, yet unique in my methods of reaching such great heights. I am who I am, and you are who you are, and this uniqueness is there to be wrapped up in party poppers, thrown a carnival infused party and rejoiced with kettledrums, not bad-mouthed, depreciated and blistered. So smile, because being different is fucking divine.

Maybe it's the contrasting change between my self-sufficient London life and the humble dwellings of North Norfolk, where my doting mother smothers me in home comforts, that affects my mood? Maybe my mood is altered by the fact I am the kind of son that has made many mistakes and despite doing my best to learn from them, I still continue to find ways to bend the rules and enjoy this hard fought and moral freedom?

Maybe it is that I was forced to experience independence and responsibility at a relatively young age that has encouraging me to continue down this intriguing individualist pavement, and as a result I struggle with hearing anything different from what I want to hear?

Whatever the reason, I have been foolish to try and break away from my past, foolish for getting riled up over what is so obviously just TLC (tender, love and care NOT tables, ladders and chairs you Team Xtreme fans.) My Mum, the same as my Dad, and how I presume any good parent to be, they simply try to prevent us from making mistakes, telling us they've been there, done that and got the perm to prove it. They believe we should from learn from the outcomes of their past. Maybe they are right. They probably are right, even if they just chucked these comments out into the open as nothing but a warning. But even if they are right, nothing has changed in my mind and nor has my outlook, for I believe I'm the one who needs to make mistakes in order to learn. I'm the one who needs to try and fail, I need to know that I've tried so that I know how to succeed after I've failed.

In my understanding you've just got to jump on that Shetland pony and live life to the full while you are able to. Go and experience everything that you possibly can. Take care of your beautiful self, look after your wonderful friends, and don't hesitate to make some silly fucking stories with these unglued, screw loose, moonstruck and nutty-as-a-macadamia companions of yours. Have fun. Be kooky and weird. Be flirtatious and frolicsome. Run a riot and make it contagious. Go out and screw up. Go out and make a mess of your life, but do it while your young, free and socially allowed to be ridiculous, and then learn from these life lessons you learnt and keep hold of the good bits.

Fuck, we all screw up along the way, it's an unavoidable blessing of life and so you may as well enjoy the process. You may as well as bounce around on the tip-top trampoline and leap feet first into frolic filled fruit bowl you little ray of sunshine you. Take the opportunity to learn from your mistakes, find the cause to your problem and eliminate it. Don't try to be what society decadently believes is perfect, just be an excellent example of a human being, because that's all we are. Know matter what others may think, you can only be asked to be the best you, and that will always remain an imperfect specimen whichever way you look at it. Just close your eyes and promise the eclectic universe that whatever you do, you won't be another brick in the wall. I need to be foolish, cordial and gregarious, but that's because no one is going to live forever, and this realisation of mortality is more than enough to dampen any reason to be forever serious, a consistent outlook of mine since 2001. What's more is I'm learning there is nought wrong with this peculiar perspective of exultation and purposeful living; at least I don't think so.

What there is something wrong with however, is fighting against the love and support of our grounding and humble routes. I mean, instead of battling these motherly or fatherly desires to help, especially during those infrequent visits back home in the months and years after you've moved out, welcome them, for all this mollycoddling suggests is that they still want to play a part in your life, and after all they are still your parents. So let them in, let them help, let them treat you like you are a child again, because you are and always will be their child. Don't let them wipe your arse, brush your teeth, pick your nose, iron your pants or wash your hair, not on every visit anyway, but accept that they will always be your procreator and you will always be the apple of their eye. I know this can be tricky and sometimes hard to swallow. I know that we often clash with our parents and sometimes hate comparisons being made between us and them, but we are sprung from their obviously awesome deoxyribonucleic acid no matter what day you question this, and thus desultory friction is bound to occur occasionally and even make some fucking sparks fly now and then. But try and understand their point of view and respect them as parents, because it is more than likely they have done more for you than you will ever know, such as lighting the candles, chucking on some Sting and the Police and making you under them warmth of a starry night sky. So get to know them at any chance you are given, as you never know when they'll be gone for good.

Of course being the main prop in any form of 'The Glowing Juniper' sex position is top of my favourite past times, but sharing laughs with those you love is a damn near second. You see I really fucking appreciate the new honesty I share with my Mum and younger brother. I love the laugh-out-loud giggles we have, and we enjoy the ridiculousness of each other's company a lot, in fact it's as if we're living the day-to-day life of any 'My Family' episode. I enjoy the subtleties of spending alone time with them, encouraging family meals and participating in one on one activity's, no matter how menial they be. I love getting to know who my family really are and this has become a priority. As Baz Luhrmann wisely poeticised, 'They are the best link we have to our past, and most likely to be there for you in the future.' It doesn't fill the obvious hole that remains after such an influential death, but it does seriously enhance your chances of moving on and enjoying what we still have, and this is where the emphasis should always lie.

I understand that we may want to manically remember those that we have lost, scared that our memories will distort our memories of them, often feeling that we're unable to prevent these reminiscences from slipping through our sieve like fingers, like sand in the wind. This is a damning realisation, and I found that the conscious decision to try and remember my Dad hindered other areas of my life and simply because I was frightened about forgetting him, afraid that letting go was the wrong thing to do. Maybe we stare blood-shot and blurry eyed at old pictures of these lovable sods we lost. Maybe we smile through the streaming tear filled rivers that roll over our cheeks and past our lips as we watch old video footage, hoping that this will prevent us from ever forgetting them. Maybe we make a shrine filled with photographs and old memorabilia that remind us of them, a place we can console ourselves in private, welcoming the pain and what it signifies. Maybe we spend hours sat in front of their headstones, wallowing in the graveyards where our loved ones lay, finally able to think, finally say our loving piece of poetic truth, a symbolic way for us to be close to the person we were so close to, understanding that we are unable to ever be as close to them as we once were. Maybe we get a tattoo as a means to remember the person or people we have lost, the people we still have left and what we have come through, all as a means to know this memory is there, wearing it proudly on our sleeve and no longer required to have it constantly etched into our frontal lobes as a harmful distraction from the here and now.

I have dabbled in all of these methods of ridiculous reminiscing. In fact I still partake in each of them now and again, similar to the proceedings of a clandestine cult. Well, all but the latter, to the relief of my Mum. This isn't to say I haven't thought about a tattoo though. I understand my Mum's point of view with regards to the almost permanent inking of the bodies largest living organ. I understand that people of her generation and upbringing see such artwork as unflattering to say the least. I understand all of her reasoning. I just wish she could understand mine. Thus, I continue this ceremony with yet another complete-nonsense-but-no-bullshit kick to the high-hat cymbal of advice, reassuringly stating that I don't believe in making permanent decisions for a temporary emotion. However, this is a fairly recent development. You see I have made a lot of rash decisions based on my feelings, without giving these feelings or decisions any worthy thought, due care or time to mellow. I've acted on the influence of rage and grief, not allowing myself a chance to sit back and secure an unclouded head and often I have learned this the hard way. However, I've learned from such mistakes. Of course, there are sometimes ultimately unavoidable reactions, but wherever it is plausible I now try my best to leave a three-day timeframe before allowing Newton's third law to naturally assume it's cuckolding control. This refers to numerous events that rear their fuck-ugly-Susan-Boyle-featured heads in the wake of such tragic loss.

However this is the point, I have thought about a tribute trinket of ink for so long now, discussing the pros n cons with the befriended angel and devil whom sit on either shoulder of mine, bickering like Jessica Simpson and Nick Lachey, or almost any other couple who have been under the same roof for far too long. But guess what, I haven't been thoughtfully perturbed by the punk-rock image of my mother's perception. You see, I remember being at home in the weeks after the plane crash and tentatively trying to approach the sore subject of tattoos with my Mum. I even approached my Goddess of a Godmother before I made the move on my ma. I guess it was a test run and a way of grasping some idea of how the woman who introduced me into this world would take the news, asking for external advice, almost seeking a guilty guidance before I took the carefully worded script to my Mum. It was still a no from mother though. It has been a no ever since my Dad died. She is against tattoo's, as is my step-dad, but it seems this is just a bitter war she has with the idea in general instead of hearing my reasons as to why I want a memorial piece of beautiful art to commemorate my beautiful Dad, as well as my Madre and bro.

More simply put, ever since my Dad died I've wanted to venerate him with a tattoo. A piece to remember him by instead of weighing myself down mentally and emotionally, understanding that every thought and decision I muster is muddied by this cognisant need to remember my Dads ever more distorted features. In my eyes, I am uniquely me, in almost everyway possible and I revel in the fact that we are all so patently distinctive and different, and this is unquestionably a great thing. But since I have experienced what it's like to exist in a place so despairingly low, previously crumbling to such an extent I was unsure if I could be rescued and having been scarred so mentally and emotionally, I may have a very different view on tattoo's than others do. You see having something so ardently passionate painted on my skin and concealed from sight, is far better than the anger infused personality that has caused so much collateral convulsions. To me, dabbling in a tattoo is the polar opposite of simplistically superficial, is far fucking better than the pain that is permanently playing fiddlesticks with my emotions and fucking up my personality.

You are right, I could just head down to the pre-planned parlour of perfection, get the delicate design I have dwelled over for what feels like decades. I could enjoy my liberty and freedom as a twenty-something year old man who loves to think he is a maverick and actually act like the kind of cheeky-chappy he is. The one that tends to never let others tell him how things are to be done. However, this would go against my very reasoning. I respect my Mums wishes, of course, for I respect my Mum oh so fucking much. But the real reason for my hasty hesitation is more complicated, possibly. You see I want my Mum to understand why I want to remember my Dad in such a fashion. I want my Mum to hopefully be there when I get it done. I want my Mum to revel in it the same way I will. I'm not a fan of shit, meaningless, any excuse to join in with the latest fad of the week type tattoos. But those pieces of art that have heart, meaning and thought behind them, they I understand. They I respect, not just as artwork, but as a healing mechanism too. I have tried almost everything to get over my Dad. I have tried almost everything to move on, but I really struggled with this vast task that causes more pain than a cock-punching-chlamydia-piss. I have tried so many different means of recovery, but I still find myself riding on the soft verges and hard shoulders of the recovery road, and this is where I struggle to see the perceptions of my loving family.

They have seen me at my lowest. They have suffered under the noxious hands and violent voice of my unrelenting wrath. They have seen me losing the fight. They have been through periods where they were unable to deal with me, always trying to help but never really knowing how. Now this, in my humbled outlook, is surely far worse, far more harmful and far more irrevocably disturbing than a meaningful, personal and ostensibly outstanding oeuvre that will allow me to move on without hesitation or fear. Sure I may be wording it in a wholeheartedly biased account, but this is what it will take to break down the walls of Jericho that is my Mums stubbornness. What's more, I am fully aware this may also be a cheeky method to get her to understand, but then this whole distasteful document is about me spilling the truth like a BP oil leak, and getting everything out in the open. This is the truth laid bare for my Mum, my brother, my formal friends, my accidental acquaintances and my one-night stands, but above all its for you, you beautiful, sultry, suggestive panther you.

Now I don't want a tattoo shrouding my lower arm in thick waves and unicorns, and I don't want my jugular to be stamped with 'lucky' after suffering at the hands of an event that is so obviously unlucky. Nor do I want my thumb inked to look like a sand worm or my face to imitate a woman's lady garden and I definitely don't want to look like I've been gangbanged by a posse of Crayola or a clique of biro's. I don't want a tattoo where the general public or others can see it unless I want them too. I want it concealed, private, personal and wonderful. It's a means for me to remember my Dad by and to use that permanent memory as a means to keep my determination unfaltering and always alight.

I believe it will allow me to open up to those significant others in my lovely life, more specifically, my step-dad and somewhat my mentors too. I have been petrified to fully open up and accept my step-dad for fear of forgetting my actual Father, another tear jerking and sacred struggle. I have been apprehensively worried since the accident that if I get too close to another Father figure I will lose the memory of my natural born blood related parent. Ah, don't get me wrong, my old man would absolutely hit the roof if I got a tattoo, fuck he may have even chased me in circles like a dog chasing his tail, with his rage fuelled adrenaline ensuring that he wouldn't tire until I had collapsed with exhaustion. But, and believe me there is a Nicky Minaj sized but here, he would also be majorly, nay, royally fucked off that he had died and left his family with such emotional turmoil. It would also sadistically allow our relationship to continue, because fuck me, Dad and I enjoyed pissing each other off, albeit this was a slightly uneven seesaw. I mean he hated my dress sense, my hair and probably my entire eccentricity. So pissing him off again with a tailored tribute kind of feels ridiculously right.

Anyway, I don't know what your method of remembrance is. I don't know whether you have a shrine spot, philanthropic photo album, veracious video library or a prodigious piece of artistry portrayed on you. I don't know whether it has helped or whether you are still fighting off the talons of the bereavement bird of prey, unable to relinquish the thoughts of these loved ones and still holding them in the forefront of your concealed consciousness. I don't know whether this remembrance ransacking hinders you or whether it spurs you on. I don't know whether it prevents you from living a full life of laughter and applause or whether it throws kindling and logs onto your internal flame of doggedness.

What I can say though, is I know how troublesome and tricky these masters of the dark arts can be. I know how easy it is for despondency and loss to take over and dominate everything, making almost all other everyday concerns tauntingly redundant. I know how devilishly these demons can play to the string quartet of your depression. I know what it is like to have so much unanswered anguish and adversity, for such misery and misfortune has the ability to make even the most prestigious medicines mourn. Fuck, I have so many silently sinister skeletons in my closet that renovations have been made to accommodate a walk-in-fucking-wardrobe. Thus, I can confidently claim that I know how harmful the mental exhaustion and head fucking can be. I know that it can prevent us from being able to convalesce, recuperate, bounce back, forge ahead or escape the woods. It is a pain that is unavailable to those who want to heal it, like a paranormal prince of pricks, hiding from the public sphere like the fame-hating Keira Knightly.

It is for this reason that I implore you to act. It is for this reason I implore you to go out and grab recovery by its rumpled foreskin, for it won't just fall into your lap like a well-paid stripper called Tarka Turnbull. Of course time is immeasurably crucial, after all time is a healer. But a remedy must also be sought. Use the support structure around you like it's mobile scaffolding, ask for help or accept it when it's offered. Go to counsellors and cognitive therapists for that extra touch of guidance and expression, especially if they look like the demi-gods Cara Delevingne and Cam Gigandet, both of who have glacial holds over the world's masochistic imagination (but that's neither here nor there). What is crucial to remember though is no progress can become success if you don't get your hands dirty and if you refuse to show life the white's of your knuckles, for everything comes down to you, and that's the bottom line because Stone Cold says so.

It all comes down to you. You maybe able to move on with these remembrances pieces that I spoke of, but only you will know if this is true. Others may not understand your methods, so if it helps you try and help them see it from your perspective. You will know what you have to do at some stage, although this will probably take some time. You know what will ensure you head towards the recognisable track of happiness and clarity, and even if you are way off, at least you'll be heading in the right direction. It is down to you though, whether it be helped by a tattoo, a job, a pilgrimage, a chat or whatever Trevor. Just remember, fight for what you are worth, and don't make permanent decisions on a temporary emotion.

So the January 3rd promise, you know the one where I had to accept I had issues, locate what the problems were and then strap on my red and gold Iron Man suit and fly through the burning gates of hell and into Lucifer's loathsome lair. You know, the day I started cracking the metaphorical but wretched whip, using my disparaging 'repulsor rays', my unrelenting 'uni-beam' and my devastating dick, all in an attempt to finally lay down the law. Well this has started promisingly, to my perplexity, marvel and willy tingling wonderment. I mean, yeah, I've got a crazy long canyon road ahead of me and considering I'm no cartoon roadrunner, this could take some time. But, the providential part of this unnerving prospect is that I have started, I have begun to make some waves, I am clearer than ever, more confident than I was this morning and less scared of my future prospects than I have been for too many rotations of this worldly globe. I guess I'm just enjoying the sunshine that is finally smashing through the usually bleak skies and dark clouds. Basically, I've got an absolute rock-on, a truly perpendicular penis and an upstanding and saluting stiffy, and quite rightly so. But this is quite simply because of the newly predicted forecast, which looks promisingly positive for the first time in a pretty prolonged period. However, this boner could quite as easily have something to with the fact the forecast predicting weather girl is one voluptuous vixen.

I know I'm still learning, and that makes this guidance of mine a little bit rich and I'm fully aware of that. But it also makes this recital an honest and bullshit free account of genuine experiences. I mean, yeah psychologists are trained and whatnot, but have they been through it all or are they just some hack that's able to narrate advice from what they learned in their revision guides and betterment books? Because if this is in fact the case, then I'll have to be honest once again, and say this is about as helpful as me giving women advice on what to expect in the third trimester. If you've got vices, drop them. If you've become closed off, open up. If you're worried, tell someone, or alternatively join the Class of '99 and listen to 'Everybody Wear Sunscreen' (at five minutes four seconds, it's the timesaver option). This whole process revolves around awareness, bravery, courage and ultimately your need to chitter-chatter with friends, whether seriously of affably. It's all about coming clean to yourself, your chummy cohorts and of course your parents, for they will all want to help, especially your folks, because, well they've got to have some uses in excess of free taxi drivers and fridge fillers right?! (I'm only teasing Mum).

What's more though, I mean on top of all these other necessities that include realising what needs to be changed, what's holding you back, what your vices are, why things have to be altered and why you need to be open and honest amid others with regards to your feelings, comes the critical concept of 'now'. I know I keep saying this prickly process takes some serious time, for we truly find out who we are over this problematic period, but sometimes I feel like I almost wasted four years of my life just mucking about in this ditch of doom, revelling in a rut and unwilling to welcome almost any form of help. Thus I now have some proper compassion and understanding that the first step in solving any problem is simply recognising there is one. Then combine this with the fact we are all mortals with expiry dates and as such we only have one chance to explore this lottery of life we've been given, and we end up with an answer that suggests the need to make actions and more importantly we need to make these actions right now. We must practically practice the present, for that's all we have. I didn't mean to slap you across the face with this prophet of a penis and this heavy open-hand of frightening knowledge, but my ability at getting serious points across comes in a fashion as shrewd as Vivienne Westwood and as subtle as a fart in the bath. But what more can you expect from a pub-going preacher man, a barstool politician and a pint-sipping prophet.

You will always be thrown an endless amount of cross roads and life junctions, but it is crucial you make your own journey. I have offered advice where I can, but at the end of the day, you must trust your heart, go with your gut instincts and try to stick with them even when the inevitable second-guessing pops up. I don't know if you've read this book and thought, fuck, we're strangely similar strange people or thought we're worlds apart. I don't know whether you've been able to relate to some chapter and verses of this chronicle, or whether you're just as lost now as you were when you got ensnared by the Venus fly-trap of a front cover, snapping you up like a moth to a flame. What I do believe however is that we, as people, are inherently good. We know the difference between right and wrong, and we also know what the impact and consequences our actions can have, and this is where your progress lies.

The consequence of my actions now lie in my desire to heal, and a little something this Lilliputian sardine learned along his caustic, laborious, grievous and vexatious river journey is that I have no intention of inflicting any type of infliction or pain upon anyone else. Of course, this can create its own gravity of problems for we begin to sacrifice everything for others out of fear. But it also means that we have innately awesome impulses, incredible inclinations, great gut feelings and a savvy sixth sense for what is best for us, as well as those around us. You just need to learn what you want from life and act upon it as soon as you come to know, if possible, now. You just need to give your decisions some physicality and stop wearing a wishbone where your backbone ought to be.

Yeah we've been unfairly bowled over by the basilisk of life, we've been unlawfully knocked about on numerous occasions and we've questioned the universe, confused by why such horrible events happen to such ultimately good people. But we're stronger for it. When I was growing up I never thought I'd be that family, the one with the hardships, the one that strayed so far away from that ever more muddied line of what is meant to be the norm. But I have come to realise that every family has their issues, big or small, for we all have our own strife. So all it comes down to is how we deal with such tormenting trepidation and this ultimately comes down to our attitude.

I've said it enough for it to now be classed as bragging, but I have changed my attitude. I have come to terms with what has happened. I am making decisions that will help me change those issues that need changing and I refuse to live in the despair of the past. I have quit the vices that held my progress firmly at the starting blocks. I have opened up to friends and families about the past, and I have begun letting them know of the struggles that present themselves in the present tense. Ultimately, I made myself a promise, one that sought clarity and happiness, and I have kept this promise in spite of all the hideous adversities that tried to fuck me along the way.

In fact, looking back and realising what has been achieved now is a miraculous moment that has made my heart and cock swell with pride. But before I go and release the pressure on my balls in the obvious manner of any young man, I want you to make a promise to yourself, a promise that you will seek the same free and awe-inspiring outcome, no matter what motorway or backstreet you end up taking, for it is when we are lost that we find ourselves.

Of course there will be numerous times where your emotions rise to the surface, moments where your temper will dominate and times where so many tears will flood out of your tear ducts it will look as though the amiable Hoover Dam has gone and overflowed. So with this intimidating battle and daunting fracas on the horizon of healing, you must be prepared to power through. You must ensure that you want to recover, you must seek a consciously controlled attitude and you must retain a powerful and positively run mindset that alleviates you from living in the past. This will allow you to live with a diurnal, imperishable and steadfast smile that will see you through any further hardships, and this will last forever and a day, which makes no sense whatsoever. But hey ho, after all it's not about how we enjoy success, but rather how we endure defeat, and this can only be realised in times of trepidation. As Philosopher Marley wisely once said to me whilst he was higher than Felix Baumgartner, "You never know how strong you are until being strong is your only choice."

The Rastafarian boss is absolutely right too, because the toughest bout you'll ever have is the one against yourself, the one that is backed up by the hammer-hitting bastard called life. As we've all learned, the world isn't all blowjobs and Bugatti's, especially when this bereavement bollocks is involved. Instead, it's a fucked up and cruel mistress and a draconian Dracula in disguise. However, I want to end on some words I heard in the most unlikely of places, and from the most unlikely of men. It draws my last breath having to draw to an end like this, not only because they are cock-suckingly clichéd words, but because they are literally from the horse's mouth, from a questionable human and a thespian superstar with almost no acting ability. But nonetheless, these words arrive via the medium of an arousing quotation that needs to be read aloud and in this actors astonishing accent, possibly concluded with back-to-back stranger wanks. My Lords, my Ladies, and all those not sitting on a silk-based cushion, I give to you the wonderful, the magnificent, the unimaginably inspiring and the completely incomprehensible, Sylvester 'Sly' Stallone:

"I don't care how tough you are, [life] will beat you to your knees and keep you there permanently if you let it. You, me, or nobody is going to hit as hard as life. But it aint about how hard you can hit. It's about how hard you can get hit and keep moving forward. How much you can take and keep moving forward. For that is how we succeed. Now if you know what you're worth, then go and get what your worth. But you have got to be willing to take the hits, without pointing fingers saying you aren't where you should be because of this or because of that, because of him, her or anything. That's what cowards do and you're not a coward. You're better than that. But you have to believe in yourself."

Now, do your upmost to escape the confines of being increasingly scornful to consensus and deaf to advice, and go and do what you have to do squire, for it is only you who knows what step has to be taken and I suggest you use your current heart pounding desire to do it right now. Lets accept life for what it is and revel in that magic understanding for life is what you make it. I mean, let's pretend there is some alternative universe out there, a universe that has people like us, a universe that has an alternative you and me. The difference is they are perfect. Their families are traditional, healthy and not plagued by a single hiccup whatsoever. Instead their lives revolve around how much they are going to spend on the new Babolat tennis racket or whether they should go on a summer holiday or winters vacation. They spend their days discussing the fact Superdrug has run out of their preferred hair spray and bickering over whether they need their cleaning lady to do the ironing every other day or thrice a week.

Maybe you're different, but I don't want to be these people. I don't want to be the alternative me, I just want to be the guy I am, I just want to be me. I want to be able to put up a fight, I want to enjoy the bumps in the road, I want to learn from the low points and soak up the highs. Life doesn't have to be perfect to be fucking wonderful, and no one can tell you what perfect or wonderful is except for you, not your parents, not your friends, not your colleagues, not society, not anyone except you. Make the most out of what you have been given in this lottery win, and this is an easier prospect than you may think, for nothing prevents us from finding the magical in the mundane.

As Bobby Dillon once croaked in my ear, 'All I can do is be me, whatever that is.' I don't know who I am yet, and I would be shocked to hear you know exactly who you are already. We're all on a jumpy, jaunty and jovial journey, and the biggest challenge we face in this life is trying to be ourselves in a world that is constantly trying to make you like everyone else. Constantly trying to remain true to who you are in a world that is constantly throwing turmoil, heartache and mayhem into your path is the toughest challenge, and life's methods are sure to be an absolute assault on your senses dude. I'm excited by to remain true to who I am through all the success and all of the failure. Trying to remain me despite every other aspect of my life constantly changing. I believe it is what you make it, you can fight it or give in to it, but what ever you choose, this is a journey that's different for everyone and unique to you. There will be exclusive crossroads and distinctive options provided throughout this trek, the kind that only you will be made aware of. All I can say is be strong, for you never know whom you are inspiring.

As Mahatma Ghandi said, "Keep your thoughts positive because your thoughts become words. Keep your words positive because your words become your behaviour. Keep your behaviour positive because your behaviour becomes your habits. Keep your habits positive because your habits become your values. Keep your values positive because your values becomes you and thus your destiny." Now go get 'em superstar.

"I've travelled the world twice and talked to everyone once. There aint nothing I can't do, no sky to high, no sea too rough & no muff too tough. I've learned a lot of lessons in my life. Anything worth doing is worth over doing. Moderation is for cowards. I'm a lover. I'm a fighter. I'm a tough son of a bitch who won't let life's lessons fade my smile."

Ballad of the Frogman

(Adapted)

'WHAT NOW' I HEAR YOU ASK

Throughout the process of writing this spiel, where I've non-verbally poured my heart out on to what started off as a painfully daunting prospect and a very blank page, I have allowed different friends to read this work in progress at deftly different stages. The only small print clause I provided was the request for a completely honest opinion. I wasn't looking for a lengthy critique worthy of 'The Guardian' for a one-word response would have made me as happy as a pig in shit. However, the acceptance of a single syllable answer was simply there as a means to wean out any bullshit excuse that they didn't have time to respond or that a technological failure had prevented their communicative abilities, for a synopsis this stupidly short required little less than Morse code.

However, I seem to be seriously lucky to have stumbled into a pack of pals who, bizarrely, seem to find me bearable enough to have provided me, a charlatan of a man, with lengthy rebuttals.

But, and as to be expected, these evaluations had a topical trend. The first observation seemed to be one of heartache, for these pleasantly peculiar people were all distraught by the fact they weren't there for me more than they were, explaining that they didn't know the true extent of my suffering. A ridiculous response in all honesty, for this coming-to-light-realisation was no one's fault but mine, for that was exactly the tact I had decided to take, and for that I apologise. The other notable craze within said comments was one of darkness, which I presume had nothing to do with them not paying their electricity bills or understanding there is a brightness setting on their laptops, but was in fact a remark based on the obviously dark overtone. What did they expect though, it's a memoir based on bloody bereavement, not a review of Finding Nemo or how tasty my Saturday morning Satsuma was.

Now it doesn't take an absolute genius to work out that these two acutely analytical common denominators happily waltz hand in hand, unlike the forever-exultant Beckham couple. I mean, as my friends, the nonsensical feeling that they weren't there for me as much as they should have been is surely just a loving acknowledgement to their new discovery. A discovery that finally shows them how hard I found these hardships, and an insight into what others in a similar situation may be experiencing.

However, there was one other question that popped up enough

for me to notice its recurrent behaviour, and that was, 'Would you want your Dad to read this manuscript?' Well to answer this curious speculation, hell yes I would. Not only because I know he would be proud of my honesty and the endgame of my attempt, but also because he died over four years ago and it would be totally tip top and utterly rad to see him again, especially to see him reading my book. Of course I know that's not exactly what they are asking or the retort they were expecting, but being affable is a coping mechanism for me, and in that sense I am very much part of the 'Cohen' clan, always making jokes, jests and witticisms too soon after tragedy.

Anyway, when reading back over this, I will raise my hand and let my head hang low like a guilty adolescent and concede to the notion that this homegrown dissertation-esque project of mine is mournful, ominous, depressing, unpropitious, abstruse, dark and a sponge for all things bright and cheery. However, let's not forget that this is a book that centres around a young man's battle with the death of his Dad, which may I add, is not the most cheery or comical of subjects for even the most screwed up and morally fucked of stand-up's, including Frankie Boyle. Instead it is the type of topic that has the ability to take the wind out of one's sails, for want of a far more superior phrase.

However its not all doom and gloom, for apart from the immediate first year after my Dad's death where smiling smothered me in a suffocating guilt, I like to believe I have been making people laugh as much as I have been laughing. You see I giggle at the slightest of things, and I cannot hold back my chuckles for I'm so easily set off and I guess I have tried to incorporate this into my writing style and into as many sentences as possible, really dipping into the perverted platitudes. I have tried to throw my affable personality into as many adjectives as feasible, crudely cursing, ruthlessly referring to sexual organs and using metaphors and similes at each and every turn. I want to show that there is space to laugh, a way to chuckle and occasionally a place to roll around on the carpet crying with laughter in stitches, all in spite of the awfully rancid pain in your stomach that feels as though some child has succeeded in connecting his foot with your balls.

I'm just a happy go lucky person who knows the importance of being exultant. There was a time where I was crazy depressed, despondent and 'Papa Smurf' blue, and I don't ever want to slip back into that coffin of morbid glowering and it is for this reason I have made sure I'm as optimistic as Floyd Mayweather is at any weigh in he's ever stormed. In any case, ever since my quiet revolution of January 3rd I have noticed my internal improvement of self-assurance, a clear direction and an intrinsic happiness with who I am. I mean forget these hallmark commercialised dates of sixteen, eighteen and twenty-one, for these are little more than just numbers to me, with this personal date in early January being the one that truly made me confident in myself and confirmed the inkling that said I am now a man. Of course I'm sure this can be taken apart by an object far larger than a fine tooth comb, with an analytical outcome that states this is obvious, but it has become more than just me overcoming my demons. It has become a platform, an opportunity and a chance for me to try and help others who are suffering with something similar. A chance for me to use my undesirable flair and help those who are feeling lost, tied to the tracks and facing the prospect of an inevitable collision with an oncoming steam train.

You see, I've always wanted to do my bit in this world of ours and help others, those less fortunate than I believe I am, because I despise the fact that life can be so random, unfair and divided, at least in certain aspects of our existence. I hate walking past homeless humans on the streets. Angry at the fact I don't have any affordable housing in my cargo pockets that I can just throw their way. I hate not being able to always subscribe to charity salesman that bug me like fucking gnats at a barbeque every fucking time I walk in or out of my office. I despise the thought that I cannot take the savage weight of everyone's problems and put them on my own shoulders, trying to ensure that no more Massive Attack 'Teardrops' dance across another person's cheek, for I know how much these variants of invisible discomfort can hurt.

There is so much piss-taking pain and sadomasochistic suffering on offer in this world and I just want to try and do my part to purposely prevent such harm where I can. I want to stretch out my middle finger and flip the bird to those intrusive issues that I have some experience and informal education in. However, I have learned that it is almost impossible to help others unless you are in a position to do so. This to me was one of the reasons I decided to imitate The Prodigy and smack this bereavement bitch up, yearning for and securing a surmounting clear head, for I knew only then would I able to think of a means in which I could help the wider audience.

I can't offer monetary assistance yet, and I think flirtatious and frivolous sexual advances would be wholly inappropriate, although much more my style. But with this in mind, I sought the meticulous means of the arts. I sought a determined route into film in order to one day produce a visual masterpiece that would be able to do some good in this ever more negative world. I decided to use my spare time to scrawl and write again, blabbering on about the dark times that make me blubber, yet the times that also make me beam with pride, for I get to see how far I have come with this documented piece de resistance. It is a piece of work that has caused irrevocable pain by stirring up feelings that have been dormant for too long, releasing the eye-watering stench of a shit storm. But, it is also a piece of work that has ensured my development as a person, and a piece of work that I hope will be able to help those who pick it off the dusty bookshelves for many a millennia to come.

I'm not delusional. It has been an unrelenting flare of fisty-cuffs to even get this worded song and dance out in the public sphere even a smidgen. I mean despite the effort to get this published, there's almost no doubt that this gutsy attempt of mine to help others will be stored somewhere behind Jordan's eighteenth autobiography, 'More' magazine and 'The Teddy Bear Times'. However, the philosophical beliefs of David Orr that relentlessly ring in my ears like the theme tune to Baywatch have always been an encouraging gravitational pull that promote morality and integrity. You see I have been hoping to provide peace-making stories for those in need of an optimistic bedtime read. I am boldly trying to bolster wider moral and ethical bravery, joining in with the struggle to ensure a habitable world of conscious triumphs.

I guess my ever more dogmatic dogfight to get the meaningful word out there is spurred on by today's pathetic fixation with the irrelevant. There is just this unneeded and crazy rise in gossip, bitchiness, bollocks and voyeurism that riles me. A rise that has been destroying the pivotal priorities of human nature, and the honourable professions of writers and journalists without due care for years, a true boner killer to say the least. You see, our urgencies and instantaneous concerns should be about civility, respect and a return to what is clearly important, concentrating on moral issues and the truth, not what colour bikini Britney's

Chihuahua's dentist was wearing in the retrenched nation of Portugal yesterday.

It is for this reason I am hoping to augment the small fleet of writers that should be known as 'The Last True Adventurers'. You know the creative genius' full of bravery and spunk, the one's with vast repertoires of stories about imperative news, relevant revelations. The one's who take risks and know what it is to dream big and beat the cynical system of society. I want to do my part to influence an audience and fulfil my ambition of seeking improvement, all of which I believe to be a rare occurrence in this day and age of feckless fame, good-for-nothing wannabes and the droves of starfuckers plaguing my morning influx of what really matters in this twisted reality of ours, but I'll try and spare you my moral indignation.

Nonetheless, this four-year struggle was heightened by my error in placing happiness hand-in-hand with my memories of life with Dad. I am never going to get to skip through meadows next to my old man again or share a Monte Cristo number Five with him, in fact I am never going to see him again, and thus I was never going to be that sublimely-happy-cheeky-chappy again, the one that old photo's suggest I was. This mentality has the ability to really get on top of you, and not in a ravishing reverse cowgirl sort of way, but more in a champion-sumo-wrestler-on-top-of-you sort of way.

You start to believe that recovery can never be done. You start to believe that happy endings are blissful parodies of bullshit that don't make it past the razor wire fences of Hollywood studios or Thai restaurants. You start to hear stories of others who have failed, given up or stopped fighting, and thus this riotous path of self-destruction becomes ever more attractive, sexy and rockstar like. Fuck, you may have even had your light-at-the-end-of-the-tunnel confidence knocked out of you by bullies, intimidating you with the prospect of an overcast future, drilling it into you until the hope has been drained out of you by the Dementors that they are.

Well I say fuck that, and serve it with a side of 'get-the-fuck-on' fries. You are more than capable of digging your heels into the ground. You are more than strong enough to become that immovable object that can't be forced back anymore. You are more than confident enough to ignore the voices of negativity and despair, more than proficient to party upon cloud nine and more than qualified to believe the impossible is possible, because impossible is just something you haven't done before. You just have to believe in yourself and remember the Chinese proverb, 'the person who says it cannot be done should not interrupt the person doing it.'

You can try and nullify the nausea and you can try and circumvent the saddening oust, but by heading down this self-destructive driveway of cutthroat cataclysm and consumptive escapism, you are only deepening your lightless hole. You will only cause yourself amplified and agonising anguish. You will only accrete the affliction and asperity of those around you, those who are also fatigued from the drudgery, and what's more you would be conceding to your lost loved one's only wish, for they would hate to see you suffering, and would wilfully want you to beguile, hoodwink, thwart and stupendously skirt self-suffering. Look, you're never going to forget what happened, and you may never going to get over it, but you will most definitely get used to it. Just let yourself feel what you need to feel, even if it hurts horrendously, even if it causes more paroxysms, malady, misery and more convulsions than an early morning cock-catheter.

But in spite of all the sentences I have constructed and all the situations I have juxtaposed, if you must remember something, then remember this. You are part of an exclusive and erotically elite group that's made up of the world's strongest individuals. Yeah that's right, you. Yes you are. You see I don't buy into the advertising techniques that media whores sell to us at every chance, but rather I appreciate what true strength is. It's getting by each and every day, one day at a time, but never giving in. You see the 'strongest' people are not those who flex their muscles in every conceited reflection and show off their visible strength in front of us innocents. Nor are these people the self-obsessed megalomaniacs that society plasters across magazine covers such as 'Men's Health' and 'Who Gives A Fitness Fuck', and they certainly aren't those individuals that oil themselves up and show off the fact their body fat percentage is the same low figure as their penis size.

No, the strongest people to grace this great planet of ours are those who win the battles we know nothing about, the one's who suffer personal tribulations at random intervals and still get on with life, singing and skipping as they make their way down the cobbled streets. It is these people, the one's like you and me, the one's that see its raining and instantly want to dance in its beauty that I get up and stand on my slightly pigeoned feet for. I enthusiastically applaud you for your strength and resilience you beautiful, ravishing, sexy, bewitching, gorgeous and radiant angel of hope you. Now go and look in that magical mirror of yours and know how stunning you are when you smile sunshine. You are an ambassador of strength, and you inspire those around you each and every day. Now get out there and enjoy this life you've been blessed with, and remember, today is a fucking great day to have a fucking great day.

ABOUT THE AUTHOR

William Hunter Howell (1988 - Present) was born on the east coast of the United Kingdom to political parents and a background of adventure, before moving to London and it's inspiring setting in his early twenties. His first years have been spent in the film industry, yet this hasn't prevented him from chasing his ambition of being an author. His debut book 'Affable in Adversity" shot to Number 1 Best Seller, and has been welcomed by both a whirlwind of readers and media interest, and enlightens its audience on the subject of being bereaved in his late teenage years. With a flair for the English language and the expanse of its offering, William Hunter Howell has a pedigree in luring his reader into a world of gritty and clever honesty, drawing out a vast spectrum of emotions with his unique perspective of all things intriguing.

Think pass further ideas

Contact Kate Tillyer ?

This week & Phillip?

Battery class? Spinning wheel!

Short Story with Philip & creating Something

July Vogue

30 sec
30 sec

4 - 5 shots
LG sec per shot
10 Credits

07864 223590

2x Am.
1x Red Led
3x Shields
Camera (tripod / cail
Sou in
macro lens

Printed in Great Britain
by Amazon.co.uk, Ltd.,
Marston Gate.